BECAUSE I CAN REMEMBER &
FROM MT. SHASTA WITH
LOVE

BECAUSE I CAN REMEMBER & FROM MT. SHASTA WITH LOVE

VOLHA ZHAMOITSINA

To all seekers of truth and the mysteries of the soul,
May these pages awaken your consciousness, inspire your journey,
and illuminate the eternal essence within you.

May the revelations of past lives, reincarnations, and sacred
encounters guide you toward love, light, and profound awareness.

May the tranquility, strength, and sacred energy of the serene and
majestic Mt. Shasta flow through these words and touch all who read
them.

With love and blessings,

Volha Zhamoitsina

Contents

BOOK I: BECAUSE I CAN REMEMBER

Introduction

Welcome to the realm where time is an illusion and the soul's journey transcends the boundaries of lifetimes. *Because I Can Remember* invites you to explore the mysteries of past lives, reincarnation, and spiritual growth deeply. In this captivating exploration, we weave together the themes of expanded consciousness, connection to the higher self and spiritual realms, and the power of inspiration and faith.

I'd like to welcome you on an unforgettable journey through the tapestry of past lives within the pages of this book. My name is Volha Zhamoitsina, I'm a hypnotherapist, past life regression specialist, and quantum healing hypnosis practitioner.

With a curious mind, my exploration of past lives and spiritual realms has led to profound discoveries and experiences that I'd like to share with you. Through this journey of self-discovery and spiritual awakening, I unraveled hidden truths and gained unexpected insights into the essence of our existence.

This book delves into the enigmatic journey of the soul's evolution, drawing upon personal experiences, spiritual encounters, and ancient wisdom. As you immerse yourself in the echoes of eternity and the veil of remembrance, you will discover the intricate threads that connect you to your past selves and the souls encountered throughout the ages. Through learning about my journey, I hope you'll find inspiration to embark on your own path of self-discovery and tap into the wisdom of your previous lives.

Additionally, you can expect to gain the following benefits from exploring the profound themes within this book:

- **Expanded Consciousness:** By delving into the exploration of past lives and the concept of reincarnation, you can expand your consciousness and gain a deeper understanding of the interconnectedness of all beings.

- **Connection to Higher Self and Spiritual Realms:** Through the exploration of past lives and spiritual encounters, you may deepen your connection to your higher selves and the spiritual realms, gaining a sense of purpose and alignment with your spiritual journey.
- **Inspiration and Hope:** By sharing personal spiritual insights, the book offers you a sense of inspiration and hope, showing you that no matter the challenges you face, there is always an opportunity for growth and transformation.

Because I Can Remember is not just a book – it is a portal to the infinite possibilities of existence, a key to unlocking the mysteries of the universe, and a beacon of light guiding you toward a higher state of consciousness. Dive into its pages and embark on a journey that will forever change the way you perceive yourself and the world around you.

1

Understanding Reincarnation

The idea of reincarnation has captivated spiritual seekers for centuries because it offers a belief in the soul's eternal nature and its never-ending cycle of rebirth in different physical forms. The soul can evolve through numerous life experiences and accumulate wisdom through this journey of birth, death, and rebirth.

Those who embrace reincarnation also recognize that our souls carry memories and lessons from past lives, which can manifest as unresolved traumas impacting our current lives. We can break free from outdated patterns and beliefs that hinder our personal growth and transformation by acknowledging and healing these deep-seated wounds from previous incarnations.

Through techniques such as past life regression, quantum healing hypnosis, and Akashic records meditation, individuals can explore their past lives to gain profound insights into their present challenges. By engaging in these practices, we can uncover past life traumas, identify recurring patterns, and address ancient wounds that may be holding us back in our current lives.

These methods provide a transformative way to delve into the mysteries of our past lives and understand how they shape our present experiences. Past life regression allows us to access memories and emotions from past incarnations, offering valuable information for healing and personal growth. Quantum healing hypnosis accesses higher states of consciousness to facilitate deep healing and spiritual awakening. Akashic records meditation connects us to universal knowledge stored in the Akashic records, providing insights into our soul's journey through time and space.

By exploring our past lives through these techniques, we can uncover hidden truths, release old wounds, and let go of limiting beliefs. This inner work can lead to profound healing, personal growth, and a deeper understanding of our soul's purpose. Through these powerful practices, we can transform our lives and create a more fulfilling and empowered existence.

"Claim now the parts of yourself that have been locked away from the pure vibration of love and trust."

– Aurelia Louise Jones

2

My First Encounter with Past Lives

A few years ago, a profound sense of longing and restlessness began to stir within me, like a gentle breeze whispering secrets of a grander purpose waiting to be discovered. It was an intangible pull, an invisible thread weaving through the fabric of my being, guiding me toward an unknown destination beyond the horizon of my everyday existence. The yearning grew more insistent with each passing moment, a magnetic force drawing me closer to the edge of a precipice, where the familiar veil of routine and monotony began to thin, revealing glimpses of a world brimming with untold possibilities and hidden truths. The feeling of incompleteness enveloped me like a cloak, urging me to embark on a journey of self-discovery and exploration as I stood on the threshold of a transformative awakening that promised to unravel the mysteries of my soul and illuminate the path to my true purpose.

I began by reflecting on my past experiences, searching for recurring patterns that resonated with my innermost being. I recalled the moments that had ignited a spark when time seemed to freeze, and I was utterly absorbed in pursuits that held deep meaning for me. Through this process of introspection, I slowly began to unravel the threads that would eventually come together to form the intricate tapestry of my purpose.

I realized my purpose wasn't some grand, elusive concept waiting to be discovered in a single epiphany. Instead, it was a culmination of my unique talents, the impact I wanted to have on the world, and the values I held dear. It was about finding alignment between my innermost desires and the external contributions I could make.

One day, I suddenly wanted to meet with a hypnotist, hoping he could help me figure out my life. I'd been caught up in the real estate world for a while, moving from place to place, but deep down, I knew something wasn't right. It felt like I was missing out on something important – there was a bigger picture I couldn't see.

So, I found myself sitting in the hypnotist's office, feeling a bit nervous but also excited to dig deep and uncover what was going on inside me. His eyes seemed to see right through me, and as we talked, it was like he was unlocking parts of me I didn't even know existed. It was my first time experiencing hypnosis, and I was clueless about its workings. But my desire to discern my life's purpose was overpowering. I was eager to comprehend why I was brought into this world and what my duties and desires were.

The session with the hypnotist proved to be a truly fascinating and eye-opening experience. As I delved into the depths of my subconscious, I was granted a glimpse into not just one but five to six of my past lives. However, this journey was far from ordinary. Rather than progressing through each past life linearly and chronologically, I leaped from one existence to another without the usual death transition. It was as if I were flickering through the pages of a book, each chapter revealing a different story from another time.

The hypnotist's attempts to guide me through the significant events of a particular life were met with unexpected resistance from my subconscious. Each time we approached a crucial moment, I would suddenly find myself transported to another life and another time, leaving me confused and disoriented.

The experience was thrilling and puzzling as I struggled to make sense of the fragmented glimpses into my past lives. Each shift brought forth a new set of memories, emotions, and connections, painting a complex tapestry of my soul's journey through time and space. It was a surreal and enlightening exploration of my existence, revealing layers of my being that I had never encountered before.

In one of the vivid glimpses into a past life, I was transported to a tumultuous scene that stirred deep emotions within me. As I peered into the vision, I saw a young girl, no older than 16 or 17, with cascading long hair. She stood amidst a field, her gaze fixed on a horizon filled with turmoil and chaos.

The setting bore a striking resemblance to the French Revolution. The air was thick with tension and the distant sounds of battle echoed through the landscape. The scene unfolded before me, with people engaged in a fierce struggle for freedom and justice, their lives hanging in the balance. The sight of people dying in the name of revolution struck a chord deep within me, stirring a wellspring of emotions I could not contain. Tears streamed down my face uncontrollably as I felt the weight of the tragedy unfolding before me.

At that moment, the boundary between past and present blurred, and I was deeply connected to the girl and the harrowing events playing out around her. The authenticity of the experience was undeniable, as goosebumps pricked my skin and a wave of realization washed over me.

All my doubts and skepticism melted away in the face of this powerful revelation. It was as if my soul had orchestrated this poignant encounter to remind me of the intricate tapestry of lives I had lived before. The vision left an indelible mark on my consciousness, a testament to the enduring legacy of my soul's journey through time and history.

Wisdom From A Scary Drowning Experience

In a different scene, I found myself immersed in a heart-wrenching moment as I observed a weathered fisherman, approximately 65 years old, battling against the relentless embrace of drowning waters. As I fought for survival, grappling with the unforgiving forces of nature, a profound realization dawned upon me: the value of life and the inherent strength within each of us to overcome adversity. The harrowing experience served as a poignant reminder that life is a precious gift worth fighting for, a testament to the resilience of the human spirit in the face of life's darkest challenges.

The sight of the fisherman struggling in the water resonated with me, bringing back vivid recollections of my scary encounter with drowning in my recent past. My sister's quick thinking and bravery rescued me from the clutches of the deep, leaving me with an enduring phobia of deep waters that still lingers to this day.

In another life, a nostalgic memory resurfaced as I was transported back to when I was a carefree little girl. Dressed in a charming floral dress, I could vividly picture myself frolicking in the sun-drenched backyard of a cozy house. The air was filled with the joyful laughter of innocence, and my heart brimmed with pure happiness as I reveled in the simple pleasures of childhood. Each moment was a precious gem, sparkling with the magic of carefree days and boundless imagination.

In a different lifetime, I found myself reborn as a solitary rock, a quiet observer in a desolate landscape. The unfamiliar terrain stretched endlessly before me, a vast expanse of emptiness and isolation reverberating with life's haunting absence. Settling into my stony existence, I embraced mindfulness, learning to embrace the present moment amidst the serene silence of my surroundings.

The spacecraft's arrival abruptly upended the quiet balance of my rough life. As the spaceship drew closer, its rounded shape becoming clearer with each passing moment, I watched in awe. The planet was a desolate wasteland, its surface scattered with jagged rocks and boulders.

I had a profound sense that the universe was offering me a glimpse into alternate realities, like the brief preview you get before starting a new chapter or embarking on a new journey. It felt like I was being shown snippets of different past lives, just scratching the surface of their stories without delving deep into any particular experience.

After exploring my past lives, I felt a guiding presence leading me to connect with my guides. I was warmly greeted by an angel, a magnificent being of pure light and ethereal beauty. Their presence radiated a sense of peace and divine wisdom, with eyes that sparkled like stars and a gentle smile that seemed to hold the secrets of the universe. Their wings were vast and shimmering, with feathers that glowed in hues of gold, silver, and iridescent blue. The angel's form seemed to shift and shimmer as if it were made of pure energy and light. Their aura exuded a sense of love and compassion, enveloping me in a warm embrace that felt like coming home. In their presence, I felt a deep sense of connection to the divine and a profound sense of awe and wonder.

The angel then turned around, signifying our journey toward the spiritual guides. The path ahead of us was glowing softly, almost like it had a magical light guiding us toward the spiritual guides we were about to meet. There was a feeling of excitement and reverence in the air as I got ready to connect with these beings who were going to help me on my journey of spiritual growth and enlightenment.

The hypnotist asked about whether the angel had a message for me. However, the angel remained silent. We were about to proceed further when suddenly, the hypnotist began to bring me out of the trance. We were running out of time. It left me without the answer I had been seeking. At that particular moment, I couldn't help but think I could have approached the situation better. The primary question remained unanswered despite leaving the session with a sense of happiness. At that moment, I continued to linger in my thoughts.

Delving into the idea of past lives was a truly enlightening experience for me, a concept that had previously been under my radar. It opened up a new realm of possibilities and perspectives that I had never considered before. I was fascinated by the idea that our souls might have had countless lifetimes, each with its own tale and lessons to be learned. It was like uncovering a treasure trove of knowledge and self-discovery, prompting me to delve deeper into the mysteries of existence and the interconnectedness of our past, present, and future selves.

I stumbled upon the College of Hypnotherapy in Los Angeles a few months later. Without hesitation, I signed up for their one-year course covering past life regression—the main reason I joined. Throughout the year, I immersed myself in the intricate workings of the subconscious mind and its profound capabilities. It was a journey filled with revelation and enlightenment as I delved into the realm of hypnotherapy, uncovering its potential to aid individuals in navigating myriad challenges. From tackling anxiety, phobias, stress, and trauma to breaking free from detrimental habits, boosting self-esteem, and achieving personal aspirations, I witnessed first-hand the transformative power of harnessing the subconscious mind. Through my exploration and practice of hypnotherapy, I gained a deeper understanding of the mind-body connection and discovered the immense capacity for growth and healing within each of us.

An Unexpected Visit From Dolores

I also began to delve into meditation, a practice I had previously dismissed as a waste of time and nonsensical. I began experimenting with self-hypnosis and, much to my astonishment, started unveiling various layers about myself. I derived great satisfaction from regression and managed to uncover multiple past lives.

During one of the deeply meditative sessions, I was graced with the presence of Dolores Cannon in a vision. Her ethereal essence shimmered with wisdom and compassion, enveloping me in a sense of profound peace and enlightenment. As I gazed upon her luminous form, I felt a surge of spiritual energy and a profound connection to the higher realms.

Dolores Cannon, a renowned hypnotherapist and metaphysical teacher, is known for her groundbreaking work in the fields of past life regression and metaphysics. She helped countless individuals explore their past lives, access higher dimensions, and heal deep-seated traumas.

Her presence was palpable, and her message resonated deeply within my soul. She told me that my current exploration of hypnosis was merely scratching the surface of my potential journey. She spoke of a path that would ultimately lead me to Quantum Healing Hypnosis, a method that delves into the realms of past lives, alternate dimensions, and profound healing on a quantum level. Her words were like a guiding light, illuminating the path ahead and instilling me with a sense of purpose and destiny. It was a moment of profound clarity and revelation, igniting a spark within me to continue on this life-changing path of healing and self-discovery.

Upon graduating from hypnotherapy college, I understood the true importance of my very first past life regression session. This experience revealed the answer to my life's purpose indeed, guiding me toward a career in hypnotherapy, past life regression, and quantum healing hypnosis. At that time, my mindset was not open to fully accepting and comprehending the message. However, as I evolved and my consciousness expanded, I could understand it clearly.

So began my journey of self-exploration. This journey was filled with discoveries, unexpected disappointments, and delightful surprises. I learned about the people in my life, and that those I met seemingly 'by chance' actually weren't random encounters at all. They held significance in my past lives.

3

The Neighbors and My Past Life in Japan

When destiny led me to the West Coast of Florida, I discovered a paradise like no other. The exquisite beaches, adorned with white sand and embraced by blue waters, exuded a magical allure. This perfect setting was the ideal place to rejuvenate and find peace. Here, I delved into my first past life regression, a transformative experience that heralded the dawn of a new chapter in my journey. I felt a sense of deep connection to this place. I knew that it was not just a destination but a soulful sanctuary where I could truly connect with my inner self. The experience was a catalyst for growth and self-discovery, igniting a passion to explore the depths of my past lives and uncover the mysteries of my soul.

Surrounded by the beauty of nature, I felt a sense of isolation from the bustling world around me. It was a time when I needed to be alone, away from the noise and distractions of everyday life. Although my friends were not by my side, I found solace in connecting with my neighbors.

There was a single father and his young daughter who lived just a block away. Often, I would take my dog to the park, where he would also bring his own dog and his little girl. She was a charming child between the ages of two and three who quickly stole my heart with her hugs, kisses, and playful nature.

Despite my usual calm demeanor around children, this little girl had a way of drawing me in. We formed a special bond from the moment we met, spending time together at the park and going for walks. She became a bright spot in my day, a companion who brought joy and warmth to my isolated moments.

Initially, I believed that the strong attachment I felt to the girl was due to a deep-seated maternal instinct within me. At my age, the desire to have children of my own was prevalent, and I thought this longing was manifesting in my bond with her. However, as time passed, I realized that the connection we shared went beyond mere maternal instincts.

It was unusual for me to feel such a strong bond with a child who was not my own. I found myself instinctively wanting to protect her from any harm, both consciously and subconsciously. Her presence awakened dormant feelings of motherhood within me, but it was more than just a desire to nurture. Our connection transcended biological ties, touching a part of my soul that I didn't know existed.

Family of Three

While studying hypnotherapy, I delved into the exploration of past lives in search of answers to my current situation and purpose. With past life regression, you have the ability to focus your attention and explore previous lives that resonate with your current desires. For instance, if you're struggling with financial issues in your present life, you can set an intention to revisit a past life where you experienced wealth and abundance. By revisiting that time, you can understand what led to your success and incorporate those feelings and emotions into your current life. Similarly, my intention was to revisit a past life where I was part of a happy, loving family with children.

Through self-guided regression, I ventured into a past life where I experienced the bliss of marriage and parenthood in Japan. In this vivid journey, I saw my happy family of three living in a simple bamboo house. It was poorly constructed, and you could see through the holes in the wall. Our son's bed was built into the wall in the kitchen, right next to the dining table.

I saw myself with my husband and our son, eating a meal for dinner. My spouse approached me, gave me a hug and kissed me. It was such a warm, loving gesture, and I really enjoyed the family time. We were not rich, but we were very happy together as a little family of three.

Another scene unfolded where I was watching my son play in the water outside, his laughter echoing through the air, filled me with joy and energy. As a mother, I patiently watched over him, waiting for him to finish his aquatic adventures. When he was finished swimming, we would walk back home hand in hand, happy and laughing. As I looked at him holding my hand, it struck me how similar he was to the little girl I used to hold hands with in the park. It was as if they were the same soul in different bodies, their eyes twinkling with the same light and their smiles equally charming.

In a stroke of luck, I unexpectedly crossed paths with my previous life's partner on the West Coast of Florida as well. Our short reunion served as a poignant reminder of the interconnected nature of our lives and how history has a way of repeating itself in enigmatic ways. Even though time and distance had kept us apart, reuniting felt like we had never been separated. Our conversations flowed naturally as if we were just continuing from where we left off. It was both sweet and sad, reminding us of the love we once had and the different paths we chose to follow.

The fact that both individuals' names were so similar in this incarnation intrigued me the most. Could it be a sign of confirmation for me, perhaps?

It is truly fascinating how connections from past lives can manifest in our present reality, even if only for a brief moment. Sometimes, we meet people and feel an inexplicable connection, unaware that we shared a history in a previous existence. Our physical forms may change, but the essence of our souls remains constant, bridging the gap between the past, present, and future.

4

Regression to the 18th Century

I was embarking on my training in past life regression with an open mind and no specific expectations. Approaching this practice with curiosity, openness, and receptivity, I created the space for profound experiences and insights to unfold naturally. I understood that past life regression can be a deeply transformative and enlightening process. By letting go of preconceived notions and allowing myself to be guided by the process, I opened myself up to uncovering hidden truths, healing past traumas, and gaining valuable insights into my soul's journey across lifetimes. Thus, the expedition to one of my previous existences started. I developed a resolution to relive a past life where I was prosperous, filled with joy, and content.

And a time travel journey began...

The first thing that caught my attention was my bedroom. I observed the drapes, curtains, carpet, and an abundance of heavy fabric adorning every corner—the upholstered furniture with floral patterns. The floral patterns seemed to be everywhere. The room exuded an 18th-century style with its massive furniture and huge windows, giving it a grand and imposing presence. My initial reaction was, "Wow, this place desperately needs some updates and remodeling."

The room felt elegant for that time but out of sync with my current minimalist inclinations and obsession with orderliness. Initially, it was overwhelming, but soon I found it amusing. Then, amidst this peculiar setting, I spotted a familiar face from my current life—a friend with whom I had once shared a romantic relationship in this present life. It was an intimate scene in my bedroom, flirting and laughing. He was dressed in the attire of the 18th century, acting as if he were some kind of lord or ruler. It felt like my friend just put on the wig to play a role game. As our eyes met, laughter erupted from within me. It was a sight to behold—witnessing someone I knew so well in such a hilarious and vastly different situation in an entirely different era.

Naturally, my first reaction to his outfit was, "What on earth are you wearing?" I found myself dressed in an extravagant, voluminous gown with layers upon layers of underskirts, giving it a fluffy and grandiose appearance. The scene before me radiated with romance. He was my lover in that lifetime, too. It was a love filled with playfulness, flirtation, and a sense of lightheartedness and belonging. I felt loved. However, It did not carry the weight of a boyfriend or a husband, and I felt more independent. It was as if we were engaged in a purposeful game, and I willingly played along, embracing the enchanting experience.

The scene then shifted to my deathbed, the last day of my life. I had a high fever, and many servants were looking after me. They were applying cold compresses to my forehead; they'd dampen a bandage or towel, place it on my forehead, and replace it with a fresh, cool one once it warmed. Most of the servants were men.

In that regression, I didn't draw any conclusions about our identities. I found the entire spectacle highly entertaining. I realized it was set around the 18th century, but, as I already mentioned, I didn't attempt to identify us by names or establish any historical links. I simply had a great time and thoroughly enjoyed this regression. It was a fun experience, and I just let it be. After a while, I put it out of my mind. It was just another experience that I ticked off my list and then forgot about for some time.

5

Madame de Pompadour and the King

Several months had passed before I found myself back in the sprawling city of Los Angeles. After spending some time exploring other states, my return remained a well-kept secret. Unexpectedly, a text message from my friend, whom I saw in my past life regression as my lover and I described earlier, broke the silence. I couldn't understand how he could have known about my presence in LA. His inquiry cut straight to the point, asking if I was indeed in town.

The arrival of this text message and the sudden reappearance of this individual stirred up memories of a past life regression I had undergone several months ago. Something about the situation triggered a deep intuition within me as if there were still hidden truths and undiscovered information waiting to be unveiled. It strongly felt like there was more to that regression than I had initially realized, and a sense of urgency convinced me to explore further and unearth the hidden depths within.

As I thought about the integration, the memory came rushing back. I could clearly remember that moment of regression, and it got me thinking. If I had many servants in the past, it must mean I was an important person in those times. It made me curious to find out more, so I looked into French history in the 18th century. I found a resemblance to the king, which gave me goosebumps. It felt like nothing had changed. In my regression, I saw him, and that led me to search for his lover. I was amazed to discover Madame de Pompadour.

The romance between Madame de Pompadour and Louis XV was a captivating tale that unfolded amidst the opulent and extravagant court of Versailles. Madame de Pompadour, born Jeanne-Antoinette Poisson, was a woman of exceptional beauty, intelligence, and charm. As the official chief mistress of King Louis XV, she became one of the most influential and powerful figures of her time.

As I was browsing pictures from that era, the lavish drapes, abundant fabrics, and expansive rooms served as constant reminders of my past life regression. It was as if I were peering into a mirror reflecting my previous existence. The memories washed over me, sending a tingling sensation down my spine. The realization struck me: I had indeed been a person of great significance in that time.

However, my skeptical nature kicked in, and doubts began to cloud my belief. It seemed too fantastical, too unreal, to be true. Maybe it was a mistake or a coincidence. Perhaps there was another explanation. But then, a memory resurfaced, reminding me of the circumstances of my fatality in that past life. As I delved into the search results, I discovered that Madame de Pompadour had indeed passed away from a high fever, exactly how it was in my regression. The realization sent a chill down my spine. It was the very same way I had perished in that previous existence. Slowly but surely, the puzzle pieces were fitting together, leaving me both astounded and filled with a sense of awe.

When I told my friends about this news, I received skepticism and strange looks in return. They seemed to think I had lost my mind. Determined to delve deeper into the mystery, I resolved to conduct further investigations on my own.

Karmic Debts Repaid

It had been some time since I last explored this subject, but a strange revelation emerged during my most recent guided meditation. As I delved into the Akashic records, information regarding the couple began to surface, adding another layer of intrigue to the unfolding story.

In my spiritual journey, I have been enlightened about the karmic debts I have cleared from my past lives. It has come to my attention that in my previous existence during the 18th century, I was entangled in a complex dynamic with a man who was married. I was his mistress. However, I made a conscious choice not to repeat the patterns of the past in my current life. I refused to settle for a relationship where I was not prioritized as the number one woman in his current life. I chose to break free from the cycle and prioritize self-love. Through this experience, I have learned a valuable lesson about not settling for anything less than a faithful and devoted partner who sees me as his one and only.

In a fascinating twist of fate, it seems that the king himself also had karmic debts to settle in this lifetime. In his past life, Madame de Pompadour had a daughter from a previous marriage whom he had refused to accept. However, in this current life, he has found himself falling deeply in love and is on the verge of marrying a beautiful woman who has a daughter of her own. Remarkably, he has embraced this child as his own, breaking the cycle of past rejection and clearing the karmic debt from his previous life. It is a beautiful testament to the power of love and growth in our journey towards spiritual enlightenment.

I received a profound message from my spirit guides, revealing that we have finally cleared our karmic debts. We no longer owe anything to each other. However, the significance lies in the fact that we have found comfort in knowing that we have a deep connection that has spanned centuries. I am genuinely grateful that we have reconnected in this lifetime, as it signifies the completion of our lessons and the resolution of our karmic ties.

Indeed, the essence of the soul remains constant throughout lifetimes, regardless of the physical form it inhabits. It is like an unwavering light that accompanies us on our journey through different experiences and embodiments. While the external appearance may change, the core of who we are—the essence that radiates within us—remains unaltered. This eternal aspect of our being allows for the exploration of various roles, identities, and expressions throughout different lifetimes. It is a beautiful reminder that our true nature transcends the limitations of the physical and embraces the infinite possibilities of existence.

6

Memories of Paris

Have you ever wondered why you feel a deep resonance with a specific era in history? What captivates you about certain historical films? Have you ever thought about how events from past lives influenced your current hobbies, including the books, movies, and media you enjoy reading and watching? We often attribute our affinity for certain creations and periods to our ancestors, but could it be possible that we are one of those ancestors?

In the past, I never entertained such thoughts. My mindset was too limited to consider such possibilities. However, with a broader perspective and an open mind, I now find myself contemplating these ideas. While there are some souls experiencing life on Earth for the first time, there are also many who have been reincarnating throughout the ages, witnessing the evolution of our planet. And I am one of those souls.

I have come to realize that I may have been a part of the very history that captivates me. It's a fascinating thought to consider that the era I feel drawn to and the stories I immerse myself in could be a reflection of my own past experiences. Perhaps I have witnessed the rise and fall of civilizations and the triumphs and struggles of humanity throughout the ages. This idea allows me to connect with and understand the world around me on a whole new level. It reminds me that

I am not just a passive observer of history but an active participant in its unfolding.

During my time at a fashion school in Hamburg, Germany, I vividly recall immersing myself in the captivating study of costume history. Our focus was on the enchanting world of Rococo fashion history, a subject that truly held me spellbound. I can still hear myself gleefully uttering its name repeatedly as if each syllable brought me joy and delight. Little did I know then that this fascination was not merely a passing interest but a connection to my past. I was studying Rococo fashion with a passion, and I had been involved in it without realizing it at the time. This seductive style, which drew inspiration from figures like Madame de Pompadour and Louis XV, was intricately woven throughout my previous incarnations. Reflecting on this realization, I find it fascinating how we are often drawn back to the places that once held our hearts and were unequivocally called home.

During my time as a fashion design student and intern at a renowned designer's atelier in Hamburg, an incredible opportunity presented itself: an invitation to join the backstage preparations during Paris Fashion Week at the Carrousel du Louvre. The mere thought of it set my heart racing with excitement. With a mix of nerves and anticipation, I gathered my belongings and set out to the fashion capital of the world.

As soon as I landed in Paris, I could feel the electric energy in the air. The city was alive with the buzz of creativity and style. As I stepped into the bustling backstage area, an exhilarating whirlwind of activity greeted me. Models, stylists, and makeup artists moved with purpose, bringing the designer's vision to life.

With wide eyes and a determined spirit, I immersed myself in the tasks at hand. Assisting with fittings, ensuring garments were flawlessly displayed, and lending a helping hand wherever needed, I felt an incredible sense of purpose. The atmosphere was charged with anticipation and the pursuit of perfection.

Paris is recognized as a global fashion capital, with its biannual Fashion Week events being of utmost importance in the fashion industry. Twice a year, fashion enthusiasts, designers, models, and industry professionals from around the world flock to Paris to witness the latest trends, designs, and collections from top fashion houses. Paris Fashion Week provides a stage for designers to showcase their creativity and innovation, setting the bar for future fashion seasons. It is an iconic event that not only influences the fashion landscape but also shapes the global fashion industry as a whole.

After the exhilaration of Paris Fashion Week, I had the opportunity to explore the enchanting city on my own terms. With the bustling energy of the fashion world behind me, I set out to experience the true essence of Paris. The day was mine to savor, to immerse myself in the vibrant vibrations that permeated every corner of the city.

I started my journey at the famous Eiffel Tower, a symbol of Paris's magical charm. Stepping onto its grounds, I was instantly overcome with a mix of excitement and wonder. The iron lattice structure soared above me, reaching toward the heavens as if inviting me to explore its secrets. The intricate architectural details, meticulously designed and crafted, spoke volumes about the city's rich history and artistic prowess. As I gazed up at the towering monument, I couldn't help but appreciate the sheer magnitude of human ingenuity that went into its creation. It stood as a testament to the human capability of turning dreams into reality, and I felt a surge of inspiration course through my veins.

When I reached the observation deck, the breathtaking panorama of Paris stretched out before me. Famous sites in the city, such as the Louvre and Notre Dame Cathedral, were visible in the distance, adding to the allure and charm of the scene. At that moment, I realized that Paris truly lived up to its reputation as the "City of Love" and the epitome of romance. The charm and allure were not merely clichés but a tangible essence that enveloped me, leaving an indelible mark on my soul.

With a grateful heart, I bid farewell to the Eiffel Tower, knowing its magic would forever remain etched in my memories. As I continued my journey through the enchanting streets of Paris, I carried with me a newfound appreciation for the city's beauty, history, and unique energy that made it truly one of a kind.

My visit to the Palace of Versailles, though, was what really lit a fire under me. I felt a wave of liberation sweep over me with every step I took toward the palace, relieving me of the burdens of daily life and enabling me to enjoy the moment fully.

Here I was, enveloped by the vibrations of history, sensing a strange connection to the past. I came to understand that this location had more meaning for me. It was more than simply a tourist destination; it was a place where my soul found comfort and resonance. It felt like my own energy and the energy of the past combined to create a potent synergy that spoke to my soul. Upon reflection now, I realized that my trip to the Palace of Versailles was more than just a visit —it was a return home. It was the reunion of a part of myself that had been quietly awaiting acknowledgment.

7

The Image of Elizabeth I: Reality or Illusion?

One day, while enjoying my coffee and relaxing on the couch, something strange happened. After finishing my coffee, I looked at the bottom of the cup and saw an image. It was a woman's profile; every feature was angled perfectly—her forehead, her chin, her nose—it was like a portrait in profile. I asked myself if it was me, and it felt like the answer was yes. The thought also crossed my mind that it was a queen.

I couldn't believe what I was daydreaming. A queen? Me? I chuckled to myself, thinking it was just my imagination playing tricks on me. But as I stared at the intricate details of the picture, I couldn't help but feel a sense of curiosity. Who was this queen?

Excited beyond my control, I hurriedly snatched my phone and began searching for images of any queens. As I compared the portraits in my coffee cup to the ones on the internet, I couldn't help but notice the striking similarities. Everything matched perfectly with the high forehead, pointed chin, and nose. I sat there, staring at the image in disbelief. How could this be? Queen Elizabeth I, one of the most influential and iconic queens in history, appears in the remnants of my morning coffee. It felt surreal.

The "Virgin Queen" of England, Elizabeth I, was the daughter of Anne Boleyn and King Henry VIII. She reigned from 1558 until she died in 1603. Strong leadership, victorious military campaigns, and the thriving arts and culture during Queen Elizabeth I's reign are among the things that people remember about her. She was a significant figure in English history.

She was known for her intelligence, determination, and strength. She defied societal norms and expectations, ruling with an iron fist and leaving a lasting impact on England and the world.

As time went on, I found myself battling with the idea that I might have once been a queen in a past life. The concept felt foreign and unsettling, stirring up fears of what accepting such a revelation could mean for my present reality.

8

Paying Off Karma: From Queen to Maid

M onths passed without much thought given to the idea until unexpected triggers reignited those buried emotions. It was as if
the universe was nudging me to explore this uncharted territory, urging me to confront the uncomfortable truths that lay dormant within
me. With each passing day, the pull towards unraveling the mysteries
of my past life as a queen grew stronger, beckoning me to delve into
the depths of my soul.

One particular moment from my early 20s came to mind: immediately after graduating from a Belarusian high school, I decided to
work as an au pair in Germany, to travel overseas to live with a host
family and give childcare services in return for housing, food, and a
meager stipend. The French word "au pair" means "on a par" or "equal
to," which captures the idea that the au pair is not an employee but
rather a member of the family. Au pairs typically assist with childcare
responsibilities including watching and playing with kids, participating in homework, and occasionally helping with little tasks at home
that are connected to the kids. The main focus is cultural exchange,
language learning, and building a relationship with the host family.

With only one suitcase, 50 Deutschmarks in my pocket, and a one-way ticket for the bus trip, I set off on my journey as an au pair in Germany. It was a leap of faith into the unknown, but I was determined to embrace the adventure and make the most of this opportunity for personal growth and cultural exchange. Despite the limited resources, I was excited about the experiences that awaited me in a new country and with a new host family.

It was a big decision that ended up shaping my life in ways I never could have predicted. Living with a wealthy host family in a beautiful mansion was both exciting and intimidating. But beneath all the luxury, I quickly realized that things weren't as perfect as they seemed. The host mother was cold and distant, and her attitude made me feel like I didn't belong in their world.

Having to wake up very early every morning to ride a bike to the bakery and pick up fresh bread was a real struggle, especially with Hamburg's reputation for cold, rainy weather year-round. It made me wonder why I had chosen this path. Feeling lost and alone in a place so different from what I was accustomed to only added to my uncertainty and apprehension.

There's a moment from my time as an au pair that still lingers painfully in my memory. I vividly recall the host mother casually labeling me as "the maid" in front of her friends during a social gathering. The room fell silent as her words hung in the air, suffocating me with embarrassment and hurt. I felt like an invisible presence in my own skin, reduced to a mere servant in their eyes. It was a stark awakening to my standing in their household, leaving me grappling with a profound sense of worthlessness and disillusionment.

But things started to look up when I moved on to a new host family. This was a fresh start for me, a chance to chase my dream of studying fashion design and working various jobs to support myself. It was a time filled with hope and possibility – a chance for me to carve out my own path. My new host family was absolutely supportive of my decision to pursue further studies.

Looking back on those challenging times, I see them as lessons that shaped me. The experience of being undervalued and mistreated taught me to appreciate my worth and to keep pushing forward. Life is full of ups and downs, and it's a journey of growth and self-discovery.

In one life, you reign as a queen; in another, you serve as a maid. Positions reversed.

9

A Glimpse into the Past

Time passed, and I would sometimes allow myself to ponder the possibilities of that past life as Elizabeth, and it would linger with me. This went on for around a year since I first saw the portrayal of the queen in my coffee cup. Sometimes, I would try to push the thoughts away and dismiss the idea, but on other occasions, I would consider that perhaps there was a reason why all this information kept coming back to me. It was as if the universe was giving me little clues, allowing me some time to digest the information, and then presenting me with more. Eventually, I began to entertain the thought that maybe there was a past life involved, or perhaps it was just an imprint. But if it was an imprint, what could be the reason for me to see it?

What is an imprint?

"They can withdraw information from the Akashic records and imprint this information into their soul, and it will then be their experience... If one were to come to this planet from another planet or dimension without the aid of imprints, one would be totally lost. One would not understand customs, religions, politics, or how to act in a social environment." – *Dolores Cannon, The Keepers of the Garden.*

Group Past Life Regression Meditation

To learn more about the era of Queen Elizabeth the First, I undertook a past life regression meditation with a group. So, it was a fun setting, and I didn't expect much. It was more about entertaining myself and seeing if I could gather any new information about that time.

As I delved into the past, I could see the scene: a carriage rolling in, with crowds of people loudly cheering on both sides of the road. I was a little girl with long hair and a flowing dress. Despite my resistance, I was taken to the palace. I didn't want to go and refused to walk, but two individuals flanked me on either side, forcing me towards the building.

Fast-forwarding through time, I saw myself as a young woman with her hair let down but clipped back to keep it off her face. This young woman was standing on the second or third floor of a building, looking down at the grounds through the window. A sense of worry was palpable; she was concerned about something. She had responsibilities that she was in charge of.

During this regression, another scene that unfolded before me was a carriage with horses and a large flag returning to what seemed to be a battlefield. The atmosphere was surprisingly joyful.

While I didn't get the significant validation I was seeking, it felt as if the universe offered me a brief snapshot of my past life, as if to say, "Here's a small preview; stay tuned for more."

Despite my initial frustration, I gradually began to understand the universe's cryptic way of communicating.

It wasn't about seeking validation or proving my worth; it was about learning and growing. It was about understanding the different aspects of my soul, the multiple lives it had lived, and the wisdom it had accumulated over the centuries.

The universe was not withholding information from me but was simply guiding me to discover it at my own pace. The brief snapshots of my past life were not meant to provide immediate answers but to stimulate curiosity and self-exploration. This journey was not about the destination but about the process of self-discovery and transformation.

I felt a profound sense of peace as this realization dawned on me. I was no longer desperate for validation or answers. Instead, I was eager to uncover more about my past life, my soul's journey, and the wisdom it had to offer. After all, as the saying goes, one step is the start of a thousand-mile journey. And this was just the beginning of my journey – one that promised to be filled with self-discovery, growth, and a deeper understanding of the universe and myself.

10

The Unveiling of a Bond

On my journey to expand my consciousness, I stumbled upon a captivating book called "Telos- Volume 2" by Aurelia Louise Jones. As I delved into its pages, a wave of enlightenment washed over me, filling my mind with the essence of knowledge and guiding me on my path of evolution. Within the ancient tome, I discovered not just words but profound revelations that resonated deep within my soul, propelling me forward on my quest for spiritual awakening.

I learned that Saint Germain, an Ascended Master, has had many incarnations; there were a few names on the list. "In one of his many previous incarnations he was Joseph, the father of Master Jesus, who lived 2,000 years ago. He also incarnated as the prophet Samuel, Christopher Columbus and Francis Bacon, the true author of the Shakespearian plays."

The name Francis Bacon caught my attention for some reason. I searched the internet for the years he was alive and came across the 16th and 17th centuries, an era of Elizabeth I. Francis Bacon, an influential figure in the 16th century, known for his contributions to philosophy, science, and literature. Born on January 22, 1561, in London, England, Bacon served as Attorney General and Lord Chancellor of England, holding important positions in the government.

Bacon is often regarded as the father of empiricism and the scientific method. He emphasized the importance of observation and experimentation in understanding the natural world, advocating for a more systematic and evidence-based approach to scientific inquiry. Bacon's work laid the foundation for modern scientific thinking, influencing prominent scientists such as Isaac Newton.

In addition to his scientific contributions, Bacon was a prolific writer and philosopher. He is best known for his essays, which cover a wide range of topics, including politics, ethics, and human nature. Bacon's writing style is characterized by its clarity, conciseness, and wit, making his works accessible to a wide audience.

Despite his significant achievements, Bacon's career was marred by controversy. In 1621, he was charged with corruption and accepting bribes, leading to his dismissal from office and a period of disgrace. Bacon spent his later years focusing on his writing and philosophical pursuits, leaving behind a lasting legacy as one of the most important figures of the 16th century.

However, the most shocking revelation came when I learned from my online research that Queen Elizabeth I had a secret son she gave away to protect her power and throne. This son turned out to be Francis Bacon, an incarnation of Saint Germain. The revelation blew my mind and added a new layer of intrigue to my quest for enlightenment.

In my newfound awareness of the connection between St. Germain and Queen Elizabeth I, I had moments of doubt, wondering if he truly was her son. Some online sources mentioned her never having a child, casting uncertainty on this relationship. However, my doubts were soon dispelled when I stumbled upon the book "Understanding Twin Flame Union: the Ascension of St. Germain and Portia" by Claire Heartsong and Catherine Ann Clemett. The book clearly states:

"Indeed, my mother was Queen Elizabeth of England who epitomized the colonization of nations, which was part of personal memory of 'star-wars'. Indeed beloveds, it is true –Queen Elizabeth was a grand fiery-haired one, to be sure, with a grand heart and a grand mind and a grand vision and a grand knowingness. She conceived that which be I and she sent me off onto other parentage, the home of the Bacons, where I became quite a boar, as it were."

"So you are confirming that Francis Bacon was the son of Queen Elizabeth, who gave her son to one of the ladies-in-waiting?"

ST. GERMAIN: "Indeed."

Another example is when Portia, his twin flame, speaks about him:

"I watched over him upon the birthing bed when he was delivered in great secrecy–a great shrouding. There were hushed whispers and dimmed lights when the cries of birthing broke forth through the dry lips of the mother with flaming red hair. My heart ached for her and for the sibling who was born. A young maiden, who was a lady-in-waiting and also a wet-nurse, took the wee babe away, at the mother's insistence, before he even had a suckle at her breast."

In this book, I discovered the profound connection between Francis Bacon (Saint Germain) and Queen Elizabeth I, confirming the truth of their bond. In the 16th century, she gave away her son to keep the throne and her power. Today, I would give it all away to have a child. The priorities have changed over the centuries.

The information I was receiving was quite heavy on my heart. It was difficult to digest, and I had to give myself breaks, sometimes for a few days or weeks, before moving forward with the next revelation. Subconsciously, I knew that it might be painful and unpleasant once I started delving into these discoveries. This underlying awareness probably led me to initially reject the idea that it could be my past life because, deep down, I knew that there was more painful information waiting to be uncovered.

In this moment of realization, I made a solemn promise to myself: to let go of all resentment, regrets, guilt, and grudges that had weighed me down. I understood that forgiveness was not an easy task, but it was a necessary one for my spiritual evolution. I knew that by letting go, I could truly embrace the beauty and potential of my present life.

Though life is not always woven with these threads, we frequently wish to see ourselves as happy, prosperous rulers. It is essential to embrace this truth without judgment. Our souls actively choose the scenarios they wish to experience, be they good or bad. Each experience serves a purpose in our soul's evolution, even if the reasoning eludes us in the present moment. The puzzle will eventually make sense once the pieces start to fit together.

I gained profound insight into why we are born without conscious recollection of our previous lives. The weight of emotions and memories can be utterly overwhelming. That's when I realized how wonderful it is to start over, free from the burdens of the past. And, remarkably, we possess the freedom to choose whether or not we wish to remember. If one finds contentment in not knowing one's past self, that choice is just as valid. We all have a free will.

"We have all been healers and we have all been murderers. It is time to forgive ourselves for all that we have done, and all that has been done in our name." – *Aurelia Louise Jones, TELOS, Volume 3*

11

Past Life with My Father

One day, I chose to engage in Akashic records meditation to seek further insights about my past life. My goal this time was to delve deeper into the life of Queen Elizabeth I and the actual events that transpired.

As soon as I reached a hypnotic state of being able to receive messages, the information began pouring in swiftly. It concerned my father, who grew up without his biological father and was placed in four different foster homes throughout his childhood, where he underwent a horrific and painful phase of his life. My grandma remarried and could not keep him in the family. A few days ago, we were actually talking about his karma and his childhood and why he had to experience it.

So the message in my meditation was that his pain in this existence stemmed from having to go through it himself to learn what it's like to be abandoned and forced to grow up without parents. In a previous life, he was Robert Dudley, the biological father of Elizabeth's son. This child was the secret child of the two and was given to the Bacon family. In this life, my father had to balance his karma in such a way.

At some point, I wanted to halt the influx of these messages. I even protested in my mind that they didn't make any sense. It felt awkward and weird, as it didn't align with my reality. However, I was told that it would begin to make sense once I started putting together all the information that I have gathered in my present life.

It is indeed intriguing to consider the possibility of interconnected relationships across different lifetimes. The concept of soulmates, soul connections, and past-life relationships suggests that the souls we encounter in our current lives may have played different roles in our past lives, such as lovers, family members, friends, or even adversaries. The idea that my father in this life could have been my lover in a previous life adds another layer of complexity to the dynamics of relationships and the eternal journey of the soul. Exploring these spiritual and metaphysical concepts can offer a deeper understanding of the connections we share with others and the lessons we are meant to learn throughout our soul's journey.

The realization triggered a memory buried deep within me—a recollection from a few years ago. I can still vividly recall a time in my early twenties when I was studying fashion in Hamburg, Germany. I decided to visit my parents in Eastern Europe, and my father picked me up from the train station. As I sat in the back seat of the car, I caught a glimpse of him in the rearview mirror. To my surprise, instead of seeing my dad, I saw an unfamiliar older man with a beard and a stern expression. This unexpected sight frightened me to the point where I couldn't bring myself to look directly at my father for the duration of my visit home. It left me with a heavy feeling inside.

I had no clue that there could be prior lives back then. I was sad and perplexed when I left home. Now, though, things are starting to make sense. The timing was perfect for their release as the intense emotions and feelings came to the surface in a wave. I was prepared.

My guides sent me a telepathic message, telling me to relax in a warm salt water bath and let the information really sink in. I was sick to my stomach and had a pounding headache from the weight of everything I had learned and experienced that day during the meditation. It was all too much for my mind to handle.

It took me several days to purge the heavy energy from my system and genuinely liberate myself from the oppressive weight. It was a task I had been evading for some time, and subconsciously, I was aware that it required my attention. Once it was brought to my consciousness and processed, I felt like I had accomplished a considerable amount of work.

I extended my love and compassion from a place devoid of judgment. I offered my forgiveness to those who had wronged me in the past and to myself for holding onto the pain for so long.

This journey wasn't easy; it took time, patience, and a lot of inner strength. But it was worth every moment of discomfort. I learned so much about myself and my ability to heal. I realized that I have the power to control my emotions and reactions, and I can release any negativity that may be holding me back.

This is my journey, my healing, and my transformation. And I am grateful for every moment of it.

12

Grandma's Visit from the Other Side

One day during Akashic records guided meditation, I saw myself jumping on a trampoline in front of a huge library structure. I was jumping so high as if reaching the cosmos, the galaxy, and the stars. It was so much fun. Then, the guiding voice instructed me to place myself in front of the library door. I thought to myself, "The fun is over," and then I felt somebody pulling my sleeve. When I looked down, I saw a little girl. She asked if she could join me on a trip to the library, and I agreed.

As we entered the library, I had forgotten about her but suddenly felt a strong urge, which confused me, to call upon my grandma, my father's mother. I called out her name, and there she was, dressed in white, walking towards me with a radiant smile. A pure energy of love emanated from her, a stark contrast to the grandma I knew in life. It was undeniably her, with the same voice, the same dress but in white, and the same charisma.

She passed away a few years ago, and I didn't have a chance to say goodbye. Unfortunately, she was not my favorite when she was alive, and her energy was very heavy on me. I tried to avoid her in any way. But it came to my awareness that someone from the other side was trying to communicate with me and had a message for me. I thought that she might want to control me from the other side as well, and I was not really looking forward to it. But one of my spiritual teachers told me that it might have been her role to play while she was alive, and her spirit is no more than pure love.

Tears of joy streamed down my face as I embraced her and apologized for avoiding her and not saying goodbye before she passed. She smiled, completely accepting and devoid of judgment or negativity. It was pure, unconditional love and light that she exuded. And she had a message for me, one about my future, my calling, and especially my future family. She also mentioned that a little girl is constantly pulling her sleeve, asking if it's time for her to go to Earth. The girl has been patiently waiting for her turn, preparing and studying for her incarnation.

I listened intently as she delivered her message. She expressed her pride in me for figuring out how to connect with her on my own and for my curiosity and desire to expand my consciousness. We expressed our love for each other, and then she was gone, leaving me to continue my guided meditation journey alone.

I spent a lot of time reflecting on this experience, and everything started to make sense. I realized that there is no separation, and it is possible to communicate with spirits on the other side. I had learned how to do it. My perspective on death shifted, and I embraced a new understanding. There is no such thing as death; there is only transition.

You Have a Visitor

Time passed, and I completed my college studies in hypnotherapy while finishing my internship for Quantum Healing Hypnosis certification. Both techniques have their benefits, and the choice between the two would depend on the individual's personal goals. I really enjoy engaging in quantum healing hypnosis, as it allows me to connect with a higher power. Even though we often label it as the subconscious for simplicity, the true essence of this energy goes beyond any specific name. In reality, we are working with a collective energy that transcends individual labels.

I had only one client left before becoming a practitioner. As usual, I was practicing energy healing myself and listening to high-frequency music to connect with my higher soul and seek answers about my current situation. Suddenly, a telepathic voice said, "You have a visitor." I was puzzled, wondering who could be visiting me. But tears of joy streamed down my cheeks as I realized it was my grandma. She had come to congratulate me on completing my internship and becoming a quantum healing hypnosis practitioner. She was incredibly proud of me.

At some point, I feared that she had come to tell me that she would be taking my father, as his health was not the best. However, she reassured me that they were not taking anyone over at that time. Instead, she revealed that a soul was waiting to come to Earth, a soul that had been waiting for quite some time. I understood exactly what she meant.

The pressure was intense, especially considering I wasn't even dating anyone at that time. But my grandma continued, assuring me that I would meet my future husband soon. I cried throughout our conversation, overwhelmed with emotions.

As she delivered the message, she paused, and I sensed she didn't want to leave as if it were our last time together. I asked if she needed to go, and she nodded. This time, she lingered as if there was nothing left to discuss or explain. Everything had been said. And then she was gone.

13

An ET-Hacked Session

In addition to conducting hypnotherapy consultations with clients, I occasionally have private mentoring sessions. These sessions are with my more experienced mentors, who sometimes assist me in my personal growth.

Recently, I had a standard, unremarkable online session with one of my mentors. I had arranged for some light, and she set up calming music to play in the background. To enhance my relaxation, I put on my headphones, and the hypnosis session began. Since I had already experienced going into a deep state before, I was able to enter a trance rather quickly. Then the voice in my headphones faded and was replaced by a loud noise that sounded like a scene from a movie if there was a coded message in the noise.

The noise increased, growing progressively louder and unbearable. I opened my eyes and looked at her. She seemed puzzled as to why I had disrupted the session. I tried telling her that I couldn't hear her, but she seemed unable to hear me as well. I unplugged my headphones from my computer, only for the noise to fill the room, echoing off every corner. I repeated, louder this time, "I can't hear you!" but she remained oblivious.

After that, I decided to record the disruptive noise on my phone. The moment I started recording, the noise began to fade, and I was able to hear my mentor again. She was confused, so I tried to explain what had happened and describe the noise. Despite the disruption, we resumed our session. Later, when I received the recording, I fast-forwarded to the part where I stated, "I cannot hear you." To my surprise, the recording only captured the music and my mentor's voice in the background, with no trace of the noise.

Initially, I thought that someone had interfered with my session. The noise sounded like a cryptic message; this was the first suspicion that popped into my mind. I also considered that it would require advanced technology to separate two distinct sounds playing simultaneously.

I decided to send the recording of the disruptive noise from my phone to my father. Upon hearing it, he became incredibly alarmed and urgently advised me to delete the recording immediately. I complied with his advice and deleted the recording. However, upon restoring and listening to the recording again later, I didn't sense any malice or danger. Rather, I sensed that there was an attempt to make contact with me. At first, I thought extraterrestrials had taken over my session.

The mystery lingered until I underwent a regression hypnosis session with Jeff at a later date. Every single one of my questions was addressed, and my concerns were indeed validated during this session.

14

Past Life as a Squirrel in
Norway

As a hypnotherapist and past life regression specialist, I am a passionate seeker of knowledge and thrilling experiences. I love to explore uncharted territories, experiment with different techniques, and uncover hidden truths in my practice. Every session felt like a whimsical journey of discovery, where I was constantly surprised and allowed to unlock the mysteries of the mind.

As I was completing the Quantum Healing Hypnosis program and preparing to start practicing with clients, a friend of mine asked me if I had ever experienced it myself. While I had conducted numerous hypnotherapy sessions and past life regressions, I had yet to undergo quantum healing hypnosis.

As fate would have it, that very night, I discovered a practitioner nearby. Without hesitation, I reached out to him, and to my surprise, someone had just canceled their appointment, making room for me the following day. It felt as if everything was falling into place as if it were meant to be. I must admit I felt a mix of nervousness and excitement. I knew this experience would be mind-blowing. Before embarking on sessions with my clients, I wanted to go through the process myself. I also had several questions about my well-being and personal life that I wanted to explore with the subconscious.

Jeff, the practitioner, and I had a small chat about my life. He asked me what I wanted to achieve and what my intentions were for the session. I also gave him a list of questions I wanted answers to.

Without difficulty, I entered a trance. I found myself in a state of comfort and tranquility, floating on a cloud toward a significant past life. As I descended, I was greeted with a breathtaking scene of lush green fields, majestic trees, and a charming village nestled at the foot of a hill. It was a small village in Norway, and the beauty of the landscape was awe-inspiring. It was a peaceful summer day, and the air was filled with serenity.

I had to ground myself and describe what I saw. To my surprise, I witnessed a transformation from an animal's nails to a baby's feet and back again. I struggled to identify who I was. However, a clear image emerged of me stretching my golden, furry body on a tree.

Initially, I felt disappointed, thinking, "Surely, I have experienced more significant past lives than that of a squirrel in Norway." I was confused. I had seen myself as a more prominent figure in history before. However, I remembered that even the most ordinary and uneventful life can still carry a profound message from the depths of my subconscious. This message may offer valuable insights into my current circumstances.

It did not take long for me to realize that I was living in a hole in the tree next to a small, old house that belonged to an old woman, and she lovingly fed and nurtured me with her own hands. She confided in me, knowing that I would understand. She was an incredibly wise woman, radiating positive energy. Every word she spoke offered guidance and insight that transcended time and space. Her wisdom extended beyond personal matters; she possessed a profound understanding of the world and effortlessly navigated through life.

Next, Jeff instructed me to leave that scene and fast-forward to a significant day, a day that held importance or had something significant happening. I was suddenly back in my house, all by myself, in the dark, and filled with a deep sense of abandonment. It was the day the elderly woman passed away. Her energy was gone, leaving behind an empty house devoid of life and spirit. I felt utterly alone.

As I witnessed this scene, tears welled up in my eyes. The profound sadness and loneliness that permeated the air enveloped me, leaving me overwhelmed with emotion.

In a moment of profound thought, Jeff asked a question that prompted me to stop and contemplate. "Every life carries a lesson and a purpose. What knowledge have you gathered from this experience?" His inquiry sparked a flurry of revelations, astounding me with their depth and significance.

The lessons I learned during my time as a squirrel resonated deeply within me:

- Embrace the freedom that life offers, and don't succumb to the pressures of conformity.
- Take control of your destiny and be the architect of your happiness.
- Let no one dim your inner light, and never forget the power you hold within.
- Write your own story and leave a mark on the world.
- Always remember who you are and what you're capable of.
- Rise above adversity and believe in your limitless potential.

These lessons, born from my unique perspective as a squirrel, hold immense value and can guide me toward a more fulfilling and meaningful existence.

Leaving my previous existence in the rearview, I found myself drawn towards a brilliant white light. I kept going up, higher and higher, until its bright brilliance completely engulfed me. The energy was unique, tranquil, and imbued with a sense of unadulterated love.

I was the one doing it. I had done it before.

My eyes were transfixed on the vast luminosity that lay in front of me. Light beings, resembling small orbs, floated around me. Pure white in color; they weren't exactly orbs but instead concentrated forms of light. They stood out against the light that surrounded me. They simply drifted past me on their serene journey.

J: How vast does this white light reach?

V: It's limitless; there's no end.

J: Do you sense yourself as part of the white light?

V: Yes. It's an amazing feeling of oneness.

J: What do you know about this location?

V: It's a waiting area.

J: What are you waiting for?

V: I'm waiting for the next step.

J: Do you know what the next step is?

V: Yes. We'll likely review my past life.

J: Who will join you in reviewing it?

V: My teachers. I'll meet them soon.

J: Do you have any spirit guides around you?

V: It feels like someone escorted me here but then stepped aside.

J: You mentioned you're going to review your life. Let's advance to the point where you   review your life. You are there now. What do you see?

V: I see a few teachers before me.

J: How many?

V: Three to five.

J: What are they communicating?

V: They are saying it was a short life. I needed it for my next life.

J: What else are they saying?

V: Don't stray from this path. There will be numerous distractions. See the path; follow the path. There will be individuals attempting to take away my motivation and distract me from my life's purpose. In the future, life will be more challenging. More trials, more distractions, and I need to recall the wisdom from the past to identify distractions and overcome hurdles.

J: It seems like a nice review.

V: They're chuckling because they're thrilled about my next life. That was just a warm-up. The real challenges are approaching now, and the true journey is beginning now.

J: Is there any one of those entities that you feel is superior, or do they all feel equal?

V: Archangel Michael is here. He has been supporting me constantly. He believes that I'm ready.

J: Is there anything else they wish to convey before you part with them?

V: Yes. Buckle up! Get ready! It's about to get exciting. Don't fall into despair because nothing seems to be happening at that moment. Gather the energy for the next step, learn to relax, and take breaks because it's merely recharging before the big step. They said I shouldn't get despondent when nothing seems to be progressing in my life, and when I feel stagnant, it's just a preparatory step.

J: Anything else?

V: They're proud of me. I've lived a good life... But they're laughing about what's going to happen to me next. They said that I had no idea what I had signed up for. They're saying they might grab some popcorn because it's going to get interesting. They're teasing me.

J: They do have a sense of humor. Don't they? They're very loving.

V: They also said, "You are never alone on this journey. We will be with you every step of the way, guiding you and nudging you in the right direction. Trust in yourself and the wisdom you have gained."

Meeting My Soul Group

With those words, a sense of calm washed over me. I knew that even though the challenges might be daunting, I had the inner strength to overcome them. The love and support that surrounded me in this realm reassured me that I was never alone.

After my encounter with my guides, I proceeded to meet my soul group. These were beings with whom I shared a deep spiritual connection, a collective consciousness. Being in their presence was like reuniting with a long-lost family; a profound sense of love and familiarity enveloped me.

J: Can you provide a more detailed description of them?

V: It appears they're engrossed in social interaction and are enjoying themselves.

J: Are any of them identifiable to you?

V: None specifically, but I do have a sense of familiarity with them.

J: Select one that stands out and describe it to me.

V: A charming young man approaches; he recognizes me and invites me to join them.

J: Can you tell me more about him? Do you remember him from this life?

V: I'm uncertain, but I believe he might be my soulmate, whom I've yet to encounter. But I'm unsure. He's a good person, indeed.

J: Who else is present?

V: My grandmother is somewhere here. She's part of my group.

J: Do you know the number of individuals in your group, your soul family?

V: Including this man, there are seven or eight of us.

J: And you've all been together for quite a while?

V: Yes, but we don't always reincarnate together in each lifetime. Sometimes, someone will choose not to return, so we take breaks from Earth. At times, they accompany me, and we discover each other in our respective lives if we reincarnate in the same lifetime.

J: Are you all following the same path, or are your paths different?

V: It varies. Not always. Some of us have our own lessons to learn in different lives, independent of me.

J: But generally, you all belong to one soul group, right?

V: Yes, that's correct.

J: What is your main area of study?

V: Our goal is to go to Earth, remember who we are, and teach others. Then we regroup and reflect on our lessons, trying to better ourselves and avoid repeating mistakes. We discuss the distractions on Earth that might prevent us from awakening. We also discuss those who fail to awaken and why that happens. Everything is a test. We come to Earth to pass a test. When we reunite, we analyze and discuss what led to failure and how we can prevent that from happening again. Then, we guide others on what to avoid and how to improve so they can awaken.

J: Do you impart these teachings while you're on Earth or back home?

V: My mission is primarily focused on Earth. We simply share our knowledge when we are back there. We all have a metaphorical 'backpack' filled with tools. When you come to Earth, you're given this 'backpack' to maintain your connection with the spirit world. If you feel disconnected, you can use these tools to reconnect and remember your true self. However, some souls fail to use it, leading to their inability to awaken. But that, too, is a lesson for them.

J: How can they access their 'backpacks'?

V: They need to quiet their minds. They need to disconnect from distractions and noises, spend more time in nature, meditate, do breathwork, be around waterfalls, visit the ocean and mountains, and listen to high-frequency music. All these activities help soothe their minds. When they connect to themselves, they reestablish this connection. This makes it easier to recall why they came here. It's similar to a newborn kitten, who is initially blind but gradually gains sight. Some people die blind, never gaining sight.

J: Yes, it's important. What is the most important thing they explain to you?

V: Always remember where you came from.

That's how you know your way; you exit through the same path you came in. Knowledge on Earth is very important for the next stage. It's essential to evolve and experience the Earth's existence because it's not only a form of entertainment but also a school and lesson for our soul's evolution. There are so many distractions—darkness, violence, anger, and fear—on Earth, and it's very easy to get swept off your feet and to flow into darkness. But those who stand their ground, discover the truth, and see through the illusions are the ones who are going to teach others.

J: Do you know how many lives you've lived on Earth?

V: I am not sure if it was every century, but I'm sure I've been here from the very beginning of everything. I have seen every step of evolution on Earth.

J: Have you ever lived somewhere other than Earth?

V: Yes, other planets.

J: Please tell me about those.

V: It's different from Earth. I don't know what kind of planet it is, but it looks darker than I see in space.

J: So how is it different?

V: There is less life, less wildlife, and fewer beings. It's hard to survive there; it's not like on Earth. I don't think there are any animals.

J: Would you prefer to incarnate there or on Earth?

V: No, there's nothing to do there. The souls go there to learn lessons, but as soon as they learn them, they leave because there's nothing to do and no fun. It's just like a stepping stone for the soul's evolution—a quick test.

The final phase of the session was dedicated to establishing a connection with SC, or the subconscious, for answers to my queries and overall health improvement. While some refer to it as the subconscious, others have known it as the source, universal energy, divine energy, the energy of the creator, oneness, or the higher soul. Regardless, it doesn't have a definitive term, as it signifies collective energy.

J: Could you please scan her body? Is there anything that requires our focus?

SC: There is an energy block in her chest.

J: Is there anything we can do to alleviate this immediately?

SC: Yes. (I was breathing heavily for a bit.)

J: It's disappeared; what's next?

SC: There's a concern in her lower abdomen.

J: Is it something you can handle?

SC: Yes.

J: Can you provide healing for her reproductive area? What did you discover there?

SC: More energy blocks, but they're not severe; they can be easily cleared.

J: So you're able to clear them out?

SC: Yes.

J: I'm really curious about how it works. Can you explain it to me?

SC: I'm sending energy to her stomach. She's doing Reiki herself, and she is doing great. But she doesn't do it every night, but she should.

J: Can you explain how she can do it?

SC: She knows she should do it, but she doesn't do it enough. She only does it sometimes, but she needs to do it every night.

J: It's like a form of meditation or something she does with her energy. How does it work?

SC: All she needs to do is listen to high-vibration music. It will vibrate and help her heal naturally. It will also help her feel better and be in her element. It will also help her stay balanced. Then she will know what to do next. She knows how to do it.

J: Thank you, thank you so much for your assistance. One of the topics she raised concerned the information she has been uncovering about her past lives. She contemplates whether to share this knowledge through a book or articles or keep it to herself. What course of action should she take?

SC: She has already taken the first steps by writing articles, and we couldn't be prouder of her. She can continue to write piece by piece, knowing that eventually, they will find their way into the world. Some may be published, while others may not, but through this process, she can introduce people to the incredible world of hypnosis and past life regression and share her personal experiences.

Many individuals are drawn to learn and practice quantum healing hypnosis, and by sharing articles and personal stories, she can spread this message to the masses and prepare them for the next stage of our collective evolution. This is the same mission that you and other practitioners are undertaking. She is making remarkable progress and has discovered a hidden talent for writing that she never knew she possessed.

J: It's truly remarkable. I've noticed that a significant number of us in this generation are being called to engage in this type of work. Even I have felt the pull towards this path, as have many of my peers. Could there be a larger shift happening that is inspiring this desire within us?

SC: The universe has called upon you, and you have answered that call. That's what it is. You have awakened to your purpose, just like others who are experiencing their awakening. They feel the calling and are instinctively drawn to practitioners like you and me, seeking to awaken their latent abilities and fulfill their life's purpose. We all agreed to undertake this journey. It's not a new concept to us; it's more like a familiar blanket. You were living your human life, and then the calling resonated within you. Suddenly, everything fell into place, and you became aware of your life's purpose: to help others awaken, heal, and believe. In due time, you will also write a book to further inspire and guide others on their transformative journeys.

I was given excellent ideas for enhancing my daily life and a detailed plan for my hypnotherapy practice. The subconscious also taught me that there is a reason why we are here. I would be able to hear my inner guidance if I tried to quiet my mind, meditate, go to the beach, spend time in nature, and practice breathwork. I was reminded to stay on course and not get sidetracked by nearby sounds. My inner self held all the answers to my inquiries.

However, the most significant question was also resolved: Was my session taken over by extraterrestrials? The response and its validation were astonishing.

J: There were just a few more questions she had. During a hypnosis session, she started hearing this weird noise in her headphones. She actually played it to me today before our session. Can you tell her what it was?

SC: It is coding.

J: What?

SC: It's coding. A coded message from another universe, another planet, to remind her where she's coming from. Now, she's living an earthly experience, and they wanted her to keep this connection to another planet. That other planet has a missing puzzle piece in her game in this life. There's nothing that she can understand with her conscious mind. Nobody can explain, neither you, nor the teacher, nor her father. Her father got scared, but she had subconsciously the knowledge that she needed to keep this message. It's also ingrained in her DNA that when she's going to need something, it's going to come automatically. It's the knowledge you cannot get from your experience, nor is it the knowledge that we can provide. It's the knowledge you can only get from this planet, and this is an amazing puzzle in her game here in life. She is going to use it when it's needed, so there's nothing you can describe with words or symbols. There is no description of it. It's nothing bad; it's a good thing. Yes, the session got hijacked; this is true, but it was the only way for that planet to communicate with her because otherwise, she could mess it up a little bit without that missing knowledge.

J: Okay...thank you. Does she have anyone in her life now or in the future who will be there to support her and help her through the tough times?

SC: She has strong support from us. She can easily reach out to us whenever she needs to because we are constantly communicating with her. Whether she's meditating or just staying quiet, she can hear and understand our messages clearly. And if she ever needs assistance or wants to do some research, all she has to do is ask us.

J: That's truly amazing. Being able to hear you directly is a special gift. In her sleep, she feels that someone is working on her body.

SC: That's us.

J: What are you working on?

SC: What she destroyed during the day, we need to restore during the night.

J: She sees you scaring away.

SC: Yes.

J: I thought it was rather amusing.

And she said she saw something above her dresser at night. Could you tell her what it was?

SC: We were teaching her to work with energy. That's what she saw above her desk. We showed her how to manipulate the energy with her hands, and that's when she saw the light ball between somebody's hands. We were just teaching her. She's going to know what to do. Subconsciously, it is all recorded. She is going to use it when it's needed, and it's going to come naturally. It's in her DNA.

J: Yeah, she was telling me about it. It is so fascinating. Is there anything specific you would like to ask on her behalf or provide an answer for?

SC: She has an additional inquiry from her list, which revolves around her family in Europe. She willingly chose this family, having signed up for it. However, they are not her soul tribe; they merely serve as a surrogate family. When she decided to leave not just her family but also her home country, she followed her instincts. They, too, are evolving and learning their lessons through her personal growth.

J: Thank you for your insight. Before concluding this session, do you have any final thoughts or messages you would like to convey to her?

SC: She is destined for greatness—on a grand scale. We are here to support her wholeheartedly; she possesses vast knowledge and resources. What she needs is to believe in herself and release any self-destructive thoughts that occasionally plague her mind, leading her to doubt the authenticity of her experiences. Everything she encounters is real; she possesses a deep understanding of her purpose. Our connection with her is strong, and she must strive to maintain a high vibrational state. She learned a valuable lesson the hard way, as we demonstrated that she could have it all, only to take it away abruptly, leaving her feeling helpless. However, this was a necessary lesson to reinforce the importance of maintaining a high vibrational state. Spending more time in nature and visiting the ocean will greatly benefit her. She will find her love soon. She's also skeptical about this. And the person she is thinking of is the one she's going to meet soon.

J: Excellent. Thank you for all the information you have given us today. Thank you.

As I slowly emerged from the deep state of hypnosis, I felt a profound sense of gratitude for the experience I had just undergone. It was like peering into the depths of my soul and receiving guidance from the wisest parts of myself. I knew that this session had unlocked a hidden treasure within me, revealing profound lessons and insights that would shape my present and future.

In the days that followed, I reflected on the messages and lessons I had received. The simplicity and yet profound wisdom of my past life as a squirrel in Norway resonated deeply with me. It reminded me to embrace my uniqueness, to trust my instincts, and to create my path in life, regardless of what others may think or expect. The passing of the elderly woman in that past life taught me the importance of cherishing the connections we have with others and the impact we can have on their lives. It reminded me to appreciate the wisdom and guidance of those who come into our lives, even if they may seem insignificant or unconventional.

As I connected with my guides in the realm of pure love and light, I felt a renewed sense of purpose and determination. I knew that the challenges that lay ahead would test me, but I also knew that I had the strength and support to overcome them. I also realized that crossing that fine line toward positive life changes requires a willingness to explore new paths, embrace uncertainty, and trust in the process. We must venture outside of our comfort zones for it and be open to the lessons and messages that come our way, even if they seem insignificant or nonsensical at first. I believe that by embracing change, trusting in ourselves, and staying open to new possibilities, we can all cross that fine line toward a better version of ourselves and create the lives we truly desire.

15

A Spontaneous Trip to Mount Shasta

Mount Shasta is a majestic and mystical mountain located in northern California, known for its spiritual significance and magical energies. It is one of the most powerful energy vortexes on the planet, attracting seekers, healers, and spiritual pilgrims from around the world. Due to the minimal barrier between the physical and spiritual dimensions, connecting with higher realms becomes more straightforward.

Mount Shasta is home to a hidden city of light, Telos. It is described as a thriving underground city inhabited by an ancient race of beings known as the Lemurians, who are considered to be the descendants of the lost continent of Lemuria.

Legend has it that Telos is a place of advanced technology, spiritual enlightenment, and harmonious living. The Lemurians live in perfect harmony with nature and each other, embodying principles of love, peace, and unity. Telos is believed to serve as a spiritual haven and healing center for those seeking wisdom, guidance, and transformation.

The myth of Telos continues to fascinate and inspire those who are drawn to the mysteries of Mount Shasta and the ancient wisdom of the Lemurian civilization.

As I prepared for my upcoming journey, the sky gifted me with a rainbow each day, a symbol of beauty and hope. The colorful arcs appeared to carry whispers of the exciting adventures that lay ahead, foreshadowing the extraordinary story that was about to unravel. It served as a reassuring reminder that even during darkness, there was always a glimmer of light and optimism waiting to break through.

Even if just one cloud lingered on the horizon, a rainbow would emerge like a sign from my guides. I could feel their unwavering support in those colorful arcs stretching across the sky. It was as if they reminded me that no matter what challenges I faced, they were always there to guide and protect me. The rainbow was a beautiful reminder that I was never alone and that my guides would always be there to light my path through the storm.

While walking with my dog one day, I looked up to see the rainbow again. I was filled with a deep sense of love and encouragement in that instant. The divine sign inspired me to act, and I hurried home to book my trip to Mt. Shasta for the next day. It felt as if everything was falling into place with lightning speed.

Setting off bright and early the following morning, I began my adventure with my faithful companion Kiki by my side. This beloved dog had been my constant companion on countless journeys, accompanying me as we explored the length and breadth of the country, creating treasured memories with each passing mile.

The drive from Los Angeles up to the Sacramento area proved to be quite challenging for me. The stagnant energy weighed heavily on my spirit, leaving me feeling drowsy and fatigued. I couldn't help but blame myself for embarking on such a lengthy trip. However, as I passed Sacramento, the scenery transformed, and a renewed sense of vitality washed over me. I began to enjoy the ride when I saw wisps of clouds accompanied by the golden tones of autumn trees reflected in serene lakes. It felt almost mesmerizing as if I had stepped into a fairy-tale realm inhabited by elves and fairies. As the road wound closer to Mt. Shasta, ascending the hills, the breathtaking views from above stole my breath away.

I arrived at Mount Shasta just before sunset. The energy enveloped me, reminding me of the familiar embrace I had felt in Sedona. It felt like coming home. Exhausted yet serene, I settled into the peaceful-ness of the surroundings.

The following day, I took my dog for a walk and grabbed a strong cup of coffee from a local shop next door. A profound sense of whole-ness washed over me as if I had found my rightful place in the world. The first item on my agenda was a visit to Lake Siskiyou, a reservoir lo-cated in Siskiyou County, California. The lake is surrounded by beau-tiful forest scenery, making it a picturesque destination for outdoor enthusiasts.

I got there early and was at peace by myself. A sense of unity and togetherness filled the air. I basked in the serenity, watching the clouds dance upon the mountain, their reflection shimmering in the crystal-clear water. It was a picture-perfect scene that captivated my senses. At that moment, I couldn't help but express gratitude to the creator for the beauty that enveloped us and for this magnificent mas-terpiece we call Earth. Numerous undiscovered treasures are just wait-ing to be found, and so many awe-inspiring places remain unknown to us.

The majority of our lives are confined inside our comfort zones. We create these boxes for ourselves to live and work in, which leaves little opportunity to fully appreciate the wonders of life beyond. However, the real magic happens when we step outside the box and discover the extraordinary.

I was spoiled by the harmony and beauty of nature while I was growing up in a small Eastern European country. It served as a contin-ual reminder of my carefree youth when I would go for walks in the forest with friends and enjoy the clean air. I cannot help but get jealous sometimes of our ease and independence during those days spent in the woods. I am incredibly appreciative of the chance to take in the wild beauty of village life, complete with fields, forests, wild animals, and birds. Looking back now, it feels like a luxurious escape from the chaotic pace of city life.

But as the years went by, I decided to leave my homeland behind. I found myself drawn to the allure of big cities like Hamburg in Germany, Los Angeles, Houston, and Miami. Each city had its own unique charm, captivating me in different ways. However, none of them could compare to the magical scenery of solitude—just me and a serene lake in a forest accompanied by my dog. This newfound luxury became my sanctuary, a place to escape the hustle and bustle of the city and the heavy traffic.

The morning was chilly, and Kiki wasn't too thrilled about the weather. So, I left her at the hotel and ventured off to the mountain alone. The day was really cold but sunny, just before the arrival of the first snowstorm. The road leading up to the mountain was awe-inspiring, and I couldn't help but enjoy the ride. I sang along to the music in my car, taking in the beauty that surrounded me. Unfortunately, the icy conditions prevented me from reaching the mountain's summit, and I parked my car and observed the activities of other visitors. Some people were meditating, others were hiking, and a few were busy capturing pictures. As I observed these diverse activities, I felt reassured that I was exactly where I needed to be at that moment.

Despite a nagging toothache, I refused to let it dampen my spirits. I must admit, I felt a bit lost, unsure of what to do during my time on the mountain. I found a cold stone to sit on, attempting to meditate. However, the stone's freezing temperature forced me to keep moving. I chose a direction and started walking, hoping to find some clarity.

Venturing deeper into the forest, a profound sense of solitude surrounded me as no other presence interrupted my journey. Suddenly, my eyes were drawn to a mesmerizing sight: two trees intertwined at their roots, growing as a unified entity. I was deeply moved by the scene and felt compelled to record the occasion with photos and videos. It was as they were saying: "We are you. You are us. We are one." Overwhelmed with emotion, I found myself hugging each tree, feeling the masculine and feminine energies they exuded. It was a powerful union, nestled in the heart of nowhere or perhaps the very center of everything.

Lost in this moment of connection, a woman with a British accent approached me, witnessing my interaction with nature. Despite a fleeting sense of embarrassment, I greeted her warmly and shared my observation about the trees resembling twin flames. She agreed, mentioning her prior visits to this spot and exuding a sense of familiarity with the surroundings. As she continued her solitary hike, I admired her fearless spirit, realizing that I, too, possessed the courage to explore these enchanting paths alone.

As I continued my journey through the forest, my mood lifted. The snow beneath my feet felt a little icy. I found solace in capturing the beauty of the surroundings through my camera lens. Like a carefree child, I reveled in the untamed wilderness that surrounded me, experiencing a newfound sense of freedom and happiness. The energy of the natural realm was nothing short of magnificent, and the snow-covered peak of the mountain held a captivating allure. I spent hours exploring the landscape, capturing the play of light and shadow and the majestic wildlife that roamed free. As I hiked higher, I felt a rush of adrenaline and excitement. The crisp air filled my lungs, and the view took my breath away.

Yearning to connect with the spiritual realms of St. Germain and Adama, I encountered a barrier that prevented me from fully communicating with them.

Entering a trance-like state usually came naturally to me, allowing me to let go and connect. However, this time, I struggled to reach that state, leaving me slightly frustrated. The persistent toothache added to my discomfort. Determined to find solace, I continued walking, channeling Reiki energy into my being. Normally, this practice would quickly transport me to a state of tranquility. Step by step, I moved forward, pausing intermittently to close my eyes and take a few more steps. Then, a voice echoed in my mind, instructing me to turn back once I finished with Reiki.

Upon reviewing the pictures I had taken, a revelation struck me. Almost every snapshot captured the subtle radiance of a violet sphere with a blue mark at the edge, shining close to my cheek in perfect alignment with the prior location of my ache. It was a tiny yet irrefutable entity, casting a soft glow of blue-violet luminance on my cheek. Astonishingly, the pain had vanished, slipping from my memory until I returned to my hotel room.

In my perception, the shade of violet mirrored the transformational might of Saint Germain's Violet Flame, while the touch of blue mirrored Adama's, the Blue Ray, essential nature. Both are spiritual entities that have left significant imprints on humanity's guidance and protection throughout history.

Adama is a revered spiritual figure, believed to be the High Priest of the ancient civilization of Lemuria. Following the demise of Lemuria, Adama and his followers retreated to an ethereal city beneath Mount Shasta, known as Telos, the City of Light.

Conversely, Saint-Germain is a mythical character who has lived through numerous lifetimes and attained enlightenment. He is frequently linked with alchemy, spiritual metamorphosis, and the Violet Flame, believed to convert negative energy into positive. Saint-Germain is also thought to be a master among the ascended masters, a collection of highly advanced spiritual entities that shepherd humanity toward elevated consciousness levels.

The realization dawned on me that I had indeed had a profound encounter with both entities. Deep within, I knew the truth.

16

Connection to Lemuria and Mount Shasta

On the way back to Los Angeles a profound sense of anticipation washed over me. It was as if the universe whispered that my return to Mt. Shasta would not be far off and that this next visit would unveil hidden mysteries previously concealed from my understanding. The time was ripe for discovery, and I eagerly embraced the path that lay ahead.

In LA I participated in a group meditation aimed at exploring the Akashic records even more. I had two specific questions that I wanted to have answered. The first question concerned my recurrent dreams, which I firmly feel have something to do with the collapse of the lost continent of Lemuria. In these dreams, I always see a huge wave heading toward the land, and then I see it all from above as the water swallows everything up and nothing is to save. It was all gone. I yearned to understand the significance and meaning behind these dreams, as well as their connection to Lemuria's demise.

The second question stemmed from a curious encounter where someone mentioned that if I feel a strong pull towards Mount Shasta, as I undeniably do, it might indicate the presence of someone awaiting me there. Intrigued by this possibility, I aimed to uncover any information regarding my past experiences during the time of Lemuria and identify the individual who might be patiently waiting for me on Mount Shasta.

So with a set intention, I started my journey, I found myself in a magnificent large library. As I took in the surroundings, a young girl of around ten, but with wisdom beyond her years, approached me and warmly greeted me. She softly grasped my hand and urged me to follow her. Together, we passed through a doorway of shimmering golden light. The little child changed dramatically as soon as we stepped inside the door. She now appeared to be a little girl of five to six years old, radiating an aura of wisdom and familiarity.

Momentarily taken aback, I paused to gather my thoughts. Sensing my hesitation, she looked at me with a cute smile and affectionately called me "mom," inviting me to join her. As the little girl continued to play, I felt a surge of curiosity and asked her about the person waiting for me on Mt. Shasta, in Telos. To my surprise, she responded with a confident "yes" and referred to him as her daddy. I was curious, so I followed up to find out what had happened to me. With a serene expression, she explained that during the fall of Lemuria, both she and I lost our lives and went underwater. However, her daddy had moved to Telos and had been patiently waiting for us to realign ever since.

For the reunion to take place, she said that I needed to raise my vibration. She mentioned that she was currently in an Angel Realm, while I was still experiencing life in 3-D. To reunite with her daddy, I needed to elevate my vibration and transcend the limitations of the physical plane.

I asked her about her father's name. But suddenly, my critical mind began to interject, bombarding me with various names and causing confusion. Sensing my internal struggle, the little girl paused. At that very moment, I sensed a comforting and familiar energy standing behind me. The powerful presence almost swallowed me with its intensity. A feeling of love surrounded me, along with a soothing voice that affectionately called me "darling." It seemed as though this presence had been silently by my side, offering unwavering support and helping to lift my spirits.

The voice assured me that indeed, he has been helping me every step of the way, guiding me towards higher consciousness and aligning our vibrations for our eventual reunion. He emphasized that he had been helping me choose the path of greater knowledge and love by giving me little prods, synchronicities, and inspirational moments.

Tears welled up in my eyes as I realized the magnitude of this support. It was a profound realization that I was not alone on this journey and that there was a divine force looking out for me and guiding me toward a reunion with my counterpart from the past. It was clear that the process of raising my vibration was not just for my benefit but for the greater purpose of reuniting with my family and soul companions and experiencing the love and support that had been missing in this lifetime.

I understood that the journey toward higher consciousness was not just about personal growth but also about reconnecting with the deep bonds that transcend time and space. It was a reminder that we are never truly alone and that there are forces at play, both seen and unseen, guiding us towards love, compassion, and unity.

As I reflected on the profound experiences and revelations of the meditation, I acknowledged that there was still much work to be done on myself. The journey toward higher consciousness and reunion with my counterpart was not a destination but an ongoing process of self-discovery and growth. I understood that to fully align with my true self and raise my vibration, I needed to delve deeper into my inner workings. This meant exploring my fears, limiting beliefs, and patterns that no longer served me. It meant embracing vulnerability and facing the shadows within me with compassion and understanding.

I also recognized the importance of self-care and self-love in this transformative journey. Taking the time to nurture my physical, mental, and emotional well-being was essential for my growth and the elevation of my energy. This meant establishing healthy boundaries, practicing mindfulness, and participating in things that made me happy and fulfilled. This process was not just about achieving perfection or reaching a final destination but rather about embracing the continuous evolution of my being.

17

Mount Shasta is Calling

Interestingly, during my journey back to LA, I had a lingering feeling that I would return to Mt. Shasta for an extended period. Though I initially dismissed the thought, over time, I found myself drawn to information about Adama and Telos, receiving his telepathic messages. He began preparing me to spend time on Mt. Shasta to write not only one but two books. Initially, I doubted my ability to accomplish this assignment, given that English isn't my native language and my writing experience is limited. I thought, "You, guys, have a great sense of humor".

But despite my doubts, I had already envisioned the titles and covers for my two books, and they resonated deeply with me. This recollection brought me back to a regression hypnosis session with Jeff the previous summer, where the subconscious encouraged me to write. Both my father and sister are writers, and even my mother has authored a few articles. I was the only one hesitating, questioning my capabilities.

After contemplating for a few days, I decided, "Why not?" It felt like the universe had presented me with an opportunity, and it sounded like an adventurous project. With my lease ending in the summer and a sense of freedom, I embraced the challenge and chose to embark on this writing journey.

After I made up my mind to go to Mt. Shasta, I started to receive more information on how to prepare for it. I began attracting people with valuable tips and information, and I also came across Paul of Venus. I will write about my experience with him in my next book. I also started getting more insides from Adama, and he wanted me to gather all available information on how to write a book quickly. He suggested bringing a recorder to record messages and finding an app that could transcribe the recordings into text. This approach seemed promising, and with support, I realized it was possible.

As I started making a solid to-do list, my doubts began to fade away. I researched the area for short-term rentals and tours. I was advised that for the first three days, I needed to clear the old energy from LA by relaxing, walking, and meditating. On the third day, I was supposed to do a four-hour tour with Paul of Venus and visit the Telos Portal. The writing process would commence on the fourth day with new energy and readiness. I was instructed to get water from a natural spring and avoid sugar and meat, among other requirements. Each day, I was to visit different places to get in a receptive state and receive messages from Adama, who had valuable information to share, and I was chosen to do it.

As I delved deeper into the topic, I began mentally packing my belongings and planning the big move. I discovered other books written in Mt. Shasta by authors who felt a similar calling. Some had relocated permanently, while others stayed for a month or a few months to finish writing. However, we all shared the common experience of being called and accepting that call.

The excitement was growing bigger with each passing day. Everything was unfolding fast. I knew the preparation was going on at full speed. They (my spirit guides) were not kidding, so neither was I. It felt like the right thing to do for me. I felt like I was coming closer to discovering who I am and my history.

But as I settled in to begin writing the chapter, a wave of doubt crept in, causing me to question my capabilities for the task ahead.

Thoughts of whether I was truly prepared or if there might be a better candidate for the job started swirling in my mind. Just then, a telepathic message from Adama pierced through my doubts, sensing my uncertainty and offering a reassuring presence:

"My darling, you are doing the right thing. You were chosen because we know that you are the right person for it. Don't worry; you have our support and protection. You are divinely guided. Together, we have a huge project ahead of us. You have been prepared for it for years. You are ready. And you will be fine. Adama."

My cheeks flushed with embarrassment as he discovered me lost in my negative thoughts, tears welling in my eyes. However, his message radiated love, care, and support, reassuring me that I had a strong pillar of support to lean on as I tackled this daunting project.

I find great comfort in the way my spirit guides call me "darling." It fills me with a sense of security and protection, making me feel never alone. This endearing term first started being used around the time I was planning my trip to Mount Shasta last year. It's a small gesture that brings me immense warmth and reassurance, especially in times of uncertainty. I am grateful to have spirit guides who show such love and care towards me, always ensuring that I am safe and supported. Each time I hear them say "darling," it reminds me of the unique connection we have and the unwavering love they have for me. I feel truly fortunate to have such a nurturing and loving presence in my life.

18

Past Life as Madame de Pompadour

It had been some time since my introductory regression session with Jeff. I had new queries and life challenges that I sought insight on. This led me to cross paths with Charbel, another amazing and gifted practitioner.

The following day, I reached out to Charbel and asked if he was open to doing a session. To my delight, he agreed, and we booked an appointment for the following weekend. The anticipation was overwhelming as I counted down the days until my session. I was excited but also somewhat nervous. My first quantum healing hypnosis with Jeff had been a profound experience, and I wasn't sure what to expect this time.

On the morning of the session, I began envisioning the kind of past life I desired to witness. I wished to see how Elizabeth secretly gave birth to her son. But quickly I realized I was attempting to control the session and needed to let go. I understand that we must trust our subconscious to choose our past lives, and we need to trust that it knows what we need to see and why. This is the advice I share with my clients: not to try to dictate the session but to trust the process and let it unfold. I caught myself controlling the session in my mind. It was unusual for me. I decided to follow my own advice and let go of all the preconceived notions.

Upon my arrival at the destination, the atmosphere instantly evoked a sense of home. The surroundings were warm and inviting, aesthetically arranged to suit the upcoming regression session. To help me unwind and soothe my senses, I was presented with a cup of calming herbal tea. In anticipation of the unfamiliarity of the new place, I had packed my cherished pair of warm socks to foster a sense of comfort.

In our dialogue, we delved into the complexities and queries concerning my present life. Strangely, though, I overlooked discussing my past life as Madame de Pompadour, and no questions were raised about it either. The truth was, I didn't seek any validation concerning that life, as its clarity was already engraved in my mind. My curiosity and questions were solely directed towards Elizabeth I. My fascination with her life, her power, and the challenges she faced was something I needed to understand, and I knew this session would provide the answers I sought.

The room was dimly lit and quiet. I closed my eyes, took a deep breath, and tried to clear my mind. I started to relax. I could feel my heartbeat slowing down, and I felt a sense of calm wash over me. I knew I needed to trust my subconscious and let it lead me through this journey. As his voice started to guide me toward profound tranquility, I could sense my awareness fading, transcending the boundaries of time and space. Concurrently, Dolores Cannon's voice seamlessly entered the session, echoing the same words as Charbel. Initially, I was uncertain about who to pay attention to, but then I realized it didn't matter.

With each passing moment, I could feel the connection with my current life fading away, replaced by images and sensations from a completely different era. I felt as though I was speeding through the air, similar to an airplane coming in for a landing. Everything below me blurred into a single streak due to my speed. But as my pace started to reduce, I could make out the green fields and the road below.

Another Meeting With Madame

C: What do you see down there below?

V: Greenfield... summertime...a lot of green grass and the road. I just saw the carriage pass by, I think with four horses and with bells. I don't see it anymore.

C: Is there anyone driving this carriage?

V: Yes. I think there was a lady...in a carriage. The type of carriage that can be unfolded for the summer.

C: Are you already in a physical body?

V: I am kind of standing by the side and absorbing this carriage.

C: Do you have a body?

V: I want to slip into that lady's body. I don't know why.

C: So you are absorbing the scene?

V: Yes. I am absorbing from above, but I have the feeling it's my body.

C: Can you look down and see if you have feet?

V: Yes, I see pointed shoes with feathers on the side.

C: What are you wearing?

V: Something fluffy, like wide fabric with a lot of volume around the arms and tight around the wrists.

C: Do you feel the body is male or female?

V: Female.

C: Young or old?

V: Young-ish.

C: What are you doing in that field?

V: We are going somewhere...We are driving...we are on the way somewhere.

C: Do you know where you are going?

V: It's a long way; I can't see. We're going to visit someone.

C: Are you still on the way?

V: We are approaching some kind of structure. A big building, like a castle, with a huge stone   wall. What I see is a protective wall, and you need to go through the gate to go inside.

C: Are you married?

V: I don't feel like it. I am feeling a little flirty.

C: What was the color of the dress that you were wearing?

V: The sleeves are white. I see cleavage...nice bust... a tight cream-colored dress.

C: Is it a fitted dress?

V: It is fitted on the top, but from the waist down, it is going fluffier, and with volume, it is a long one. I'm not sure, but I think I see the life of Madame de Pompadour. That Rococo.

At that moment, I felt a little bit confused. Why was I being shown the same past life that I had seen before? I was aware of my past life as Madame de Pompadour, and I didn't need proof of that. However, there must have been a reason why the subconscious was showing me this exact past life but in a different setting.

C: Have you been there before?

V: Yeah, I had a life there that I am aware of. Based on the dress and carriage, it might be it.

C: Let's move backward to before that happened and see what got you into this situation. We are moving backward now, and you can tell me about it. You are there now. What do you see?

V: I'm alone somewhere, walking. Forest or field...forest. I have no idea what I'm doing there by myself.

C: What is there around you?

V: Nothing. Just wildness. I'm singing. It feels like I am flirty...bubbly...bubbly and flirty, that kind of...maybe silly, but smart. I think I have a plan. I don't know why.

C: Do you know what the plan is?

V: No, but I'm feeling very intellectual and wise, and I am using my fluffiness for something. I don't know what yet.

C: You don't know what you're doing there?

V: I have a feeling that I have a plan, but I don't see anybody. In my mind, I have a plan. I am singing and just being happy.

I was instructed to leave that scene and move to another important day.

C: What is happening?

V: I am part of the kin...I am in the castle.

C: Are you already inside of it?

V: Yeah, I am one of them. I live there.

C: What do you do there?

V: I think the plan I was thinking about has worked out perfectly.

C: So, what were you thinking about in terms of how to get inside the castle?

V: I don't know. But it seems the plan has already worked out. What I wanted to do. Now that I am in this palace or castle, I am very important...one of the important people in the castle. She is dressed nicely. Wealthy.

C: Do you know where this castle is located?

V: It comes to mind that it's Versailles, the Palace of Versailles. I see gardens in front of it.

C: Describe the gardens for me.

V: Well-kept, when you see the palace from afar, a well-kept beautiful garden, green beautiful trees, and all together with a garden palace make a beautiful, almost surreal picture.

C: Are you alone? By yourself now?

V: Now, when I'm looking at the palace from the side, I am alone, yes...but it seems like the adrenaline is kicking in because the vibe is different. It's a higher level than I had before. It's almost giving me shivers that my plan worked out. And I got it.

C: So, what was the plan?

V: I think...to get into the royalty life or something.

C: Are you married?

V: No. I have a lover.

C: Does he live in the castle?

V: Yes.

C: What does he do in the castle?

V: He is a king.

C: So, are you a mistress?

V: Yes.

C: Do you have a name?

V: Yes. Madame de Pompadour.

C: How did you get to meet a king?

V: In the forest, in the bush where I was.

C: How did you meet him?

V: Being silly...he paid attention to my silliness. Being fluffy and flirty, just enjoying myself. That's what caught his attention.

C: What's the king's name?

V: Louis.

C: What is the number?

V: XV.

C: Are you happy?

V: Yeah.

C: That's what you wanted?

V: Kind of. I had to sacrifice some things.

C: What did you have to sacrifice?

V: My daughter.

At that moment, tears welled up in my eyes, and feelings of guilt washed over me. I became overwhelmed with emotions, and my voice became shaky.

C: You had a daughter?

V: Yes.

In my mind, I saw a portrait of a little girl with rounded cheeks, and I had the feeling that this was my nephew in my current life, my godson.

C: Was she from a previous marriage?

V: Yes. The king didn't accept her. When I was accepted to be his mistress, I already had a little girl, and I brought her to the palace. He didn't show his disapproval, but he did everything to push the child away and get her out of the way. He was kind of jealous that I spent some time with my daughter.

C: What happened to the father of your daughter?

V: We got divorced, he just stayed out of the scene. He could not do anything against the king. He just accepted it.

C: And what happened to your daughter?

V: She was sent to school, but the main reason was just to get her out of sight.

C: Were you able to see her or check on her?

V: No, I was involved in the court. I had things to do; I had responsibilities. I didn't give much time to my child.

C: How does it make you feel?

V: Horrible.

C: So, you never married the king?

V: No. He was married.

C: So you were only a mistress?

V: Yes. Kind of a favorite mistress.

As the scene shifted to another significant moment in the life we were observing, my attention was immediately drawn to a unique piece of adornment. Instead of the usual jewelry, it was a delicate woven fabric accessory with pearls designed to accentuate the cleavage, adding a touch of elegance and charm to any special occasion. I'm not entirely certain if I can take credit for this masterpiece, as I only truly saw its beauty when I carefully draped it around someone's neck to admire how it looked.

C: Are you still living in the castle?

V: Yeah.

C: How old are you now?

V: 38.

C: How long have you been there for?

V: Not sure, but it feels like home. I have been there for a while, and it feels like I know everything already and how it works.

C: Is there anybody who is causing your problems?

V: Yeah, some people don't like my attitude. I don't pay attention to them. I just do my job because I have the support of the king. So they're just obstacles. Some people don't agree with my vision, and since the king is also observing my vision and projecting it to others, they see me as a bad influence. Not always, but in some parts, yes. The king appreciates my vision, respects it, and listens to it.

C: Do you love the king?

V: We do have a connection, but it's more like a flirtatious one. I do like him, but I don't love him. I like him a lot, and he feels very close to me, but there is another part: I'm doing it for a reason.

C: Are you still in love with the father of your daughter?

V: I feel sorry for him.

C: Have you loved him?

V: It was more like childish love. Not sure.

C: How do you feel when I mention him to you?

V: It feels pure and innocent.

C: So, there were no hurt feelings?

V: I just had a big vision. I left everything behind just to pursue this big vision, which I am currently working on.

C: Do you know where this vision is leading you?

V: When you have a plan, you just go for it. That's what I did to get a king. I think I just had this vision. Nothing could stop me, and it feels right to do so. I don't feel guilty...

It feels right; it feels like I was supposed to do that.

Then I was moved to the last day of that life, and I was asked to describe what I saw. All I could see were white clouds all around, nothing else. Often, people go through the experience of death, but for some reason, I chose to skip that part. Later on, I understood that I saw my death experience in the previous regression I described before. There was no need to see it again.

C: Can you feel your body?

V: No.

C: Are you outside of the body?

V: I think so.

C: How did you leave the body?

V: As I always do.

C: Did you die?

V: Yes. The vehicle is no longer needed. I am done.

C: How did it end?

V: I just exited...I left my body on Earth. I see pure light now.

C: How does it feel?

V: Home, finally.

Then Charbel replied that there is a lesson and a purpose to every existence. What lessons did that life teach you, and why did you have to live it?

V: When you set something in your mind, you just go for it.

No obstacles can stop you; just have the vision and follow every step to achieve it.

Go for it. Don't look to the sides; there are always obstacles and distractions. Go forward.

When you set the goal, hold it in your mind and don't get distracted or demotivated. If something is not going the way you want it to go, eventually you're going to go and get it.

C: What is the purpose of that lifetime?

V: To experience power and influence and to create a history that will be admired and cherished for many years to come.

Deep Conversation with the Subconscious

Moving forward, Charbel will engage in direct dialogue with the subconscious or SC (referred to as "they"– the collective energy). To proceed to the final stage of the session, he began addressing my questions from the list I brought with me. He was also curious why they were highlighting that one specific life among all the others and what kind of hidden secrets and meanings were waiting to be uncovered in the details of that past.

SC: Because she needed to see that when she doesn't belong to a certain level or community, she can still manage to be a part of it. Even if she thinks she doesn't belong. She came from being a normal woman and became a part of the court. She became one of the most important people and part of a group that you might think she doesn't belong to, but she made herself a part of it by working hard. In this life, she refuses to climb higher up the ladder because she is afraid of becoming famous and has some fears, but that life is a great example that showing that from nowhere, she can go somewhere, be somewhere, and create history.

C: But what is causing her fear?

SC: That people are going to judge her. Judgment.

C: How are you going to help her?

SC: She is writing a book right now. She is clearing a lot of her issues by writing, and she is also realizing that when she's writing, she is recalling her past memories and the lives that she's really proud of, that she was powerful. So she's basically collecting all those pieces, piece by piece, getting herself together into one piece. All her past lives—that's who she is today—are basically like she's collecting one missing piece after another and creating her own entity in this life.

C: Since you mentioned she is writing her book, what else can she write about other than the things she is writing about now?

SC: The first book is based on her own experiences. It's going to be more like an autobiography about her past lives and also her experiences during the guided meditations or Akashic records where she found out about her past or other parts of herself. But there are going to be more books to follow. She already has an idea she loves, but the first book is mainly about her own experiences.

C: So, is she on the right path with this project?

SC: Yes.

C: And why are all those challenges facing her?

SC: To make her stronger and see if she truly wants to do this, she should hold on to it or give up and say it's maybe not something for her.

C: What about the financial struggle?

SC: She needs to set priorities, determining what is most important for her at that moment. As soon as she sets all the priorities, everything is going to fall in the right direction. What is most important for her? She is asking for help, and she wants a shortcut; she wants the answers right away, but we want her to go inside and think for herself. She is creating her path.

C: Are there any money blocks?

SC: Not really; she has already worked on them. There are just a few obstacles in her way.

C: Obstacles like what?

SC: Money. Lack of money.

C: How is she going to solve this?

SC: She needs to learn how to set intentions and priorities, focusing on what is most important. Money can be a great distraction for everyone because a lack of money can divert you from your life purpose.

C: True.

SC: And if you feel weak, think, "Maybe this isn't for me." You might consider finding a side hustle to help you survive. What is the purpose of your life? What is your life's goal? What do you want to achieve? Therefore, you may need to step outside your comfort zone and find a side hustle for a few hours or days to overcome those obstacles. Some people are willing to take risks and focus on their main goal. For example, she is determined to continue pursuing her passion for writing a book. She believes that distractions are inevitable, but she perseveres and continues writing regardless.

C: How are you going to help her make an income?

SC: There is money coming. There might be a time when it's going to be tough, but it's not for a long time. Once she moves to Mount Shasta, she is going to do quantum healing hypnosis from Mount Shasta while working on her book.

C: So, you want her to move to Mount Shasta?

SC: Yes. Yes, and she agreed to it. It's not forever, but she needs to spend some time there. Consider it a continuing education in her life. She needs to be closer to the Masters. She needs to spend more time alone, meditating. She is going to receive messages, which she will share in her books, but we need her there physically.

C: How are you going to help her find the right apartment and the money to move?

SC: Exactly the way she has moved from the East Coast to the West Coast with $200 in her pocket. And here we go; she made it. We are always helping her. The right people and the right circumstances are always going to make themselves present.

C: Can you do a body scan?

SC: Yes, she is complaining about her vision.

C: True, what can you do about that?

SC: She is refusing to see some things for what they are, but we're showing her something she's refusing to accept. That's why she is losing her vision.

C: Things like what?

SC: That she is powerful. She has a God inside of her. She is the universe. She became a little more open to this concept through her clients, but there is still a little resistance. Once she accepts that she has power, she can create rain, and she can stop the rain. She has already done that. She changed the path of the hurricane so it didn't hit Miami when she was there. She did it; it was her job. Just face it and see it for what it is.

C: Are you going to heal her vision today?

SC: We can improve it a little bit.

C: Why not all?

SC: She needs to do her homework.

C: So you can clear it for her, and after this session, she will continue with her homework. You know vision is very important, especially for someone who is writing and spending a lot of time in front of a computer.

SC: Yeah.

As I paused to catch my breath, I felt the air filling my lungs deeply, almost like I was inhaling pure vitality. Charbel began to move on to the next question, but the

subconscious urged him to wait just a moment longer until the healing process was complete.

C: What about her dizziness?

SC: She is getting a lot of downloads. It's okay. It's going to settle. She has been prepared for the next level, so...stay grounded. That's something she needs to go through to reach the next level. Her body, her physical body, is also expanding to accept bigger downloads, and there are more significant downloads coming, step by step. Sometimes she's stressed out and doing all the earthly stuff that keeps her out of balance. When she gets her next download, it's kind of too much for her. That's when she feels dizzy. However, when she keeps herself grounded, she doesn't feel dizzy but still receives the downloads. Just stay grounded and be aware of the energies she is receiving.

Continuing with the body scan, a few issues were detected and cleared.

SC: Her neck.

C: What is causing her neck to be stiff?

SC: Her posture. She is not using the right posture to read and write and has been sitting for hours.

C: Will you fix it for her today?

SC: Yeah, we can remove that buildup and adjust a little bit. (At that point, I turned my head to the sides and up and down.) She needs to stretch more. She is not sleeping on a good pillow. She has a better one. I am sending light to soothe her neck, but first, she needs to replace that pillow. That will make her feel a lot better.

C: Thank you. What else?

SC: Feet, not feeling the ground underneath, she is like flying and not finding the right place in her life. Also, she needs to walk barefoot at times, as the shoes she was wearing were not right for her. It's good that she threw away the slippers. They were not right for her, either. By walking with just her socks on or barefoot, she will notice an improvement.

C: Can you fix this issue as well?

SC: The improvement will come with time. We can alleviate cramps. She needs to use the massage ball with needles she has at home and just put it under her sole. There are some spots she needs to activate on her feet. It's also going to improve her vision. She can do it on her own. She has some massage tools. Right now, I'm touching that spot with a big toe—that spot she needs to work on. It's going to improve her foot health; her headaches are going to go away; and it will also improve her vision.

I could feel the pain from a toe pressing into my sole; they were showing me the spot.

C: What about her hormone levels and diet?

SC: Hormones are fine. Her diet is good. It is great that she removed meat from her diet. We are proud of her for that. She might want to include some juices and smoothies for added vitamins.

There was a little bit of unhealthy bacteria in her stomach; it came from the water. The water in her apartment building is not good. But once she moves, it is going to improve by itself. We already told her to drink only spring water on Mount Shasta and not to consume bottled water at all. The tap water on Mount Shasta is healthy. However, the tap water in her apartment building is not good at all, and even the filter doesn't help. She is buying bottled water to drink, which is fine, but she still uses tap water for cooking. This is creating bad bacteria in her stomach.

C: What about her chakras? Are they balanced?

SC: The root chakra is a little bit out of balance.

C: Can you balance it for her?

SC: Yes...her heart chakra is also.

C: Can you work on that as well?

SC: She needs to watch her thoughts and her feelings. She has been managing well lately; she became more aware of her emotions and thoughts and started to control them. But once something happens, like bad news, they still throw her off her feet. She needs to find the balance to get back into her element and not allow bad energy to take over for too long. This is for everybody as well. Bad emotions, fear, and stress are all low-vibration energy. You lose connection with the source when you allow those negativities to take over. To restore the connection, you need to keep your balance and find your inner core to connect again. And when you feel connected you won't panic.

Her ears. That part is a little bit blocked (I was showing which part). That's because she allowed herself to hear what she was not supposed to hear, like negativity and being around negative influences. That's why she feels pressure in her ears. Just accept it and let go; it's in the past. Allow yourself to make mistakes and let them go. What's done is done. Also, there is some fogginess in her brain.

C: Are you going to remove that?

SC: Yes...it comes from her thoughts that are causing the fog. We are removing it as if with a vacuum, sucking it out. She is going to have more clarity.

C: Are there any energy blocks?

SC: Yes, her knees. She is refusing to walk forward.

C: Can you clarify that?

SC: Yes, but she needs to work on that as well. She needs to remove the fear that she might be punished for spreading out the information that she signed up for before she came here. Eventually, she will need to cross that river of fear and insecurity, align with herself, and fulfill her mission and her life purpose.

C: Why did she feel the vibration in her body and the feeling of nausea?

SC: She experienced stress and received downloads. When she is stressed and receives a lot of new energy without alignment, it causes her to feel like vomiting. As we mentioned before, she needs to maintain a high vibration and stay in alignment. More downloads will continue to come. When she is stressed, she is out of alignment, and the downloads still need to occur. If she allows herself to become stressed, she will not be able to handle it.

C: What are all those issues with her apartment? What is this for?

SC: If she were comfortable there, she would renew the lease and stay. The same goes for the clients: if she had a lot of clients, she would be busy at this location, but she needs to move. It might take her until summertime when her lease expires, but she is not going to even think about renewing it. She will be happy to be out of there.

C: But why do you want her to move to that area? What is special about it that is not here?

SC: Mount Shasta. She knows about it. There is Telos underneath Mount Shasta. She's aware of it. Adama has contacted her as well. Mount Shasta is calling people. You need to receive a call to move there. She can call you, and she can also kick you out of there. She can make your life miserable, and you have no choice but to move away. But she is going to call certain people at a certain time for future education, evolution, and a learning experience. And she needs this learning experience to better do her job on Earth. This is when we are approaching the deadline for her to do that. And she has accepted the call. She is not going to be there forever, just for a certain period of time. We cannot say how many months or years; when she is done, she's going to know she's done.

C: Is there any connection between her and Adama?

SC: Yes, he is her teacher. She's going to be working closely with him.

C: So, that's why she was called to go to Mount Shasta?

SC: Yes...Saint Germain will also be present. He will teach her many things during her time there. She will have the opportunity to see him in physical form. Additionally, she will meet people who are not widely known. To truly learn about and connect with them, she must be present in that community. These individuals are incredibly valuable and important in her life, playing a crucial role in her next steps and personal evolution.

C: Why is she receiving all that information about Saint Germain?

SC: Because he is her master. He is preparing her to impart the information he knows, which she can then share on Earth while she has a physical body. Together, they are going to write a book. Saint Germain, an Ascended Master, will guide her as she uses her body to write and share knowledge with people. And he has been preparing her for years in different incarnations.

Even if it was for a short period, there was an activation made that now, once she's going to meet him, she's going to be prepared. Also, her physical body is adjusting to the energies that she can handle.

C: What is her mission exactly? Is she on the right path with her mission?

SC: Yes.

C: Could you tell her more about it?

SC: Her mission is to expand consciousness on Earth. She is aware of it, but she doesn't want to admit it. She is part of the awakening process. While she doesn't believe she has the power to assist people in their awakening journey, she does possess that ability.

And that life as Madame de Pompadour, Elizabeth...we showed Elizabeth because Elizabeth yelled at people that she had power, and now Volha says that she doesn't have power. Who am I to do that? We want her to know that she used to have that power. She had a great influence and people are still writing and talking about her. She has already had other incarnations, but people are still talking about her previous incarnations. She does have power, and she has the power now to help humanity expand consciousness on the planet.

C: So, was she Elizabeth in her past life, or was it just an imprint?

SC: It was her life, her father was Robert (Robert Dudley). Yes, she got it right.

C: What can you tell her about that past life?

SC: She had great power; she led wars, managed people, and created history as a woman. And now she is a woman, and she cannot even open her mouth.

C: Why did she have to incarnate with her father?

SC: To learn the lesson...and her mother.

C: What is the lesson behind it?

SC: The lesson is to love each other. They are a family, so they have to love each other. There is no choice. They have to learn to love each other...and her mother as well.

C: Was her father Robert Dudley?

SC: Yes.

C: And what about her mom?

SC: Amy...Robert's wife...who had an accident. It was not an accident. She was standing in the way between two lovers, and they got rid of her. That's why she feels heaviness. She feels guilt. That guilt has been following her for years and many incarnations. And that she doesn't get along with her mother as well. She needs to learn to forgive, ask for forgiveness, and learn to love and accept her mother as her mother in this life...you agreed to it!

C: Could you tell her about the relationship between Elizabeth and Francis Bacon?

SC: Yeah, that's her son.

C: He was her son?!

SC: Yes.

C: Was she a part of his life?

SC: Partially. She was so afraid to get her mother's feelings involved that she acted very cold. But on the side, she was following his life, yes.

C: What could you tell her about Elizabeth's life that has an impact on her life now?

SC: Lonely. The lonely life of a powerful woman who could have created a loving relationship, had a child, built a family, lost everything, and simply been a woman. She could have experienced the feelings of being a woman, a lover, and a mother, but she refused to embrace them. Instead, she pushed them away, becoming cold like a robot, suppressing all emotions.

C: But why is a woman like Elizabeth so powerful, but in this life, she's not the same? She doesn't have the same power.

SC: Remember karma: you want to be powerful, and you want to experience what it means to not have the power to even karma. In one life, you want to be wealthy, and in another, you want to be a beggar. You want to experience every side. You want to experience feelings and emotions from everybody on each side. So in that life, she was powerful, but in this life, she is not powerful yet. She has the potential to be, but she needs to work towards it. She must awaken the power within, tap into the memory of that power, a memory of strength, and move forward. She questions why Elizabeth would choose to incarnate in a village somewhere in Eastern Europe. It is to follow a path, evolve, experience, grow, and believe in her power. She needs to realize that whatever she dreams of, she can achieve it, but she must first be born into a poor family. She chose to be in that family, knowing that she wanted to see the other side of the coin.

C: You know that she has doubts about her past life. Why is this so? How can we give her more proof?

SC: She is going to make more discoveries about her past that will confirm it. For example, she recently received information about her father out of nowhere, which took her by surprise. She even asked us to stop revealing details because it felt awkward. She had dreams of being intimate with her father when she was in her 20s, and it turned out to be a recall from her past life. At that time, she wasn't aware of it, but once she learned about her past life as Elizabeth and her relationship with Robert, the dream started to make sense. It wasn't just a dream; it was a memory from the past life that now makes sense. There are more things she will understand later that will start to make sense, and all the pieces of the puzzle will come together. Saint-Germain is helping her by presenting all those books to read for confirmation because he knows. He is part of this game as well...Saint-Germain was a big part of her life during King Louis XV's time. They had a connection in that past life too.

C: Does she have any other historical past lives that she needs to know about?

SC: Not that she needs to know at this particular time. We cannot provide her with any additional information, as she needs time to digest the information she already has.

C: Did you give her too much information to digest?

SC: Those two lives are enough for now.

C: Why is she still single?

SC: She needs to finish some projects because she knows who he is, and he is very handsome. She would throw everything away just to be with him and would not follow her path. So we want her to do her project first, and as a final surprise, she's going to get him...as the cherry on the pie, not the cherry first. She needs to get the pie first and then comes the cherry. She has projects to do without him – alone. He's there; he is not going anywhere, but she needs to do her homework.

C: Can you give me a time frame?

SC: Around six months, up to a year.

C: You promised...you promised it before, and it didn't happen.

SC: Well, we didn't promise her anything; we just informed her. However, we don't have a specific timeframe. The timing will depend on when her current project is completed and she can move on to the next one. If she remains stuck on the current project for years, she will only meet him after that. If she continues working on her project as planned, the meeting could happen within a few months to a year. It's not as simple as saying she will meet him in six months and then take a vacation to Hawaii during that time. That would not be beneficial and would postpone the meeting. It's not about the time; it's about how you use the time. What are you doing with the time that is bringing you closer to him?

C: Does she have a home planet?

SC: Yes...Electra. A purple planet.

I Am Electra, One of the Seven Sisters

A few years ago, as I was taking my dog for an early morning walk, a thunderous inner voice resonated in my mind, declaring, "I am Electra, one of the seven sisters." Instantly, an energetic surge seemed to spring from my chest and solar plexus area, triggering a wave of goosebumps across my entire body, causing me to spin around in awe. It was an incredible, potent experience. It felt as though some dormant part of me had been activated. Every time I affirmed, "I am Electra," it seemed to trigger this energy activation, enveloping my entire physical form.

The same sensation rippled through me each time I affirmed this newfound identity as if I was both the caller and recipient of a cosmic message. I was in awe of the transformation taking place within me as if I had connected with an ancient force—a lineage lying dormant in my soul for countless generations.

My curiosity led me to research the Pleiades, the seven sisters, and specifically Electra. In Greek mythology, Electra was the offspring of Atlas, doomed to hold up the world, and the nymph Pleione. I was beginning to grasp that this was more than a spiritual awakening; it was as if a part of my soul, long buried, was being unearthed. I felt a deep connection to the cosmos, a sense of belonging that surpassed the material world.

My bond with Electra deepened. My intuition was sharper, my dreams became more lucid and prophetic, and my senses seemed to harmonize with the world around me. By embracing my bond with Electra, I had awakened a part of myself that was ancient, potent, and deeply connected to the cosmos. It was a journey of self-discovery, self-empowerment, and spiritual awakening.

I never thought I could be from that planet. Yet the birthmarks on my right arm, forming the shape of the seven sisters, provided a profound insight. The birthmarks were not just peculiar skin pigments but a constellation, a sign of my celestial lineage. They were my guide, my compass pointing towards home—a home I never knew I had but somehow always longed for.

C: What are the characteristics of that planet? Can you tell me?

SC: It is similar to fairies and fairy tales—something magical, surreal, almost childish.

C: So...it's a beautiful planet?

SC: Yes, but she wanted to have an experience with all the negativities and emotions, so she's experiencing them now.

C: So...there are no negatives and no emotions?

SC: They are always happy; they're playing. Sometimes it is boring...they're always happy and all the same.

C: So, do you mean the emotions are for entertainment?

SC: Like stress and fear, we don't have it, but she wanted to experience it. She's getting it now.

C: What is the purpose of experiencing all those emotions?

SC: This is for soul evolution. You have different incarnations, and in each incarnation, you experience different emotions. They are also important for your soul and its history, essentially collecting various experiences from different incarnations.

C: When does the soul graduate?

SC: Never – You are always expanding. There is infinity. You can reach higher levels, but there is always room to grow. As you grow, you also teach.

C: Why do they (spirit guides) call her 'darling'?

SC: Saint-Germain calls her 'darling'. He had also spent a lot of time in Europe. It comes from the British.

C: Does she have to move this mid-March or stay longer to finish what she has started?

SC: Keep working on the book. Forget about it for now.

C: So, she doesn't have to move in the middle of March?

SC: Not yet. We will inform her of the exact date later. However, she should start preparing for the move. It is likely to happen between mid-March and summer, but not immediately.

C: How did Elizabeth feel about giving her son away?

SC: Horrible, she suppressed all her emotions and became a very cold, emotionless lady. But deep inside, she was regretting and blaming herself for pushing away all the motherly feelings. She screamed and yelled a lot just to kill that feeling.

C: Are they preparing her for her ascension?

SC: If she wants to...she has done a lot, and she has evolved a lot. If she wants to, she can ask us, and we will guide her, but we know that she doesn't want it. She wants to keep working on the planet, on Earth, and she wants to have a baby. She wants to experience it. She wants to balance her karma. She wants to give birth to a baby. She wants to create a loving relationship to experience what it feels like to have a husband and a child, and she has a right to do that. She doesn't have to ascend. She can keep going and just balance her karma; what Elizabeth could not create, she can create now in this life.

C: What is her relationship to Jesus?

SC: She will come to it later, but they do have a connection.

C: Is there anything she needs to know about Sharula Dux?

SC: It was her on Mount Shasta...she's going to be around. She (Volha) can reach out to her anytime she needs help; she's going to hear her and help her, and once Volha is in Mount Shasta and needs help, she can reach out to Sharula for guidance to connect her with people who can help locally.

I was prompted to ask about her after a recent telepathic encounter where a voice introduced herself as Sharula Dux, a Princess of Telos, during one of my meditations. Her presence intrigued me, and I wanted to know why she had come. She reminded me of a prior agreement with my spirit guides to notify me when it was time to move. After confirming my recollection, she said that she was here to deliver a warning that the time for action was drawing near.

I typically receive guidance from my spiritual guides as a heads-up when it's time for me to relocate, allowing me to prepare, pack my belongings, and plan for the transition. Sometimes, the exact timing of the move is uncertain. However, these moves usually signify a shift to a new location for a specific purpose, such as embarking on a new project, learning something new, or fulfilling a commitment that I made before coming to Earth.

C: How is she evolving on her path since she started practicing quantum healing hypnosis?

SC: Greatly, we are proud of her. Her consciousness is expanding and will continue to evolve, with the next step on the horizon.

C: You know that she has an ex-lover?

SC: Yes.

C: How is he affecting her life?

SC: He is draining her energy.

C: How can she stop that?

SC: Stop communicating; cut the cord.

C: Just like that, so easy?

SC: Yes. Don't answer his messages; just ignore him.

C: Is it going to be easy for her to do so?

SC: No, he's kind of the stronger one, but he has a mission to distract her from her purpose. Sometimes he does it well, and sometimes not. Occasionally, he shakes her, making her feel unsteady on the ground. He is also teaching her a lesson on being grounded and cautious about where her energy goes—her communications, her surroundings—so she does not lose her energy and then asks for our help. When she stops giving away her energy to people who are unnecessary and do not help her in her life, she will have more energy for herself and her projects, and she will ask for help less often. Of course, we are helping her, but she also needs to be aware of where her energy and focus are directed.

C: How is she going to feel after the healing process is complete?

SC: Lighter. Much lighter.

C: Does everything look okay?

SC: Yes. She needed this reset to clear any obstacles from her path. We want her to just keep going forward without looking to the sides or behind. The most important thing is what is now and in front of her; everything else is not important.

C: Do you have any last messages for her?

SC: Keep going. Don't stop...we are always supporting you. We are always here to help, even turning the impossible into possible. Even if it's not your turn to receive something, we can manipulate digital numbers and make it your turn now if necessary. We can manipulate time, shift realities, and do whatever it takes for you. But if it's not meant to be, we will do everything to prevent it and you need just to accept it. If we are blocking something for you, trust that there is a reason behind it. Some things may not make sense now, but they will become clear later... just trust.

The session was intense yet enlightening. I gained a deep understanding of the life of Elizabeth I, her resilience, and her fears. I discovered the power she held, the sacrifices she made, the challenges she faced, and the loneliness she endured. I learned about her strength, her wisdom, and her unwavering dedication to her kingdom.

These insights not only quenched my curiosity but further assisted me in recognizing my advantages and disadvantages. The session gave me a fresh perspective and a new lens through which to view my current life. It made me realize that I was much stronger than I believed and that the trials and tribulations I currently face are just a part of my journey, just like they were for Elizabeth I.

As I emerged from the hypnosis, I felt a deep connection to Elizabeth I and Madame de Pompadour, two powerful women who left a lasting impact on history during the 16th and 18th centuries, respectively. Both women have defied societal expectations and wielded power in their respective spheres, leaving a lasting impact on the history of their countries and the world. Their legacies as strong, independent women who navigated the complexities of politics, power, and influence continue to inspire and captivate people to this day.

The session ended, leaving me with a sense of peace and clarity. It was as though a weight had been taken off my shoulders. It was a unique and enlightening experience, one that I will cherish for the rest of my life.

This experience was a powerful reminder that it's essential to trust the process and allow the subconscious to guide us. It's not about fulfilling our fantasies or curiosities, but about understanding our past lives in a way that can help us grow and evolve in our current lives. I felt humbled and grateful for this enlightening journey, and I was ready to share this insight with the world.

19

Symbolic Dream: Key to My Soul

The dream I had the other night was truly extraordinary. In the ethereal world of my slumber, I found myself transported to the familiar setting of my grandmother's old bedroom. Though she has long since passed away, I have always felt a deep connection with her that transcends the boundaries of life and death.

As I stood in the room, I was immediately drawn to her bed, where an array of keys of varying shapes and sizes were strewn about, mingling with a heart-shaped hanger. It was as if a mysterious puzzle awaited my deciphering.

At that moment, the realization dawned on me that uncovering the matching key would be no simple feat. The task seemed daunting, as though it would require an eternity to find the one that fits just right. Yet, almost as soon as I embarked on my quest, my eyes fell upon the perfect key. It was as if it had been waiting for me all along, a key that held the power to unlock something profound within me—my very heart, the deepest secrets of my soul. The sense of discovery and connection that washed over me was nothing short of transformative. It felt like my grandma gave me a confirmation of my self-discovery and that I was on the right path.

This dream experience reaffirmed my belief in the interconnectedness of all beings, not just within the tangible realm of our existence but also across the vast expanses of time and space.

We are all interwoven in the grand tapestry of life, our threads crossing and intersecting, creating a beautiful pattern of relationships, experiences, and lessons. This realization is not just about my personal journey but serves as a reminder that we are all part of a larger, universal narrative. Our lives, our stories, are not merely our own but are interconnected with those of every soul we come across.

This energy is not confined by the constraints of time or space. It is eternally flowing, eternally evolving, connecting us all in an intricate dance of life and death, joy and sorrow, creation and destruction. We are one.

BOOK II: FROM MT. SHASTA WITH LOVE

Introduction

Greetings, I am Volha Zhamoitsina, a hypnotherapist and quantum healing hypnosis practitioner. My journey to Mt. Shasta began with a profound calling from my Spirit Guides, urging me to share the transformative experiences I encountered in this sacred place. This book, *From Mt. Shasta with Love*, emerged from a deeper purpose—a response to a call from the universe that I couldn't ignore.

My initial visit to Mount Shasta in November 2023 was nothing short of life-changing. The profound energy of the mountain, the serenity of the landscape, and the spiritual awakenings I experienced marked a pivotal turning point in my journey. The memories of that trip still reverberate through my mind, each one a stepping stone toward deeper self-awareness and spiritual enlightenment. Following this transformative trip, I authored my first book, *BECAUSE I CAN REMEMBER: The Tapestry of Time: Reincarnation Memories and the Soul's Journey of a Hypnotherapist*. This work laid the foundation for what was to come, reflecting on my early revelations and insights. Soon after, my Spirit Guides extended an invitation to return to Mount Shasta for an extended stay, where I would work on my second book.

From Mt. Shasta with Love delves deeply into the extraordinary experiences and spiritual lessons encountered during my time in Mount Shasta. This book offers readers not only a narrative of my personal journey but also a guide to their own spiritual awakening. It illuminates the path to a deeper connection with the divine energies that pulse through Mount Shasta. By sharing my journey, I aim to assist others in expanding their consciousness, raising their vibrations, and embracing the transformative power of spiritual growth.

20

Crossing the River of Uncertainty

I could feel it building—subtle at first, like the whisper of wind before a storm. A quiet nudge in my chest, asking me to let go. It began with a sudden urge to declutter—not just my home, but my entire life. I started releasing what no longer felt aligned. Physical things. Energetic ties. The weight of the past.

Something within me knew: a shift was coming. I needed to travel light.

I couldn't explain why, but Los Angeles—once a place that nurtured me—had begun to feel heavy. Stagnant. As if the walls were closing in around me. I wasn't breathing fully anymore. The city that had once held me now felt like a shell I had outgrown.

And somewhere in my dreams, Mount Shasta began calling.

At first, it was just an image, a thought, a feeling. Then it became louder. More persistent. A pull I couldn't ignore. Shasta represented something I couldn't quite name—freedom, perhaps, or the remembrance of something ancient and sacred that lived inside me.

Yet the idea of leaving everything behind filled me with equal parts excitement and fear. I was standing at a threshold—one foot still in the life I knew, and the other hesitating above a path I couldn't yet see.

The comfort of the familiar is powerful. It wraps around you like a warm blanket, even when it suffocates. I had been walking in circles, repeating lessons I thought I had already mastered. The patterns were so subtle, so cleverly disguised, that I didn't realize how deeply I had been looping.

But the soul always knows when it's time.

There's a moment—often quiet, but unmistakable—when the heart says—Enough.

That moment came. And with it, knowing: If I wanted something different, I had to choose differently.

Stepping into the unknown was not romantic or easy. It felt like standing before a river of uncertainty, it's dark waters swirling with everything I didn't yet understand. The what-ifs, the doubts, the stories that told me I needed to be "sure" before moving forward. But I also knew that clarity would never arrive at the edge. It would only come from the crossing.

So I chose. I chose to listen to the part of me that remembered what freedom feels like. I chose to trust that my longing for the mountain wasn't random. The decision didn't come in one dramatic moment. It was a series of small, brave choices. Saying no to what drained me. Saying yes to intuition. To the path that had no roadmap, only resonance.

Mount Shasta wasn't just a location on a map. It was an initiation. A turning point. A portal into a new way of living and being.

21

The Student Has Arrived

"*When the student is ready the teacher will appear. When the student is truly ready... The teacher will disappear.*"
— Tao Te Ching

During my last Quantum Healing Hypnosis session, the Subconscious reassured me with a calm certainty:

"When the time is right, all necessary arrangements will fall into place—transportation, housing, and the right circumstances."

I held on to that message. It lived inside me like a quiet promise. And yet, as the days passed and my departure from Los Angeles drew near, panic began to surface. Affordable accommodations in Mount Shasta were becoming harder to find. The remaining listings were well beyond what I could justify. The pressure of logistics—the very human side of this leap—was growing.

Still, I kept listening. Though anxiety crept in, I never stopped trusting the presence of my spiritual guides. I knew they were working behind the scenes, orchestrating something I couldn't yet see. I stayed aligned with the knowing that the universe would lead me to the right place—my sanctuary.

And then it appeared.

A secluded guest house, nestled in the forest among the towering pines, quietly revealed itself. I knew the moment I saw it—I had found my haven. Each room offered a view of Mt. Shasta, her snow-capped peak visible from every angle. Her presence filled the space, not just through the windows, but in the atmosphere itself. I could feel her welcoming me.

To my delight, a friend of mine—who had always dreamed of visiting Mount Shasta—decided to join me. It felt like the perfect arrangement, the ideal companion for this unfolding adventure. As we drove toward the mountain, I received a lighthearted, telepathic message from my guides:

"We even arranged a private chauffeur for you."

I laughed. Of course they had. The orchestration was perfect.

Leaving behind the dense buzz of Los Angeles, I felt the shift immediately. As we entered the forest, I could breathe again. The air was rich with pine and damp earth, grounding and alive. The silence was thick and comforting. Everything felt slower, softer. I had arrived at the edge of something sacred.

We reached the guest house just in time to witness a breathtaking sunset. The sky turned violet, casting a magical glow over the landscape. The fading light touched the peak of Mt. Shasta, and for a few suspended moments, the snow turned shades of purple—radiant, ethereal, otherworldly.

I knew this was a message from Saint-Germain, my beloved master guide. This was his signature—his way of greeting me.

This was the sign I had been waiting for. The violet flame above the mountain, signaling the start of a summer filled with growth, teachings, and transformation.

The student had arrived.

As I settled into the stillness of my new surroundings, the forest wrapped itself around me like a protective cloak. The tension I had carried melted into the earth. I surrendered to the rhythm of nature, allowing myself to be held by something ancient and wise.

Everything had unfolded just as it was meant to. I trusted. I had listened. And now, I am here.

22

The Blue Light Beneath the Snow

On our very first day, we made our way toward the mountain herself—Mount Shasta. The drive alone felt like a ceremony. We wound through dense green forests, each bend of the road lifting us higher into thinner air and deeper stillness. The further we climbed, the quieter we became. There's something about ascending toward Mt. Shasta that silences the mind—it softens the edges of thought and prepares you to listen.

When we reached the parking lot, I blinked in surprise. It was full—overflowing with cars, every space taken. I had last visited in late November, when the air was crisp and quiet and only a handful of cars dotted the lot. But now, summer has brought the seekers. The lot pulsed with life.

We set off on the short hike to the entrance, eager to stand at the foot of the mountain and see her famed stone steps once again. The trail wound through a snow-covered landscape, quiet and bright. I pointed out the twin flame trees to my friend as we walked—a pair of tall evergreens, standing side by side like mirrored souls. I've always felt their energy. They remind me of sacred partnership—the kind that transcends time.

Though the air was cool at first, the movement quickly warmed us. We shed our layers as we went—jackets tied around waists, sleeves rolled to elbows—until we were hiking lightly, our steps quick and joyful, breath matching the rhythm of the mountain.

And then, something caught my eye. At first, I thought it was water—maybe someone had spilled something on the snow. But the blue shimmer was everywhere. Subtle, but unmistakable. A faint light, emanating from beneath the snow. I knelt down and touched it. Not cold. Not wet. Just... light. My friend saw it too. We looked at each other, both wide-eyed. It felt like a portal had opened just beneath our feet—quiet, hidden, and humming. I still don't fully understand what we witnessed that day. Only that it was real. And it was beautiful.

As we climbed, we passed dozens of hikers making their descent. Some moved slowly, heavy with gear and stories. One couple paused to speak with us. They told us they'd set out from the parking lot the day before at 3 PM and had spent the night at the summit. "There were over a hundred tents up there," they said, the excitement still fresh in their voices. "Everyone came to sleep beneath the stars."

I pictured it—the top of Mount Shasta lit not just by starlight, but by the soft glow of lanterns and shared dreams. The mountain draws them in—pilgrims, mystics, adventurers. And She holds them all.

By the time we returned to the car, I felt alive. Light. Energized in a way I hadn't felt in a long time. It was more than just a hike—it was a homecoming. The mountain and I, we had reunited. And in her presence, I remembered something I hadn't realized I'd forgotten: that the Earth is speaking, always. That beauty can stop you in your tracks. That mystery still exists.

I left that day full of awe and gratitude. For the snow. For the forest. For the strange blue light and the twin flame trees. And for the mountain, always, for welcoming me back.

23

Mystical Encounter at Pluto's Cave

On the second day, we decided to explore the neighboring town Mc Cloud's, eager to visit all three waterfalls nestled in a pristine forest setting. The scenery was simply breathtaking—lush greenery, the thunderous roar of falling water, and the crisp, fresh air made for a perfect getaway. What impressed us most was how well-maintained and clean the area was, despite being a popular tourist spot. There wasn't a trace of litter, which added to the serenity of the place.

As we wandered through the forest, admiring the picturesque views and capturing countless photos, I received a sudden message to stop and observe a particular tree. As I focused on the tree, I sensed a distinct personality, a consciousness emanating from it. Then came the message: "Envision an entire forest filled with this consciousness." It dawned on me that the tranquil and calming effect of being in the forest stemmed from each tree possessing its own consciousness, collectively creating a forest of awareness.

The message continued, prompting me to contrast this with a bustling city where each person could be seen as a parallel to these sentient trees. In cities, especially living in high-rises, one can feel surrounded by a mix of energies—below, beside, and above—both positive and negative. It struck me deeply how these contrasting environments affect our sense of peace and harmony.

This realization felt like a profound teaching from nature—a reminder of the interconnectedness and consciousness present in all living things. Just as I was reflecting on this, about to leave the forest, I noticed a stone with a naturally formed smiley face, its features clear and joyful. I felt compelled to capture this moment, a simple yet poignant reminder of the high consciousness that can be found even in unexpected places.

Then we decided to visit Pluto's Cave. It was a short drive from our guesthouse near Mount Shasta. Expecting a prominent sign to mark the location, we were surprised to find only a small, nearly invisible sign on the side of the road. It was nothing like the flashy "Welcome to Las Vegas" signs; just a simple marker that we drove past, prompting us to turn around.

We found ourselves on a narrow, broken road in the middle of nowhere, or perhaps, the center of everything. Parking the car, we noticed a red arrow pointing in one direction. We began walking, absorbing the scenery that felt remarkably like Sedona, AZ. The landscape, with its twisting juniper trees, exuded a surreal, high-energy aura that made me feel at peace, at home – much like how I always feel in Sedona.

After some time, I decided to check our location on my GPS, which surprisingly indicated that Pluto's Cave was in the opposite direction. Trusting the GPS, we turned back towards the parking spot. We wandered for 10 to 15 minutes without finding any signs of the cave, finally realizing we were going in circles.

Back at the parking lot, we encountered a few other explorers. Asking for directions, they pointed us towards a different path, assuring us it was only a 10-minute walk. With renewed determination, we started walking in the suggested direction, leaving behind our water bottles, backpacks, and any belongings in the car. All I had was my phone.

We walked for about 20 minutes when I felt a sudden pull to glance back at a spot along the path. At that very moment, as my eyes settled on it, a man appeared. It was surreal – one moment the trail was empty, and the next, he stood there as if materialized from thin air. There were no trees, rocks, or shadows nearby for him to hide behind; he simply wasn't there a moment ago, and now he was.

The man told us we were heading in the wrong direction, explaining he had already tried that path and found nothing. He pointed us towards the correct route, and without questioning, we followed him. Despite the strange circumstances of his sudden appearance, his friendly demeanor and conversation distracted me from my initial assumption.

As we followed him, I couldn't shake the feeling of how strange his sudden appearance had been. But as he continued to talk, guiding us with confidence, my thoughts were redirected. He led us through the field, deeper into our adventure, and I began to feel a mix of curiosity and excitement, wondering where this unexpected guide would take us.

It took us only a few minutes, and suddenly, we were standing right in front of Pluto's Cave. The mysterious man had guided us directly to our destination. He accompanied us down into the cave entrance, but his demeanor remained oddly detached. It was as if his sole purpose was to bring us to the cave, not to explore it himself.

On the way, he asked where we were from. When we mentioned that we had just left Los Angeles, he casually mentioned that he was born in the San Fernando Valley. It seemed plausible, yet something about the encounter felt strange. For someone who claimed to be searching for the cave, he showed no interest in taking photos or exploring the surroundings. Instead, he merely pointed us in the right direction, wished us well, we made eye contact, and then he turned around and left.

It struck me as peculiar that someone who had seemingly been on the same quest would abandon it so abruptly. His behavior was

strange – almost as if his presence was orchestrated for the sole purpose of guiding us. As he walked away, he seemed to vanish into the
landscape just as mysteriously as he had appeared.

Left to our own devices, we began to explore Pluto's Cave. The air
was cool and the space echoed with an ancient silence. Shadows played
across the cave walls as we ventured deeper, feeling a mix of excitement and curiosity. Despite the initial confusion, we were grateful for
the man's guidance, though his sudden appearance and disappearance
lingered in my mind, adding a touch of the surreal to our adventure.

As soon as I stepped into the first chamber of Pluto's Cave, a
smaller, somewhat musty space, I was immediately struck by an overwhelming sensation of busyness. The air buzzed with activity, energy
swirling and darting about like a bustling airport terminal. I began
recording, and to my astonishment, I captured glimpses of light beings
flitting past, their movements quick and purposeful. This area felt
alive, teeming with energy.

We then made our way to the main entrance of the cave, a larger,
more imposing space. The temperature dropped noticeably, and the
sound of water dripping from above echoed through the cavern. Massive stones lay scattered about, some having fallen from the ceiling,
creating a chaotic yet intriguing scene. My friend, however, hesitated
to venture further into the darkness.

Determined, I pressed on, knowing that the true exploration lay
deeper within. The cavern felt ancient, each step reverberating with
the history of the earth. Later, I shared my experience with a friend of
mine on social media who had visited the cave before. He showed me
photos filled with energy orbs, vibrant and full of life. It was clear that
Pluto's Cave held more secrets and wonders than I had discovered in
my brief visit.

Despite not venturing as far as I would have liked, the trip left me
feeling elated and energized. The high vibrational energy of the cave
stayed with me, lingering in my mind as a place of profound spiritual significance. I resolved to return one day, better prepared to delve

deeper and fully immerse myself in the cave's mysterious and powerful energy.

24

Secret Visitors Behind the
Lenticular Cloud

I woke up a little later than usual that morning, just after sunrise. The sun had already risen above the mountain, casting a radiant golden glow across the sky. As I stretched and looked out the window, my eyes were immediately drawn to the summit of Mt. Shasta. Its peak was wrapped in a thick, brilliant white cloud, glowing as it reflected the morning light.

I had seen this very same phenomenon exactly a week ago, but somehow, it slipped my mind when I tried to write about it. The cloud had the unmistakable shape of a spaceship—its edges smooth and rounded, perfectly still in the sky. It was one of those famous lenticular formations the locals often talked about, the ones said to carry messages or visitors from beyond. I remembered how, just last Sunday, the cloud had hovered for hours in the early morning sky. Now, here it was again—another Sunday. Was it a coincidence? Or was there something intentional about this weekly appearance?

"It has always been rumored that Mt. Shasta is a fueling station for spacecraft, and that they hide in the strange lenticular clouds which frequently form a perfect halo over the mountain."

— Emilie A. Frank

Those words echoed in my mind as I watched the cloud linger. There was a stillness in the air, but not an emptiness—rather, it felt charged. Like a silent gathering was taking place just beyond what I could see.

Each day, I found a deep sense of peace simply sitting in my back-yard with Kiki, my little dog, curled at my feet, and gazing at Mt. Shasta. No two days ever looked the same. The mountain was alive, not just with weather or light, but with presence. It seemed to show me something different each time I looked at it—like an artist reveal-ing a new painting with every passing hour.

As the summer sun melted more and more of the snow from its slopes, the ground beneath was slowly revealed, and with it, new pat-terns and shapes appeared. A few days earlier, as I recited my affirma-tions—calling in my power, abundance, and clarity—I saw something that made me pause. There, in the rocky silhouette of the mountain, stood the form of a woman. She seemed to be listening. Her head tilted gently, as if receiving the words I was speaking. I felt that she heard me. That she knew. And in her stillness, I felt validation—like the mountain itself was nodding, affirming the truth of my path.

Then came a new vision.

As I sat in quiet contemplation, letting my thoughts dissolve into the view, something new emerged from the mountain's face. I saw a man and a woman locked in a tender, passionate kiss. Their embrace was soft, but full of strength—a meeting of equals, a merging of essence. It wasn't just romantic; it felt sacred. The kind of union that speaks of more than just two people—it was masculine and feminine, sun and moon, yin and yang, coming together in perfect harmony.

It was the image of divine union. Of twin flames.

Of sacred balance.

I watched, motionless, as the mountain offered this vision. I didn't need to question it. These moments weren't born from imagination—they were messages. Whispers from something ancient, sacred, and aware. The scenes Mt. Shasta revealed they weren't coincidences; they were communications. Symbols meant for my heart to decode, reminders of the deep interconnectedness of all things—and of the power of Presence.

25

Merging with the Light of the Land

The first week in Mount Shasta felt raw—like I was caught in a tug-of-war between the energies of my past and the frequencies of this new land. One moment, I was overflowing with love and serenity; the next, I'd be hit with waves of anger and frustration. It was an emotional whiplash—back and forth, back and forth—for several days. But little by little, I felt the old layers being peeled away, making room for something unfamiliar but invigorating: new thoughts, new visions, new excitement.

Looking back, I'm grateful I didn't interact much with the locals during that initial adjustment period. I needed that time to detox energetically. I could have easily projected that unsettled frequency onto others, unintentionally affecting them—like walking into someone's pristine home with muddy shoes. The "mud" was everything I carried from my time in Los Angeles, and I realized it was essential to clear it on my own before authentically engaging with anyone new.

After ten days of surrendering to the rhythm of this mountain town—its stillness, its open skies, its pure water—I felt a noticeable shift in my energy. Something within me had softened and opened. I began to recall my dreams with stunning clarity. In one dream, I was using my hands to manipulate energy and stop a natural disaster. I could feel the currents moving through me—vivid, intentional, empowering. Another night, I saw celestial beings dancing across the sky, their presence oddly familiar. What once might've seemed paranormal now felt perfectly natural.

This clarity stirred a desire to explore further, so I decided to finally go into town. Even though it's only a ten-minute drive, the four-mile walk in 86-degree heat didn't appeal to me. I messaged a friend, who graciously offered to drive me around for a small gas fee. As we drove, he casually mentioned Peter Mt. Shasta.

Hearing Peter's name again sparked something in me. I had encountered his work years ago—read a few of his books and even watched some interviews. But somewhere along the way, I had lost that connection. My friend's mention of him acted like a cosmic nudge, prompting me to reconsider what I had set aside. Maybe it was time to revisit Peter's teachings. Or at least attempt to reconnect with his energy—whether through his words, his presence, or perhaps even directly.

After being dropped off, I wandered into town alone to soak it in on my own terms. Mount Shasta's downtown is small but radiates charm—cozy and colorful. As I strolled past the storefronts, one place called out to me: a shop filled with singing bowls. I stepped inside, instantly drawn to the resonance in the air. A kind woman greeted me warmly and handed me a mallet, inviting me to try a bowl.

I hesitated, explaining that a year earlier, I had experienced severe ear pressure, and the sound of singing bowls had been physically painful. She smiled gently and assured me I'd be fine. So I took a chance.

I struck the first bowl. The sound moved through me—clear, strong, alive. Then another bowl, and another. One bowl kept singing as I started a new one, and soon I was surrounded by cascading tones. The room filled with harmonic waves, a symphony of frequencies. The woman encouraged me to continue, inviting me to create music of my own. I felt like a child again—curious, uninhibited, joyful.

We talked as I played, and she shared her story: she had also recently left Los Angeles and followed an inner call to relocate to Mount Shasta. Her eyes sparkled with purpose and peace. Her journey mirrored my own. It was affirming—reminding me that this magnetic pull to the mountain wasn't just mine; others felt it too.

After the singing bowl shop, I made my way to the Blue Star Child Gallery. I had heard about the place and its connection to the consciousness community in Mount Shasta. Visiting felt like another important stop along the path. The moment I entered the gallery, I was captivated. The artwork was multidimensional—filled with sacred geometry, light codes, and otherworldly beings. A massive dragon drawing caught my eye. Every piece buzzed with energy.

The gallery's owner carried a quiet power. As we spoke, I felt an intuitive resonance between us. Oddly, the questions I asked were ones I already knew the answers to. It felt less like learning something new and more like confirming what I already carried within.

At one point, she looked at me with an unwavering presence and said, "If you already know the answer, why are you still searching for it? You already know. Just listen. Look inside."

Her words landed deeply. I had been seeking confirmation from the outside world, when everything I needed was already within me. That moment was a mirror, reflecting my own wisdom back to me. I left the gallery feeling both affirmed and energized.

As I wandered through town, I became more familiar with its corners and characters. There was a softness to everything—a high-vibrational friendliness that made it easy to feel at home. When my errands were done, I called my friend for a ride back. Returning to my guesthouse, I was greeted by Kiki, who had clearly missed me. We sat quietly in the garden, watching the light shift on the mountain as evening settled in.

And then I saw her again—in my mind's eye, on the mountain. The feminine figure. Her silhouette is shaped by rock and shadow. Her fingers stretched gently forward, as if saying, "Just a little farther. Keep going."

That night, I reflected on how much had already changed in just a few days: the emotional detox, the dreamworld openings, the spontaneous connections, and this quiet inner call to seek out Peter Mt. Shasta again. Not out of spiritual desperation, but from a more grounded curiosity. A readiness. Maybe this time, the connection would be clearer.

This day was a gentle turning point—an attunement. To the mountain. To myself. And to the subtle guidance waiting patiently for me to notice.

26

The Keeper of Wisdom

Afew months back, I had sent Peter Mt. Shasta a friend request on Facebook. I was intrigued by his work with Saint-Germain—my beloved master and guide—and felt a resonance with Peter's dedication to the teachings of the ascended ones. But our first energetic exchange didn't go quite as I had hoped. Peter had expressed a clear disinterest in past life regression, which I found a little surprising at the time. It left me with a subtle feeling of rejection. Only later did I realize that my own social media presence was flooded with content and ads related to my regression work. Without context, it probably looked like I was trying to pitch something to him.

Looking back, I can understand why he might have assumed that. It was a gentle reminder of how important it is to curate our online spaces in a way that genuinely reflects who we are—not just what we do. Our vibration speaks through our digital presence too. Still, despite the initial misunderstanding, I couldn't shake the feeling that I needed to reconnect. There was something about Peter's connection to Saint-Germain that continued to pull at my heart.

So I followed that inner nudge and took a leap of faith. I reached out to Peter again. To my surprise, he responded with warmth and kindness. Not only did he agree to meet, but he also offered to come into town so I wouldn't have to make the full 25-minute drive. His energy felt clear, understanding, and welcoming. The apprehension I had felt just dissolved.

Peter Mt. Shasta is a spiritual teacher and author known for his deep connection with the Ascended Masters—especially Saint-Germain, the Master of the Violet Flame and transformation. His path began after a series of powerful inner callings and outer synchronicities led him to Mount Shasta, a place long revered as a vortex of spiritual energy and a meeting point for higher consciousness.

Peter's teachings are rooted in the ancient wisdom of the I AM Presence, a practice made more widely known through the work of Guy Ballard in the 1930s. His books, including *Adventures of a Western Mystic* (Volumes 1 & 2), *I Am the Open Door*, and *Lady Master Pearl*, chronicle both his personal spiritual experiences and the timeless messages of the Ascended Masters. Through his writings, he invites readers into a deeper relationship with their Higher Self and the divine beings who assist humanity from higher dimensions.

As I prepared for our meeting, I remembered a printer I had brought with me from Los Angeles—a brand-new one that I no longer needed. No one else had use for it either. On a whim, I offered it to Peter. I wasn't sure if he'd want it, but he quickly replied that his printer had recently broken. The timing was uncanny. In that moment, I saw yet again how perfectly the pieces of life can align when we surrender and trust. What I no longer needed turned out to be exactly what someone else was silently asking for.

The meeting with Peter went beautifully. He carried a soft, radiant presence—so light, so pure. I felt the openness of his heart immediately. What I hadn't known until that day was that his father was born in Belarus—my own home country. That little synchronicity made the world feel even smaller, more connected, more magical.

We sat and talked for a while, and although I had so many thoughts, so many questions, and stories to share, I held back. My guides had been gently reminding me to listen more and speak less, to be more present and receptive in conversation. So I listened. I let the stillness between words carry as much weight as the words themselves. And still, the exchange was rich, layered with meaning, and full of insight.

One moment that truly stood out was when we spoke about the printer. Peter shared that just recently, while considering buying a new one, he had received a clear inner message: Do not buy a printer. At the same time, I had received my own message—to offer mine. That kind of synchronicity goes far beyond coincidence. It was a beautiful example of divine orchestration, of how we are guided to fulfill each other's needs in the most unexpected and graceful ways.

I also shared with him the story of my visit to Pluto's Cave—and the mysterious man who appeared behind us, seemingly out of nowhere, and vanished just as quickly. I described how his presence had shifted the energy so profoundly. When I recounted this to Peter, he paused, then said, "That sounds like Saint-Germain. That's his style." The moment he said those words, I was covered in goosebumps. My whole body tingled with truth. Deep down, I had already known. I couldn't accept the story that he was just some random guy from the San Fernando Valley. I knew what I had felt. I saw through the veil. And now, hearing it from Peter—who knew Saint-Germain intimately—was the final confirmation.

That meeting wasn't just a pleasant conversation—it was a powerful activation. A reminder of how deeply interconnected our paths are. How divine timing arranges these seemingly small moments that leave such a deep imprint on the soul. I left feeling lighter, affirmed, and grateful.

Peter is someone I now hold in the highest regard. Not just because of his teachings, but because of his humility and heart. That day, I didn't just reconnect with a fellow seeker—I reconnected with a thread of my own soul's journey. A reminder that we are always being guided, even through Facebook friend requests and broken printers.

Sometimes, all we need is a moment of courage, a spark of intuition, and a willingness to follow where the current leads. Because when we do, we find the right people, the right signs, and the right confirmations—exactly when we're meant to.

27

The Masters Appear – St.
Germain & Mary Magdalene

On a cool morning at Mount Shasta, I prepared for another profound session using the Quantum Healing Hypnosis, developed
by Dolores Cannon. This method guides clients into a deep hypnotic
state, unlocking access to the subconscious mind, past lives, higher
realms of consciousness, and profound healing insights.

My client had traveled from out of state, drawn not only to the session but also to the magnetic, mystical energy of Mt. Shasta itself. She
expressed a deep longing to connect with the transformative energies
within her. As I gently guided her into hypnosis, I watched in awe as
layers of emotional and physical blockages began to dissolve, guided
by the wisdom of her higher self.

During the session, she suddenly gasped, sensing Saint-Germain's
presence. She described being wrapped in a luminous violet energy—a
radiant flame of transformation and healing. His energy flowed
through the session, opening doors to clarity, emotional release, and
deep spiritual insight, infusing the experience with a profound sense
of peace and elevation.

Another session with a different client proved equally extraordinary. As she drifted into the hypnotic state, Mary Magdalene ap-

peared, offering a healing elixir that seemed to cleanse and restore the client on every level—mind, body, and soul. Then Joshua joined them with a message: "Never forget that balance between Divine Feminine and Divine Masculine energies is essential for true healing."

The room seemed to hum with unity and harmony, a living tapestry of sacred energies weaving together around us. The client emerged from the session transformed, carrying a luminous sense of balance and renewal.

Reflecting on these experiences, it became clear why Mount Shasta is a magnet for seekers and healers alike—it is a portal of spiritual awakening and profound transformation, offering a unique and sacred space for soul-level healing.

28

Gateway Peace Garden

*"R*evelation reveals
heaven's hurricane steals
all the small things,
except for our wings,
Away."

—Douglas Rubel

Today was another special day, marked by a chance meeting and profound realizations. I met with a friend who had personally known Dolores Cannon, the renowned figure behind the technique of Quantum Healing Hypnosis.

As we talked, my friend introduced me to a breathing technique. I knew that deep breathing could elevate one's state of consciousness, and indeed, it did. We both engaged in the breathing exercise in his garden, and I felt a shift. I was curious if he was receiving any messages, given our shared heightened state. Afterward, I thanked him for his kindness and started my walk back home, a 10-minute journey.

As I neared home, a truck stopped next to me, and I saw my friend waving for me to get in. He felt a calling to show me a special place, a sanctuary I might never have found on my own - Gateway Peace Garden. He believed it was perfect for activating my Divine Feminine Energy. We arrived, and he suggested I explore the trails alone for some quiet time, offering to pick me up later. Though initially resistant, I embraced the opportunity.

I left one of my crystal bracelets at the main entrance, feeling a connection to Mother Mary. I took pictures, meditated, and reflected. Then, I came across a medicine wheel, a spiritual experience I had longed for. As I walked towards the center, where an angel figure stood, a message came to me: "Spread your wings." I opened my arms, felt a surge of energy, and began to cry.

Today was another day of learning and experiencing another energy exchange, just being in this beautiful place where no one but a little bird was following me, watching what I was doing. It was a moment of peace and solitude. This hidden place is a symbol of unity and oneness.

29

Back to Reality

As my one-month rental agreement in Mount Shasta neared its end, I began searching for a way to stay longer. I wasn't ready to leave. I had envisioned spending the entire summer there—walking the trails, listening to the stillness, letting the mountain recalibrate me in ways only She could. But the little guesthouse I had been staying in was already booked; the host's family was coming to visit, and they would be taking my place. I could extend for a couple more days, but after that, there were no viable options.

I looked around, tried different listings, asked locals—nothing felt right. And with the 4th of July weekend approaching, everything was either sold out or wildly overpriced. The town, so quiet and mystical when I arrived, was now filled with travelers, noise, and high demand. Nothing aligned. I felt a creeping sadness. It was as if Mount Shasta herself was gently closing the door behind me.

I sat in silence one evening, asking the mountain: Why now? And what I felt in response wasn't resistance—it was release. A soft message settled in my heart: You've received the downloads. You've gathered the pieces. Now go. Rest. Integrate. Come back when you're ready.

It wasn't the ending I imagined, but it felt orchestrated by something higher. A spiritual nudge that my time—at least for now—was complete.

So I packed up my things, with a mixture of gratitude and quiet reluctance, and made my way back to Los Angeles.

The contrast hit immediately. Returning from the serene expanses of Mount Shasta felt like diving from the heavens into a dense, buzzing hive. In Shasta, the air had been thick with silence and spirit. Nature spoke clearly. I had been living in the frequency of presence, connected to the pulse of the earth. Back in Los Angeles, everything was loud, fast, and heavy.

The stillness I had cultivated seemed to vanish the moment I crossed into city limits. Sirens, car horns, screens, advertisements, distraction. I found myself surrounded by people glued to their televisions, endlessly scrolling, numbing. It was a jarring return to a collective rhythm I no longer belonged to.

I felt out of place—like I had come from another world, only to be dropped into a timeline that didn't match who I had become. And yet, I knew this was part of the process too.

I remembered what my guides had taught me: that reality is not fixed. That timelines are fluid. That I have the power to shift, to choose again, to align with a version of reality that reflects my inner truth.

But at that moment, I didn't need to make a grand leap. I needed to breathe. To rest. To let what I had received on the mountain sink deeper into my bones.

Maybe this return wasn't a step backward—but a necessary pause. A time to integrate.

Mount Shasta wasn't done with me. But for now, she has released me.

And I had to trust that when the time was right, she would call me back.

30

Journey Between Lives with Jeff

The invitation to experience a Life Between Lives session with Jeff came at a time when I was truly ready for deep exploration. I had worked with him before and was always amazed at how the sessions provided profound insights into my soul's journey, my higher self, and the deeper meaning of my life experiences. When he suggested we do a regression session, I agreed right away. There was something about his presence that allowed me to relax deeply and feel safe in the space of vulnerability that comes with such transformative work.

I had always been curious about what lies between lifetimes, those moments in the spiritual realm where our souls go after physical death but before they reincarnate. What happens there? How do we prepare for the next incarnation? What guidance do we receive during this time? These questions had been lingering in my mind, and now, I had the opportunity to uncover the answers.

As the session began, Jeff guided me into a state of deep relaxation. His calming voice, always so soothing, took me deeper into my consciousness, and soon I was drifting into a peaceful, serene state.

Jeff: Can you find a place like that?

Volha: Mm-hmm. Under the pine tree.

J: Under the pine tree. And as you're under the pine tree, what do you notice around you?

V: I am walking, or I am moving circles around the tree.

J: How does it feel to be there?

V: It's like a meditating state. Like a ritual.

J: Like a ritual?

V: Uh-huh. I am moving clockwise around the tree. But I am not touching the ground. I am flying around the tree. I see the medicine wheel.

J: You see the medicine wheel?

V: Yes, and as I fly, my path is creating it. Like a pattern of the medicine wheel.

J: Your path is creating the medicine wheel. What is it about the medicine wheel?

V: Healing.

J: Healing?

V: Yes. Healing, recovering... energy and power.

J: Energy and power?

V: And a connection with the source. It's creating a connection with the source.

J: Beautiful. Healing, recovering, energy, power, and creating a connection with the source. That's incredible. As you focus on that, allow the energy of the medicine wheel to guide you even deeper into this state of connection.

V: Yes, I can feel it.

J: Wonderful. As you feel this connection, let's go even deeper. I'm going to count down from five to one. With each number, allow yourself to sink further into this healing energy, deeper into the power of the medicine wheel.

Jeff gave me a few suggestions about what I would experience in the next part of the session. He explained that I would be entering the realm of my soul-mind, a sacred space I always carry within. I would begin by revisiting joyful moments from my childhood, the journey back to the womb to connect with the reasons for my birth and purpose. From there, I would explore a past life to uncover valuable lessons, and finally, I would enter the realm of light to connect with my guide and receive higher wisdom.

J: Now, I want you to imagine yourself standing at the top of a beautiful, safe staircase—a staircase unique to you, reflecting your personal style. Can you tell me how you're experiencing that staircase?

V: In the mountains. In the background, there is a huge, huge, huge mountain. And I'm standing on the top in all white. And there are flowers, like Hawaiian flowers, around my neck. And the dress... a long, flowing dress in white. I think there's something on my head, like Hawaiian style.

J: How does it feel to be in that white dress with the Hawaiian style?

V: Free and flowing.

J: Free and flowing. As you stand there, you might feel a sense of anticipation and comfort, knowing that each step down the staircase will bring you closer to a place of deep relaxation, deep peace, and higher wisdom. You're safe, you're comfortable.

With each step, you'll find yourself becoming younger and younger, going deeper and deeper into relaxation, feeling more at ease. As you descend, you'll revisit some of the happiest moments from your childhood. These experiences will bring you joy, warmth, and positive emotions.

Jeff guided the journey, counting down: Deeper and deeper down with each and every step. 30... 25... 23... 20... 19... 18... 17... 16... Younger and younger... seeing yourself at 15... 14... almost there... 13... And now, as you take the next step, you're at 12 years old. At this age, a happy childhood event awaited, filled with joy and warmth. J: What are you experiencing?

V: I'm in a field. On one side, there's a forest, and I'm getting food for my rabbit. Gathering grass—green, juicy grass for my rabbit.

J: You're getting food for your rabbit?

V: I had a rabbit, yeah.

J: And what are you noticing around you as you're gathering food for your rabbit?

V: The grass is so green and juicy. There are some flowers along the field. There's nobody else here. I'm singing.

J: You're singing?

V: It feels good.

J: Feels good to sing with your rabbit?

V: Yeah.

J: Just allowing yourself a moment to really feel into that—singing, being with your rabbit, and feeling good. And when you're ready, we're going to step back onto that staircase. Continuing our journey down... going back to 11 years old... further and further back... 10... 9... 8...Younger and younger... seven. And at six years old, there's a happy event waiting for you. A time filled with joy and laughter. Just allow yourself to be surrounded by it. And what's happening?

V: It... it wasn't really a happy event.

J: No? What do you see?

V: There were... there were ships...on crops. They were leaving behind crop circles. I heard my parents talking about the... spaceships. And I got... sad that they were there. They didn't pick me up. And I really wanted to go with them.

J: You wanted to go with them?

V: Yes. And I said, I have no idea who these people are (my parents). Please pick me up. I promise I'm going to behave on the ship. And I was sad that they were so close... and they didn't pick me up.

J: Yeah... you were sad that they were close but didn't pick you up.

V: They left me there. With my family.

J: Yeah... What's your sense of that?

V: I was left alone. To be... to do it on my own. Without help.

J: Left alone... to do it without help. Is that right?

V: Mm-hmm.

J: Let's step back on that staircase, and we're going to continue our journey down. It's getting easier and easier as you go down... further and further... younger and younger... five years old... going further and further down... three years old... and sometimes around one or two years old, there's a happy childhood memory waiting for you. Just allow it to surround you. And what's happening?

V: My sister is laughing. I can hear her voice so clearly. I think we got dolls from our grandpa to play with.

J: Yeah? You got dolls to play with?

V: Uh-huh.

J: Uh-huh. What do you notice about those dolls?

V: They're huge, almost my size.

J: Tell me about them.

V: Big eyes. They look like humans—like child-sized humans.

J: And do you play with them?

V: My sister does.

J: So what's it like seeing your sister play with them and smile?

V: She's having fun.

J: And how about you?

V: I'm watching and observing.

J: Uh-huh. What's it like to watch and observe?

V: She's really having a moment. She's enjoying it, like a carefree child. No worries. Just a happy child.

J: And what do you notice as you're watching her?

V: I have big cheeks. Chubby.

J: Uh-huh, you have big chubby cheeks?

V: When I get angry, I just put my lips together, start to shake, and my cheeks get bigger. It's so funny. I look almost like a grandma.

J: And are you angry?

V: Uh-huh.

J: What are you angry about?

V: I don't know. She's so happy, and I'm angry.

J: Focus on that anger.

V: I don't like something.

J: What is it that you don't like?

V: I don't know. She's playing, and I'm watching her.

J: But you got angry?

V: Uh-huh. It's like my whole body gets intense.

J: Your body's intense. You're getting angry, and you're screaming.

V: I'm moving my hands. Like protesting something. I'm not happy about something.

J: And what is it? You're not happy about something. You're screaming. Your body's tense. What do you notice about that?

V: Something about how my sister's playing with the doll.

J: What is it? Your sister's playing with the doll. You're angry, you're tense, and you're screaming.

V: I think I don't agree with how she's holding the doll.

J: How is she holding the doll?

V: Normally. I got frustrated. Maybe not the way I wanted her to hold it. And she did it her way.

J: So let's move on and get back on that staircase and continue our journey back. Going even further back now. Back into the womb as a soul. Looking at the soul's perspective of this time in the womb. Just allowing yourself to go back there now. Three. Further and further back. Two. And one. Be there now. In the perspective of your soul, what are you noticing about it?

V: A dark place.

J: What do you notice about your hands and arms? Are they reasonably comfortable?

V: Uh-huh. But the space around me looks like a virus. Like a virus you would see in a picture. It's weird.

J: And what is it about that virus?

V: A lot of negativity. A lot of negativity. It's not a happy place.

J: Where is the negativity coming from?

V: They're showing me the cord with my mom. Like from my... uh-huh... from my stomach, connected with my mom.

J: And what do you do with that negativity?

V: I'm just swimming in it.

J: What's it like to swim in negativity?

V: I see a few lights coming through from outside. Which on the side, it's a little bit brighter than inside, so it's kind of breaking the darkness. And like a wave, covering my body in that light, like a vibrational spiral or something. And it's enveloping my body and breaking the darkness.

J: What is this light breaking the darkness?

V: Source.

J: And what is Source doing?

V: Transmuting the negative dark energy into the light.

J: And so this negativity that you're swimming in, does it affect you? Do you take it with you in this life?

V: Not anymore. I think they pushed it away. Because right now, I feel like I'm swimming in white water. I see a wave of high frequency. So we pushed it away. It's no longer there. They make me feel comfortable.

J: Yeah, so they pushed it away for you, making you feel comfortable.

V: Uh-huh. Like they created a space, like a source, that feels like home.

J: So you're there, comfortable in that space. It feels like home. I wonder if you ponder the life you're about to live. What is it about the life you're about to live?

V: I'm resisting it.

J: And where's this resistance coming from?

V: The family I chose.

J: Tell me about the family you chose.

V: Karma to pay off. It's not going to be a smooth ride. And I'm resisting it. It's uncomfortable.

J: So it's uncomfortable, this karma that you have to pay back.

V: Uh-huh.

J: So in addition to the karma that you have to pay back, what other things are you coming to learn about or to do?

V: To do it on my own terms. I have to bypass the family system and create my own. Because there will be a lot of teaching and brainwashing from my parents, and I have to bypass it and follow my own path. Do not believe in it. I'm going to be caught up in this life for a while until I wake up and go my own way.

J: Once you get past that critical point of waking up and following your own path, what's the plan?

V: To create.

J: How will you create?

V: Create peace on Earth. High vibration. Share the knowledge, share the information. Download from the source and share it. Share the knowledge.

J: Create peace on Earth. High vibration. Share knowledge, download from the Source. Is that right?

V: Yes.

J: Very good. What else are you noticing about this life? Maybe something that you need to remember about this life.

V: They're showing me a dog. My dog.

J: They're showing you a dog? What's that like?

V: That I have a companion. I have support, so that I don't have to do it alone.

J: You don't have to do it alone.

V: Yeah. It's Kiki.

Tears slipped down my cheeks. But it wasn't sadness. It was love. It was the deep, aching comfort of knowing—some bonds are never broken.

J: Kiki, yeah.

V: My soulmate. She's from my soul group.

J: She's here with you. You don't have to do it alone.

V: Yeah. She knew it was going to be hard, so she came with me.

J: She came with you to support you.

V: Yeah.

J: When you're ready, let's continue our journey back. Only when you're ready. Just give me a nod when you're ready.

V: Yeah.

J: Okay. Let's continue our journey back.

Jeff instructed me to drift away from my mother, feeling calm, weightless, and peaceful. He encouraged me to become aware that my soul had existed long before this moment, carrying memories, knowledge, and wisdom from past lifetimes. All those experiences were a part of me, waiting to be remembered.

As I rested in this serene and safe space, he guided me further, urging me to journey beyond this life—to another time, another place, another existence where I had lived before. A lifetime that held significance for me. He asked me to tune into a life that still echoed in my present experience or perhaps one from long ago that carried valuable lessons. Most importantly, he told me to trust that my subconscious knew exactly what life to reveal.

J: Just drift back through time—before this body, before the womb—floating effortlessly and naturally... How are you feeling right now?

V: Relaxed.

J: Okay. So just allow yourself to go back now. Five... The veil of time gently lifts. Memories begin to surface—fragments of lifetimes long before this one. Four... drifting effortlessly back. Three... sensations or images begin to emerge from that most appropriate time, that most appropriate place in your past. Two... stepping into the essence of that life. One... be there now. Just take a moment to observe, to understand. And when you're ready, just let me know what you're noticing.

V: It's like a wall. Then suddenly, a crack forms, and the wall begins to split apart.

J: What's behind it?

V: Light. The sky. It pushes through the opening as the two pieces drift apart. And on the wall, before it breaks—a face of a woman. Maybe a Native Indian or some kind of god. It was engraved in stone, and then the wall cracked in the middle and started to open up, and the sky came through.

J: Okay...

V: Now I see a lot of realities, like different layers of realities, and there are a lot of them in front of me, like cards.

J: Different layers of reality like cards?

V: Uh-huh. Like when you have cards in your hand and you play with them—that's how I see realities. But nothing stands out from those realities—just many, many, many... A huge collection, all blending together.

J: And what's your sense of all these cards, all these many, many cards with all these different realities?

V: That's my database of the soul. Like data storage, my biography. It's huge. When you see it from afar, it stretches out long... like a snake. And that snake has many layers of different realities.

J: As you really focus on all of these cards—like a snake— what do you notice about it?

V: You can tune into any of those realities anytime you want. It's like an all-you-can-eat table—you can choose whatever you want and be there... Wow... How do you choose?

J: And help me understand, give me more context about these layers and layers of cards. Are you in a place? What do you notice around you?

V: It's space. Just space. But when you look at it, it's like cards. You can compare them to cards, but all together, they're one after another, after another, after another. And it forms a shape, like a snake. It's long. But when you look closer, you can see that they are separate pieces, like layers. Which, all together, forms the shape of a snake. The life scene—reality—is like a card. And when you choose any of them, you can be there. You can live that reality.

J: You can live that reality?

V: Uh-huh.

J: And so, have you lived these realities before, or are there some that you haven't lived?

V: I think it's all together. That's my database.

J: Uh-huh, your database. And is there anything in particular that's standing out in this database?

V: They're showing me some kind of spaceship, like a rocket. It's already the third time during the session that they're showing me a spaceship. They show me, and then it disappears. I have no idea what they're trying to tell me.

J: Uh-huh.

V: I'm behind that rocket. I don't know where we're going. I'm just following it.

J: What do you notice as you follow the rocket?

V: Space. Space. We are going somewhere. I don't know. It's taking me somewhere.

J: Where is it taking you?

V: To a planet. Space...

J: Help me understand.

V: It looks like a mothership now, with a lot of windows on the bottom.

J: And are you inside or outside?

V: I'm under it. They're showing it to me. The picture is constantly changing. That's a bigger ship, I think. It has a lot of small, rounded windows on the bottom. Windows that you can open. But they're so small. What can you even do with them? There's glass, and then there's metal—a huge, rounded metal frame around it.

J: Uh-huh.

V: And it's just a tiny, tiny window. I have no idea what's the point of such a tiny window.

J: As you're looking at this window, I wonder if there's anything or anyone that could help you understand it.

V: Something is spiraling, working. There's so much metal. I don't understand the metal stuff. It's like technology. It's part of the huge ship. There's so much metal in it.

J: Uh-huh.

V: Everything is made of metal, like heavy metal. Are they showing me technology? I don't understand anything about technology.

J: And what is this technology? Describe what you're seeing.

V: Now they've opened the bridge. It's like the bridge is falling down from above so I can walk. We are going up, and it's dark—like a tunnel. The bridge is taking me to the tunnel. It's dark and made of stone. Hmm.

J: So you've walked up and into this spaceship, is that right?

V: Uh-huh.

J: And then the spaceship turned into a tunnel?

V: Uh-huh.

J: And can you see inside as you're going through this tunnel?

V: It looks like a portal. It's just nothing. Like a whole black hole. I think it's a portal. I cannot see anything inside the ship. I only see the stone walls and this bridge going up to the opening up there, which is also dark. I go inside—it's a tunnel—and I follow it. There are more tunnels. I think it's a portal to somewhere. Yeah... yeah, it must be a portal.

J: And as you're sitting there on that spaceship, with a portal in front of you, I wonder if you can get a sense of yourself.

V: I'm already in the portal. I'm moving somewhere through the tunnel. I think we've already left the spaceship. So I'm moving through the tunnel. It's just darkness. But I keep moving. Something is pushing me.

Visiting The Inner Earth

"Just as the long night of the Arctic ends, the brilliant sunshine of Truth shall come again... and those who are of darkness shall fall in its Light... for I have seen that land beyond the Pole, that Center of the Great Unknown." — *Admiral Richard E. Byrd*

J: And what happens next? You've been pushed through this tunnel—this portal.

V: It looks like volcanic lava. Hot. I see spring. Water. Or is it lava? I see green grass, it's somewhere outside. I see a few stones and a river, a small river.

J: So there's a volcano, stones, and a river?

V: Uh-huh.

J: And do you feel planted into the ground? Are your feet on the ground?

V: Floating.

J: You're floating?

V: I think I'm going through portals more and more. Where are we going? They're showing me to look up. I see the trees, but the trees form a rounded portal. I think it's also a portal. Why so many portals? It looks like Earth—pine trees and a blue sky. Looks like Earth, yeah. Are we having sightseeing now?

J: Is there someone there you can ask? You're mentioning "they." I wonder if they can help you understand what we're seeing.

V: There's some being floating like a fish (jellyfish), moving like a fish, but it's not a fish.

J: Can this being, that's like a fish but not a fish, help you understand what we're seeing?

V: It's showing me another tunnel. Also, like an underground tunnel with stone. It's pretty dark. I don't know. It's not scary, but it's unpleasant. And there are endless tunnels underground with stones around—almost rounded tunnels. Is that Inner Earth? Oh, it might be the Inner Earth!

J: Ah, Inner Earth. What are you noticing as you're seeing this Inner Earth?

V: Yeah, because it was like Earth, but the colors were a little bit different than Earth.

J: Yeah.

V: They showed me the Inner Earth. There is also life, and you get to Inner Earth through the tunnels. Underground, there are portals and openings.

J: So what do you notice about this Inner Earth?

V: It's like us, but happier. Like no worries, no stress, no problems. But it's like us. It's nature like ours—water, stones, forest, sky. But the colors were a little bit different from Earth. I would never say that it's Inner Earth, because it's just like us, but so pure. It's pure, it's happier. No worries.

J: It's pure, it's happier. No worries. And what is it about this place?

V: Everybody has access to it. You just need to open up to receive the key to heaven on earth. I see the waterfalls. Beautiful.

J: And have you been here before?

V: Not with that awareness. Pure nature, not destroyed. So peaceful.

J: Yeah, so peaceful. Pure nature. No worries. And what is it that you do here?

V: Flying. Oh, that ship was really cool. I see the opening, and I'm flying on a ship. You can't even tell the difference between the two worlds. There's just an opening—you fly through it, and you're here on Earth. Wow.

J: And did this ship take you to this Inner Earth?

V: Uh-huh. Now I've left Inner Earth. Now I'm on Earth. And they're showing me this—like you really wouldn't be able to tell the difference. Just energetically. It's the same nature. I'm flying above the forest now. This is Earth. But they showed me the opening—it was like a crack in the wall. When you leave the Inner Earth and go to Earth, it's so simple. And I see a lot of forest underneath. This is Earth.

J: And this ship you're on, have you been on this ship before?

V: Not with this awareness. But it was a white ship, like a cool, cool technology white ship.

J: And have you been on this ship with another awareness?

V: Oh, for sure, yeah. I just have amnesia about this. So beautiful. They show me in my dreams, they show me the forest I was flying above. It looks like this one. But it's so easy to get to the Inner Earth.

J: And how do you do that? How do you get to Inner Earth?

V: You just go through the opening. It's so easy; you're right there.

J: And do you need a spaceship to go through this opening, or can you do it on your own?

V: They show me two ways: one through the underground tunnels, and another by spaceship. The tunnels are so long, and they're not scary, but they're not pleasant either. But on a spaceship, on a ship, it's a beautiful view, and you have this opening, like a crack in the wall. You don't even notice that you're already on the Inner Earth. It just seems brighter, and the energy is much lighter. So they showed me two ways to get there. The easiest and most pleasant is by ship. The information is coming to me now that there was a plane that flew into that place through the exact same opening. And they showed him around, but nobody believed him. But it's possible.

J: It's possible. And those who are showing you this, can they present themselves to you so you can get an understanding?

V: Collective.

J: What do you notice about them? Do you see, feel, or experience anything?

V: I feel their energy, yeah, but I don't see them.

J: You feel their energy. Uh-huh.

V: I don't see them in a physical form.

J: And are you able to communicate with them? Can you ask them questions?

V: Telepathically.

J: Ask them about this snake, this snake and all of these cards. What is that place?

V: Akashic Records. It's a database of the soul, where all the information about that particular soul is stored. What you would call the past life, future, and parallel—all exist at the same time. That's why you can tune into any layer, any reality.

J: And are the Akashic Records located in the same place as the spirit? Where spirits go between incarnations?

V: Yes.

J: And what do you do here at Akashic Records? What can you do?

V: You can ask questions and receive answers. You can see a life preview if you want to. You can see what you signed up for. Working, learning, teaching. It's like home for the soul.

J: And do you come here as a soul?

V: Yes.

J: What do you come here as a soul for?

V: To talk to my Spirit Guides about the challenges I'm experiencing on Earth and how to overcome them. We have small meetings once in a while.

J: I wonder if you can find yourself meeting with your spirit guide there at the Akashic Records? What's your spirit guide like?

V: Mary Magdalene.

J: Just notice the energy. What do you notice about the energy?

V: Female... That's what we're working on.

J: That's what you're working on?

V: Uh-huh.

J: Help me understand that.

V: Mm-hmm. That's the hard part. Divine feminine energy. I have to activate divine feminine energy. And we have been working on this. Mount Shasta was also to activate female energy—yeah, there was some activation done on me.

J: And your spirit guide there, presenting as Mary Magdalene—does she have a name you call her by?

V: Master Mary comes to mind.

J: Master Mary?

V: Uh-huh.

J: And does she have a name she calls you—your soul name?

V: Tevry.

J: Tevry?

V: Uh-huh.

J: And so, Master Mary was telling you about working on your feminine energy. What does she say?

V: We are not done yet.

J: What lies ahead?

V: Twin flame activation—where the female and male energies merge. But before that happens, I need to fully activate my divine feminine energy. It's not activated yet.

J: And will you know how to do this? Will you do this on your own, or will you have help?

V: I started after Mt. Shasta, for one session with Mary Magdalene, and then I stopped. I have received messages that I need to do it, and I kind of pushed it to the side. I ignored that. I didn't know Mary Magdalene was my master.

J: And so now that you know, what's next?

V: I need to do the work.

J: What is the work?

V: Clearing the womb—mother womb trauma before having any kids. Generational trauma. Forgiving all the women in my lineage, the generations before me. They messed it up. They had no idea what they were doing.

J: So I just want to make sure I'm getting this right—clearing the mother womb trauma, the generational trauma, forgiving all the women, back through generations, is that right?

V: Yes, they created many issues. Some did black magic. On the father's side.

J: And is this something that Master Mary wants you to do as a soul?

V: Yes. In this body.

J: Ah, in this body as Volha.

V: Yes. Once she clears it, she clears the generational path too.

J: How will you, as a soul, help Volha to do this?

V: I send her information. She needs to listen to her instincts. She's been guided. Don't ignore it. Mt. Shasta is coming again, once again, for more work. Deeper work. She's not done yet.

J: And does Master Mary have any advice for you as a soul, or for Volha, as the personality you've incarnated in?

V: Ask for help and you will receive it. You don't have to do it on your own. We are here to support you. It's hard, but you will do it.

J: And I wonder if you can ask Master Mary, why did you show me all of those portals, the spaceship, the Inner Earth?

V: That's where she travels. Like what you call it, commuting to work... Teachings.

J: Teachings? Ask Master Mary, what is it about teachings?

Now, as I am putting this in writing, it comes to my mind that recently I was doing a guided meditation with Archangel Michael and St. Germain. I could vividly and clearly feel that Archangel Michael was standing on my right side—he tickled the sole of my right foot, and St. Germain tickled the palm of my left hand. So I knew exactly who was where.

I asked them for guidance, to teach me how to manipulate energy, just to teach me and give me knowledge. At some point, I literally heard them laughing, making fun of me, saying that I was teaching myself and now I was asking them to teach me. I said, "Guys, I can hear you," but I did not understand what kind of teachings they meant. I could clearly hear that they were making fun of me. It was like, "Sorry, guys, I do have this amnesia. I don't remember what I am doing while I am asleep, but with this awareness, I did not know that."

V: I'm teaching something. What am I teaching? Energy. Frequency. Higher dimensions. Parallel realities. Wisdom, knowledge, ascension, sharing the knowledge.

J: Yeah, sharing the knowledge. And you do this as a soul, as Thevry? Or do you also need to do this in the life of Volha?

V: Oh, different forms. Same time, different forms.

J: Same time, different forms. Help me understand that.

V: Pleiadian. Arcturian. Lemurian. Telos. Mermaid. What is it? Crawling. Looks a little bit like... My gosh, it's not on Earth. We don't have it on Earth.

J: And are these also incarnations?

V: Uh-huh. A being, yeah. It looks like Reptilian, but it's not Reptilian, it's not on Earth.

J: You do this through all these incarnations?

V: Yeah. Different forms, different tools, same concept.

J: Ah. Do you also teach there in spirit or is it all in incarnations?

V: Incarnations. Spirit is wise enough.

J: Ah. And what is it that you're teaching as Volha?

V: How to ascend, remembering, sharing the information on Earth and other dimensions and planets. Love, pure love, love and light.

J: I wonder if Master Mary can help you, as a soul, remember what you were supposed to do—what was planned for Volha in this life to help people ascend, remember, and share knowledge about other dimensions and planets. Can Master Mary take you to a place where you can remember?

V: She showed me Queen (Queen Elizabeth 1).

J: What is it about Queen?

V: She has killed her femininity. She needs to shed that layer of being a strong woman. Open the heart. Heart chakra is closed.

J: And how does one open the heart chakra?

V: Release the resistance, fear of rejection.

J: How does one release the resistance and fear of rejection?

V: Through imagination and visualization.

J: I wonder if Master Mary can take you to a place of higher wisdom.

V: Yeah.

J: If she takes you there, what do you notice?

V: Crystal. In the middle of the room. Purple crystal.

J: Tell me about the room.

V: It's a cave, a rounded cave, and in the middle of the room there is crystal. It's constantly changing shape and form. It was purple, now it's white, and broken into many, many small crystals. It looks like a sun, but white crystal.

J: And how do you get knowledge from this crystal?

V: Place your hands around it. Tune in and ask to download the information you need to download. You are like merging. You ask for access.

J: And do you do this as a soul? Or does someone assist you?

V: As a soul. You can do that. You have the right.

J: So, Volha had some questions she would like for you to ask on her behalf this crystal. We were talking earlier about soul contracts and agreements with New Orleans. Can you ask the crystal about New Orleans?

V: Spreading the light. She signed up for it.

J: She signed up to spread the light in New Orleans?

V: Yeah. She took New Orleans as her territory to cover.

J: She was expressing concern about that and wanting to do hypnotherapy instead. Help her understand.

V: She's almost done.

J: Ah, hmm. And when she's almost done there, can you give a time frame?

V: Soon. She will know. She will feel it. And the doors in New Orleans will be closed.

J: Contract complete?

V: Yes, the contract will be complete, and she will be pushed out of that zone. We will tell her when the job is done completely.

J: Can you give her any sense of time? A month, a week, a year?

V: No.

J: She was also telling me about siren triggers. What can that crystal help her understand about her triggers with sirens?

V: It's a past life memory. A revolution. The French Revolution.

J: Can you show her that live—just a glimpse—so she can understand?

V: We showed her before. It was that connection. She knows it. She thought it was going to trigger something in New Orleans. But it's the French Revolution.

J: So, is this trigger still important in her current life?

V: There is some fear stuck. She needs to release that fear. She was a young woman when she saw the battle and felt fear. That fear is still in her blood. The French Revolution is no longer there. Let it go.

J: Is this something she can heal in spirit, or does she need to do this in the physical world?

V: She can do it during meditation. Separate your lives. Let it be. Let it go. Leave it in that life. Don't bring it here. Don't bring it over here.

Mother-Daughter Soul Contract

J: What about her relationship with her mother? She feels it might be preventing her from meeting her soulmate and attracting more clients.

V: Correct.

J: What can you help her understand about that?

V: She needs to release her mother's influence. Her mother still has an effect on her.

J: How can she release this?

V: In meditation, forgive her mother. And grow up, you can do it on your own without your mother, you are an adult now, take responsibilities.

J: Sometimes it's easier to understand and forgive when you can see it from the other person's point of view. Is this something that you can help her with? Can you help her see her mother's point of view, or is there something else you can help her to forgive?

V: Her mother is just playing her part. Volha's part is to deal with her own karma around her mother. The past life she knows about has not been processed yet, and there is a block preventing her from meeting her soulmate, and blocking her financial income.

J: I think this would be really important for Volha to know how to remove this block. Can you help her with specifics on how to remove it? I know we talked about meditation, but is there more than that? We talked earlier about the forgiveness of her mother, forgiveness of generational trauma, and forgiveness of women in the generations. Is that the same forgiveness, or is there something else?

V: Her mother doesn't love her. She felt it. She knew that. But her mother also yells a lot. She forces people to love her, like demanding that love. Let her play her role, her part.

J: What are you learning from this, as Tevry - the soul, with the mother playing her part?

V: Love comes from her heart, not from people outside. Love comes from within; it's always there. You don't have to rely on others for love or to feel loved.

J: And is that part of the agreement?

V: Yes.

J: Are there other parts of the agreement between Volha and her mother? You, as a soul, and the soul of her mother?

V: She doesn't want to have her mother's soul in any other incarnations. But she needs to learn the lesson in this life, not to repeat it. Just accept her mother as she is. Don't focus on negativity. Focus on your own love. Pure heart.

J: So, what about this cyst, this ovarian cyst?

V: Mom's.

J: Help me understand that—mom's.

V: Her mom has a really strong personality. Very controlling and very dominant. And Volha got her influence from the very beginning. She still has that influence—until she does the work of removing her mom from her system.

J: Mm-hmm.

V: And this is a reminder of that outsider energy. She has to set healthy boundaries. She doesn't have to agree or disagree with anything her mother says. Just let her be. But you need to learn to separate the energies. Your mother is not your soul. They are two different souls. Even if we are all one, her mother has her own lessons to learn.

J: Is her mother learning lessons from this relationship as well, or is it just Volha?

V: She is learning in her own way, but she is way, way, way behind Volha's development. She is far behind—like a baby in kindergarten. Volha is much more advanced.

J: And is there anything that Volha—or you as a soul—can do to help her mother advance, or does she need to do this on her own?

V: She has her own guides she needs to connect with, but her mother's religious influence makes it a bit harder. Still, she is on her own soul evolution. Don't get frustrated if someone isn't moving at the same speed as you. Just let her follow her own path.

J: Volha was also asking me about her current living situation, wondering if you, as a soul, could ask the power of light and knowledge—what is this about? Why doesn't she have a home right now?

V: She doesn't need to have a home at the moment. There are a few travels she must take. If she had a home, she wouldn't be able to leave for two to three months at a time. We need her to be in different places for a certain period. Financially, this is also easier.

J: And where are these places?

V: She needs to go to Mt. Shasta, New Orleans, Sedona, San Diego, and other places she will recognize when the time comes.

J: And what will she do in these places? What is her mission?

V: Activation. She receives activations, and she also activates these places with her energy. Mount Shasta is not done yet. She needs to return for more teachings. But she had to leave because she had received enough downloads for that period of time. She will go back when she is ready.

J: And will there be a home in her future?

V: Yes.

J: Can you help her understand that more—maybe a time frame, a place, or some other insight?

V: It's not about the time frame; it's about the project she needs to finish in a certain location.

J: So she needs to finish the project in a certain location?

V: Yes. And when she is done with traveling, we will find her a home. A nice one. She likes nice homes—comfortable ones. We found her one in New Orleans and one in Mount Shasta, which felt like a miracle. She loved that. And she knew we helped her find those homes. Don't panic. You are protected.

J: What about this Electra...? She'd like to learn more about that. She had a glimpse...

V: She is Electra! (The voice declared—powerful and commanding, like the voice of divine authority reverberating across dimensions, leaving no room for doubt.)

J: What is this about Electra?

V: That somewhere in a parallel life, she is Electra—a powerful, beautiful goddess.

J: And is this Electra—this life, this parallel life—influencing her current life as Volha?

V: Yeah.

J: In what way?

V: It's pushing her to embrace her femininity. And also...she's moving around like a comet...and getting what she wants to get. Very determined.

J: And why is there a push to be feminine?

V: To be able to reconnect with masculine energy. This is very important for the ascension. For the energy they will create together, and the impact on the people around them. This is very powerful—when feminine and masculine energy unite, it's a very powerful force. But she's not ready for it yet. She's complaining, but she's not ready.

J: And what is her complaint? What is she not ready for?

V: She hasn't completely activated her Divine Feminine Energy, which involves working through her mom's trauma, her mom's relationship, and continuing her work with Mary Magdalene. She's helping her.

J: And this trauma with her mom, is it just this lifetime, or does it extend to other lifetimes?

V: The past life too. The Elizabethan one.

J: Are there more?

V: Yeah. But it's enough for her to know as an example. She doesn't want her parents to incarnate with her anymore, but they have more to go through. They're not pleasant characters around her—neither her father nor her mother, both of them. But they're playing their part. She doesn't like it.

J: Yeah, they're playing their part in incarnations.

V: They are like a trouble-couple, teaching her lessons, but she doesn't like it.

J: And is this something they've planned together, these lessons?

V: Yes.

J: Mm-hmm. Would it be possible to help her see the planning of those lessons with the souls of her mother and her father?

V: She sees that it was in Elizabethan time. That was one of the hardest, and it's still echoing in her life now.

J: And what was it in that life that was difficult?

V: She was a very lonely woman in that life. She had problems with a man, and she fell in love with a lover who was married to a woman, her mother in this life. And they murdered his wife to be together. That guilt of winning, but winning through the death of some other person. And now she is her mother, and they both don't love each other. They play like they do, but they don't. They can't. The guilt is still there.

J: Carried over from that lifetime?

V: Yes. Forgive. Forgive.

J: And is there some way that we can forgive in this session today? Is there some way that we can accomplish this today?

V: Yeah. Imagine hugging your mom. And forgiving her everything, asking her for forgiveness.

J: What does she do?

V: Resisting. Uncomfortable.

J: Yeah, uncomfortable. I wonder if there's a place you as a soul, Tevry, and your mother's soul can meet together. Soul to soul, not person to person, but soul to soul.

V: Yeah, they're smiling when you say soul to soul. Like I told you, it's going to be hard. Oh my god, they are laughing. They are laughing and crying at the same time because her mom told her that it's going to be hard. And she said, no, no, no, we can handle it. And now she is saying, I told you...She (her mom) is not that cold.

J: Yeah, she is not that cold as a soul. I wonder if she could share her name with you, her soul name.

V: Mary. Like her mom, Volha's grandmother.

J: Yeah. And is there forgiveness? Can forgiveness be asked and given at this level of the soul?

V: No, it's not necessary. They know it.

J: And so when you shift your focus back to Volha and you're seeing all of this, how is that for you?

V: Much lighter. Much easier to do it on the soul level than on Earth. Physical form is harder.

J: Yeah, it's much harder.

V: So much resistance.

J: And do you feel forgiveness?

V: Yeah. She is such a bright light. Pure. She is just playing her part.

J: Yeah. She is just playing her part.

V: It looks so real. Believable...on Earth.

J: And so now I'm wondering if you can shift back to your perspective as Tevry, the soul, and ask that light. Now that forgiveness has happened, can we move forward? Life, the unblocking, are there any other things that we need to do to unblock?

V: No, that was the hardest part, that she could not do on her own.

J: Yeah. And so now that this block has been lifted...

V: She is going to move to another challenge.

J: Another challenge.

V: She is not done yet.

J: And what advice can you give her for the next challenge?

V: Get ready, you might need some help.

J: And what about attracting more clients and booking her calendar?

V: Yes, and she needs to focus on spreading the word—doing more advertising, writing more. Put it out on the internet that she is there. News, news, news, news, news. Open your mouth...do podcasts.

J: Mm-hmm.

V: She's afraid of podcasts. She needs to share with people—sharing the knowledge, sharing the wisdom. That's her assignment.

J: Yeah. Sharing the knowledge, sharing the wisdom.

V: She's afraid of the camera. Oh, child. Make yourself pretty and go out there. Big stage. Big stage. Big stage.

J: Mm-hmm. Big stage.

V: Big stage. Big lights. You're meant to be on a big stage. No more hiding. No more hiding.

J: No more hiding.

V: No.

J: And how can you help her not be afraid to stop hiding, to be in front of the camera, and do podcasts?

V: She is almost ready for that. Step by step, we are pushing her closer to the cliff...that she is not scared. But soon she will have to fly—fly high.

J: And when she goes over the cliff to fly, what will happen?

V: She will not have any other option. She will just do what she was supposed to be doing—spreading all the knowledge. Sharing the wisdom—so much wisdom, so much knowledge—that needs to be shared. There are a lot of people looking for that knowledge. She is not sharing it. She promised to share it.

J: Can you give her a glimpse of the future? When she's gone off that cliff and she starts flying. Can you show her what that will be like?

V: She's blocking it. There's some fear. She's fearful that people are going to recognize her and some will judge. Of course. That she will need to hide somewhere in the forest. Darling, you don't have to hide in the forest. Oh my God, child.

J: What is something that she can do, even tomorrow, to begin to get past the fear?

V: Record yourself on camera. Start speaking on camera, even if you delete it later. Start. You are going to be on a big screen anyway. She is so afraid of a big screen. She is so afraid that the Brits are going to go after her.

(Both laughing).

Oh, darling, you are safe. They're not even going to believe in that. You are so safe. They are going to make fun of that, and that's it. You're good.

J: Yeah, you're good. Is there anything else this light, this crystal, wants to share with you before we move on to another area?

V: Some downloads. Give us a second as we download some information. (I started breathing deeply for a few seconds).

V: That's it.

J: Very good. So, Tevry, I wonder if Master Mary is around. Can you find her?

V: Yes.

J: When you find her, just let me know. And I'd like for you to ask her to remind you, what do you do for fun there in the spirit world, in between incarnations?

V: Do you remember yourself as being a child? There are no worries. You just can be whatever you want to be. You can play, relax, study, watch some situations on Earth like on a big screen, learn from that. There are no limitations. What your human mind cannot even imagine, or what you would think is too magical to be true, it's all possible there. Infinity of possibilities: learning, growing, playing, expanding, socializing, being alone, whatever you want to be.

J: Beautiful. So before we begin to close the session, we have one more question and then we'll continue on. What about this Prophet Samuel? If you, Tevry, can ask Master Mary about this Prophet Samuel?

V: She is resisting this information, so we will wait until she is ready. She will not believe in that anyway. It's too soon for her to know. We gave her a glimpse. She is rejecting it.

J: Oh, okay. Leave that for another time.

V: Yes.

J: So, Tevry, I'd like for you to look one last time around. Just look around and see if there's anything else that you'd like to explore before we make our way back.

V: My Pleiadian Family.

J: Mm-hmm.

V: My sisters. They're so supportive.

J: Yeah. So supportive. What do you notice about them?

V: High energy, wisdom. They're watching me on Earth. They are always there for me. My mom. They are there. My star family. I miss them so much.

J: Yeah. Just take some time to be with them.

V: They're saying I'm not alone. I wanted to do this, and they're supporting me. And I'm doing this really great.

As this session came to a close, I was overwhelmed with emotion. I cried more than I ever have during a session in my life—perhaps one of the most emotional experiences I've had. The tears flowed freely, but it felt necessary. The release, the cleansing, and the deep healing were all part of the process. It was intense, but it was so needed.

In that moment of vulnerability, I knew that the work being done was transformative. The weight of some of my most lingering questions had been lifted, and I felt a sense of peace and clarity. I had received exactly what I needed at this point in my journey, and while there was a profound sense of closure, I knew that this experience would continue to unfold within me as I integrated the wisdom I had received. It was deep, it was healing, and it was worth it.

31

A Portal Between Missions in Asheville

My soul began to whisper of movement again. This time, toward Asheville, North Carolina — a place I had heard about for years. A spiritual epicenter nestled in the embrace of the Blue Ridge Mountains, said to hold energy portals, sacred waters, and a magnetism that called in those on the path of light.

It was finally time.

The occasion? A Quantum Healing Hypnosis reunion. Practitioners, seekers, old souls. People who, like me, remembered that this work is not just a modality — it's a soul contract. A remembering. A movement of light.

The night before my trip I still hadn't booked my stay in Asheville. But I knew exactly what I wanted: something quiet, surrounded by nature. No upstairs neighbors. No walls on either side. Just space. Just peace. Just me, Kiki, and the trees.

And the Universe delivered, as it always does when you trust.

In the middle of the night, I checked Airbnb. One listing stood out — the only one left. A small house, tucked away in the forest, about twenty minutes outside of downtown Asheville. The photo showed a two-bedroom cottage, embraced by trees, with a tiny creek out back. It looked a bit eerie at first — isolated, wild, and a little too quiet.

But I booked it immediately — eight days. Enough time to settle, to walk, to integrate, to feel into the mountain energies before the re-union began.

When I arrived, the scene was surreal. Only two homes along a quiet road, right across from a gas station — and yet it felt like another world. The forest wrapped around the property like a secret. The house welcomed me like it had been waiting. The air was heavy with silence and the scent of wet leaves.

And then, the message came:

"We know what you like. We always find you beautiful places. It may seem unrealistic. It may seem magical. But we are always guiding you."

My heart softened at that moment.

The house was perfect. The birds sang each morning. The creek whispered its song into the backyard. The green surrounded everything like a cloak of love. One night, I woke up to let Kiki out and stood barefoot in the darkness as rain poured through the trees. It was so alive. So soft. So mystical.

Asheville felt like an initiation into a new frequency. A home-coming after a long, karmic mission. A gentle reminder that after every cycle of service, there is replenishment. That the soul who gives must also receive. And that sometimes, the forest itself becomes your teacher — quiet, patient, and filled with signs if you know how to listen.

I didn't know it yet, but this place would mark a turning point — not just in my journey, but in the book of my life.

The forest embraced me like a veil — soft, protective, wise. Each day I spent walking among the trees, listening to the creek, and letting Kiki rest beside me felt like a slow unraveling. I wasn't just resting — I was preparing.

When the reunion began, I felt the shift immediately. Over 700 souls from across the globe, all connected through the legacy of Dolores Cannon. We were there because something ancient lived inside each of us — a knowing that transcended time and form. You could feel the power of it in the air: the quiet excitement, the soft tears behind people's smiles, the recognition in strangers' eyes. Souls remembering each other.

One of the sessions offered was a group past life regression — using the Dolores Cannon method. I had experienced deep journeys before, but this one... this one opened something in me I didn't know I had forgotten.

As my body relaxed and my consciousness drifted, I suddenly found myself in another world.

I was a priestess, or perhaps a goddess. Clothed in a free-flowing dress, my entire being radiated elegance, freedom, and light. My arms moved with divine grace — and my hands... I remember my fingers gently touching one another in a mesmerizing pattern, like they were casting blessings or holding a frequency through simple gestures. There was so much intelligence in that movement — not the mind's, but the soul's.

Everything was sacred.

Even eating — yes, food itself — was a ceremony. A sacred offering. An act of connection, not consumption. It wasn't about nourishment alone. It was about reverence. I had known this before. And in that moment, I remembered.

It felt like the part of me that had waited lifetimes to be seen again finally stepped forward.

And that... that is what Asheville gave me. Not just rest. Not just rain and solitude and the whispering trees.

It gave me a portal of remembrance. It gave me me.

32

Failed Mission in a Forgotten Lifetime

Magic attracts more magic. And in the stillness of those days, I met another quantum healing hypnosis practitioner who offered me a session. Of course. The Universe was orchestrating everything, as always. And all I had to do... was say yes.

When the session started I had this clear vision. I saw myself leaving the Earth very quickly, moving at a high speed. I remember seeing the tops of the trees as I shot upward, leaving everything behind. In an instant, I was traveling through space, moving at high-speed.

I arrived on another planet. From far away, it looked like a black disco ball — round, shiny, and dark, with a metallic sheen. As I got closer, I realized the surface was flat, black, and smooth, like metal. It felt empty. Lifeless. Cold. There was no sign of life, nothing to welcome me — just a vast, black, flat surface stretching endlessly beneath me. It wasn't a place meant for life. It wasn't a home. It was just... emptiness.

Surrounding this planet was the blackness of space. As I looked more closely, I noticed something moving out there in the darkness — tiny, see-through bubbles. They moved together, almost like they were

connected. There were many of them, countless, and they stayed together as they stretched and shifted. They never fully disconnected.

Watching them made me feel... free.

Even though the planet felt cold and empty, there was a strange
sense of freedom in simply observing these bubbles drifting through
the darkness, sticking together yet always moving.

I was asked to look further, deeper, and see where these bubbles
were coming from. And they were coming from everywhere— from
space. I saw this dark spiral of something above me, and it's endless. It
has infinity. Then I was asked, where do these bubbles come from in
this black spiral? And I saw that they created themselves... like gases.
Just forming. I was asked what I would describe myself as, and the answer was—fast-moving energy.

P (Practitioner): Do you have any image at all?

V (Volha): It shows me... like when you press the steamer on an
iron and the steam comes up. That's how it looks. That's what I'm seeing.

P: Are there any colors?

V: Now, when I'm talking about the steamer, it comes like white...
I see white steam. But I'm not sure that it's me.

P: Do you feel like it's you?

V: Part of me.

P: Where's the other part of you?

V: Everywhere.

P: How do you know it's everywhere?

V: I feel it. It's like... we're all one. The bubbles... Now they have
disappeared.

P: Where did they go?

V: I don't know. But now I see another kind of energy moving. It's
not like bubbles anymore. It's more consistent.

I was trying to describe this energy... it was fast-moving, but not
like bubbles. It looked more solid. Solid, but fast—like it's leaving a
trace or a blur behind as it moves.

P: Where is it coming from?

V: Also from the same space. There are many different forms of energy flying around.

P: How do you feel seeing this?

V: It feels good. But I don't understand why there's so much darkness.

P: Where is the darkness?

V: It's everywhere. The energy is flying in the darkness.

P: Where are the energies coming from?

V: Source.

P: What is Source?

V: It's everywhere. That's all that is.

P: How do you know it's there?

V: I just know it.

Something was preventing me from moving forward. It almost looked like the back of a spaceship. I couldn't tell if it was metal, but I was pressing up against a large, solid wall. I didn't understand what it was exactly—was it the back of a ship, or simply a barrier? Its surface had unusual shapes, and all I could sense was that something needed to be opened.

I looked around to see if there was anything I could open. Everything looked sealed. I moved to a place where I could find a way. It was just a lighter space—one area was kind of lit up, with some little white steam coming from it. It felt like I needed to go through something to get to the other side. Then I saw a rounded window.

P: What color is the window?

V: Black, everything is black.

P: Can you see through the window?

V: No, it's all black and shiny.

P: How do you open it?

V: Like a screw to the side.

P: Is it inviting you in?

V: Something is releasing, something is going out through this opening.

P: What do you see?

V: It looks like a big bug. Now it's going somewhere. Picking up speed. And flying. Something has just been released through the opening.

At that moment, I saw an insect-like being curled up, sliding down, and then flying away—and something told me it was a Mantis. It went into space.

I thought I was in front of a spaceship. I was outside of it. It wasn't moving, and something had just left that structure through the opening.

The opening was still ajar. I wanted to sneak in, but it wasn't easy. Something was holding me back—like a mind game telling me it was impossible, even though I knew I could get through. Then I truly believed it was possible to enter, and suddenly, I was inside.

Around me was dark but open space. The air smelled like metal. It was completely silent. I realized I was at the back of some kind of structure, maybe a spaceship. There was nobody, no life inside. It seemed designed to release something from that structure out into the vastness beyond. The controls must have been somewhere in the front. Where I stood was the very back of the ship—used only to send something out, but otherwise, no one went there.

P: What is it like in this space?

V: It's like... empty space. Huge empty space.

P: And what else can you see inside there? Can you see the walls?

V: Yes... they're black. Just plain black.

P: How did that thing get into space? Where did it come from before it went out?

V: It was stored there. Like... a storage area.

P: And who stored it there?

V: I don't know.

P: Look around carefully. What do you see?

V: There's nothing to see... not in there. I feel like I need to go to another structure. One that's more used. It's at the very back.

P: And how do you get there?

V: There's a little door.

P: What do you want to do with that little door?

V: I want to open it... and go through.

P: Good. So you've opened the door and now you're through. What colors do you see around you?

V: It feels lighter. Warm. Not white... but beige. Light beige. Warmer, and not so empty.

P: And what is this place?

V: It's another structure.

P: Where does that structure go?

V: It seems like... a middle structure. Between that storage space and something in front. It's like a passageway.

P: And why is this structure here? What do they do here?

V: Preparing. Preparing to go out... for the project.

P: What kind of projects?

V: To fly somewhere. To see.

P: And why are you there? What role do you play?

V: I'm not sure yet.

P: Do you feel like you belong where you are?

V: I don't have that feeling yet.

P: Where do you want to go now?

V: There is another sector in the front where all the technology is. It's like sectors—sector one, sector two, sector three.

P: Tell me about them.

V: The first sector is technology. The middle sector is the preparation area. The third one is an empty area, where they prepare to take off and where things go out into space.

P: And how do you get to sector one?

V: There is also a door.

P: And what do you want to do?

V: Go check the technology.

P: You're there now. What do you see?

V: It's all on the wall. I don't know what it is.

P: What does it look like?

V: Like odometers, almost like you have in a car. And there are many, many, many. The entire wall is covered with them—small and rounded.

P: Is there anybody else around you?

V: There are a few people standing in the same position as I am, and we are looking at the same wall.

P: Do you know them?

V: No.

P: What's your feeling toward them?

V: They are not surprised that I am here.

P: What are you supposed to see?

V: I'm supposed to work.

P: What do you do for work?

V: Technology.

P: So you work in sector one?

V: Yes. I am a Technician.

P: Do you work alone?

V: No, there is a crew.

P: How many are in the crew?

V: Three or four, plus me.

P: How do you communicate with them?

V: We just understand what everybody thinks.

P: Do you have bodies?

V: Yeah.

P: What do you look like?

V: Like human beings.

P: What are you wearing? Do you have anything on your feet?

V: I'm not sure about my feet, but everybody is wearing the same... like a beige uniform. Like pants, an overall—or what do you call it?

P: Overall?

V: Yeah, overall. Two pieces in one. Beige.

P: Are you carrying anything? Do you have anything on your head?

V: Some kind of cover-up.

P: Does it cover your whole head?

V: Just the top.

P: Just the top?

V: Everybody has the same.

P: Would you say that you are more of a male or a female energy?

V: Female.

P: And what about the others?

V: A mix—female and male.

P: How long have you been doing this?

V: For a while.

P: How old would you say you are?

V: There is no age.

P: And what else do you do with this technology?

V: Cleaning. Making sure it's working properly.

P: So you clean it. Who made it?

V: I don't know. I didn't.

P: Is that person still there?

V: Yeah. Everybody is looking at the same wall, which has so much technology. I'm standing on one side, and three or four people are on the other side. We're all facing the same wall, which has so much technology on it. And we're just... patiently looking at it.

P: And what does this technology do?

V: It's like measuring something. These are measuring devices installed in that wall. Like odometers, like in a car. But there are many, many of them—all across the wall. They're responsible for some kind of measurement of temperature somewhere.

P: Why are you there? What's your purpose for being here?

V: To fix things if something fails.

P: Has anything failed?

V: Not yet. But I have to be there.

P: Who tells you that you have to be there?

V: The commander. Like a captain.

P: And where is he—or she?

V: He's up front.

P: Are you allowed up there?

V: No. That's not my responsibility. My responsibility is to stay with that technology and fix it if something fails. I have to do it right away, so I cannot wander around.

The practitioner advised me to move away from that moment and focus on an important day in that lifetime, where something significant happened—the most appropriate moment to explore. He asked me to explain what I saw around me.

V: They're rushing around. Something happened.

P: What happened?

V: The temperature got too hot.

P: And what are you doing?

V: I'm not doing my job. Frozen.

P: Why are you frozen?

V: I don't know. Everybody's rushing around. Something happened, and I'm standing here, not knowing what to do.

P: Why don't you know what to do?

V: Like I failed to do my job.

P: What was your job?

V: To fix it.

P: Let's move back to that moment where something happened. When you started to freeze, what happened?

V: Something hit us. Like something flying in space that struck the spaceship.

P: Were you hurt?

V: No, but it caused overheating. The temperature became too hot.

P: Where did that object come from?

V: From space. It's kind of a meteorite or something.

P: Was the strike intentional?

V: No. It was an accident.

P: And your job was to...?

V: To monitor the temperature, which is now overheated. I don't know what to do because it's beyond my control.

P: What are you supposed to do when it overheats?

V: Cool it down.

P: How do you do that?

V: Adjust the temperature to cool it, but now it's too late. I wasn't prepared. It came too fast and overheated the entire system.

P: So what happens now?

V: They are rushing. They are panicking. I think we are going to die. It's too late. There's nothing to save. Everything is melting.

P: How does that feel?

V: Like failure. It feels like failure.

P: So if there was nothing you could do, how did you fail?

V: There was nothing I could do. It's just too late.

P: What do you see?

V: They've given up fighting.

P: Why did they give up?

V: Because there's nothing left to save.

P: What were you trying to save?

V: Our lives.

P: And you can't save anything right now?

V: No. We just have to wait until it burns.

P: What's happening now? What do you see?

V: I'm sitting there, shivering from fear.

P: Where is everyone else?

V: They went to another sector—the last sector, actually. I stayed behind with this one, the technology sector... alone.

P: And what are you doing?

V: Just sitting there... waiting for death.

The practitioner asked me to move forward to another important moment. I found myself in a quiet, empty corner, a soft, rounded space. I was looking for an exit, trying to make sense of my surroundings, but there was nothing around me—just emptiness. It felt disconnected from the chaos I had just experienced; it seemed like an entirely different scene, removed from the moment the ship was struck.

As I focused, I became aware of myself rising, floating high above the Earth. Below stretched fields of green, with distant mountains faintly visible. I was alone, immersed in the vast, vibrant energy of the planet beneath me.

I felt a purpose guiding me—a search for a specific spot on Earth, though I could not yet locate it. As I scanned the landscape, my attention was drawn to water. A massive waterfall appeared, powerful and alive, cascading with unstoppable force. Its sight was breathtaking, its presence magnetic, and I sensed that this was the place I had been seeking.

The waterfall originated from a river, tumbling down the hillsides with incredible strength. The water crashed against the stones as it plunged down the mountainside—white, cold, and relentless. I stayed there, observing, taking in every detail. The sun reflected off the rushing water, creating sparkles that danced across the surface, adding a luminous energy to the already powerful scene. Being near it, I could feel its vitality; it made me feel alive.

Looking toward my lower body, I noticed sandals—but they were empty, with no feet inside. My hands, when I looked at them, appeared see-through as well. There was no visible clothing either; my body seemed transparent, like a delicate, ethereal form.

I allowed myself to simply enjoy the Nature of Earth—the beauty of the landscape, the flowing water, the vibrant life below. Nothing else mattered in that moment. This was the spot I had been searching for. And I found it.

I was sent there to recharge. After recharging, I would return to the spaceship—the same one as before. The ship waited patiently until I completed this process. This was before the incident, a necessary pause to restore energy. To recharge, I had to be on Earth, by the water, drawing strength from its flow and vitality.

P: How is the water recharging you?

V: It's giving me energy and storing knowledge.

P: What knowledge are you gaining?

V: The knowledge I need for that project.

P: What project are you working on?

V: A project on the spaceship—fixing things, monitoring the temperature.

P: And why are you on Earth?

V: Something is connected with overheating and cooling off with water. I think I was supposed to collect water to cool off if something happened on the spaceship.

P: Did you collect the water?

V: No.

P: Why not?

V: I was distracted by the beauty. I think that was the problem—I didn't do the preparation needed for accidents.

P: What were you supposed to do?

V: I was supposed to bring cool water to the spaceship to prevent the equipment from overheating.

P: And you didn't do that?

V: No.

P: Alright.

I moved forward in that lifetime to another important moment. What I saw was stillness—complete stillness. There was no movement, no sound, just quiet. When I turned into myself, I realized I was no longer in the body. I had shifted into another form—pure energy.

Looking down, I felt lighter, free, yet there was also a lingering heaviness inside me: the sense that I had not fulfilled my mission. It was too late now. My next step was clear—I needed to return "home"-to the spirit world, to go back to my Guides and discuss what had just happened.

The practitioner asked my subconscious why it had shown me that particular lifetime. The answer came clearly: it was chosen to remind me of the consequences of distraction. In that life, I allowed myself to become absorbed in beauty and wonder, but in doing so, I failed to fulfill my mission. The subconscious explained that the same risk exists now—I am surrounded by many distractions, and if I lose focus, I may once again miss what I came here to do. The message was simple yet powerful: to stay on my path, I must cultivate unwavering focus.

The practitioner asked whether it would be easy for me to stay focused on my path. The subconscious answered that it would take discipline. I already carried that strength within me, but there were still small distractions that pulled at my energy. Little things—like people around me sending videos or reels—seemed harmless, yet each time I gave my attention to them, I lost energy that could have gone toward my real work. These distractions drained the focus I needed to fulfill my purpose. The guidance was clear: to complete my mission, I must give my energy only to what truly matters and cut away everything else.

The practitioner asked how I would know what I needed to focus on. The subconscious responded simply: I already knew. There was no doubt within me, no uncertainty about my path. And yet, I still allowed distractions to enter. Why? Because I wanted to be nice. But the message was firm—being nice in this way was not serving me. The distractions were not random; they were placed before me with the purpose of preventing me from becoming who I was meant to be. To move beyond them, the guidance was clear: I must focus, and only focus.

S (Subconscious): It seems simple enough, but she's still giving in to little distractions. And little distraction by little distraction...

P: They become bigger.

S: Exactly.

P: But you can help her—you can give her a push to avoid these distractions, right?

S: We are already doing it all the time.

P: Then why doesn't she hear you?

S: There are still remnants of her being "too nice." She's still learning the lesson of setting boundaries.

P: So she still has more to learn about boundaries?

S: Just a little more. The people who used to distract her. They
won't be in her life anymore, but they were around until recently.

P: I see. Wasn't it going to be hard for her not to have them in her
life anymore?

S: No. Some people are not going to be part of her life any longer.
Her family will remain, but she must learn to set healthy boundaries—even with her parents.

P: Let's continue the body scan. Starting from the head and moving
down—what do you notice?

S: The chest. There's pressure in her chest.

P: Pressure in the chest. What is that related to?

S: It comes from her living situation in New Orleans.

P: But she has already closed that chapter, right?

S: Yes. It's finished now. She doesn't need to feel it anymore.

P: Good. What about her eyes?

S: She was checking herself out in the darkness.

P: Can you clear that out and improve her eyes?

S: Yes, but she resists. She believes she doesn't deserve it.

P: But she does deserve it, and you and I both know that.

S: Yes. She is worthy.

P: Why does she think she isn't?

S: Childhood trauma. She grew up believing she wasn't enough.

P: Does she carry any karmic debt?

S: From her mom.

P: From her mom? Why?

S: It isn't hers. She accepted her mother's debt as her own.

P: So she doesn't need to carry it? Can you help her release it?

S: Yes. It's already done. She has cleared all debts with her mother.

P: Beautiful. And she has nothing else left to carry from her mom?

S: That's right.

P: What about her dad?

S: There is something sexually connected to him.

P: Where does that come from?

S: Unfulfilled desires from a past life.

(My father and I were secret lovers in one of our past lives. Through many regression sessions I gathered that information and wrote about it in my first book *Because I Can Remember*.)

P: But she isn't living that past life now, is she?

S: No, but she is still experiencing it.

P: Why?

S: Because it hasn't been cleared yet.

P: And how can we clear it?

S: We leave it in that lifetime, and we close the chapter.

P: And that's something that you can do right now?

S: Yes.

P: Because she doesn't need to carry that anymore, right?

S: No.

P: So does she have any other debts to either her mom or her dad?

S: No.

P: Can you check one more time? So she knows that those debts, they're paid.

S: The guilt is no longer there. No shame, no guilt. She released them. We are helping her to release her mom's influence completely, like leaving her body. She can do it on her own. She has been carrying it for too long.

P: Yeah. What about her sister?

S: Anger.

P: Where does that come from?

S: Past Life.

P: So much like her dad, what can you do?

S: Release the anger.

P: How does she release it?

S: She needs to understand that some things have to happen the way they happen.

P: You can help her see that, correct?

S: Yes. There were different lives before that past life, and they had unfinished business.

P: So, they kept carrying it forward?

S: The last past life involved the pain of returning karma. She didn't know about lifetimes before that. So, that's why she felt guilty toward her sister. But she paid off the karma.

P: Moving forward, is there anything left that she needs to clear?

S: No.

P: So we've worked on her mom, her dad, and her sister.

S: Sister—she's cleared her karma in her past life, but she didn't understand that. And she still felt anger, because she sees only a small part of the whole concept.

In one of my past lives, my sister had been my cousin, and she was executed on my behalf. I had known about that life, yet in this current life, there was always a sense of coolness between us, a subtle tension, as if we were quietly competing, each trying to be the best. What I hadn't understood at the time was that by executing her in that past life, I had actually been "returning a favor". Something had happened in yet another timeline—she had caused me great harm—and this act had been part of the balance being restored.

S: We are removing that coldness between the two sisters.

P: Let her breathe that in—the connection that she and her sister truly have. Allow her to fill herself with that love she carries for her parents. To actually feel all that love without any debt. Now let's go back to the body scan, since we've already worked through the head. What's going on with her teeth?

S: She doesn't have lineage support.

P: So, what can you do for that?

S: Restore the connection.

P: You're doing that now?

S: Yes. They're holding hands now.

P: Okay, closing the gaps. And how's her heart?

S: Most of the issues with the heart came from relationships with her relatives and her roommates. But with the roommates, she needed to learn the lessons. And just check that part of the chapter—she did complete it.

P: And what about her cousin's family?

S: The relationship with her cousin is causing pain in her heart too.

P: How does she heal that?

S: She has to accept that it's not the timeline for them to awaken.

P: And you can help her see that?

S: Yes, she understands it now. She has to accept the fact that it's not their time to awaken yet. She gets so frustrated that they're stuck. Everyone has their own timeline and their own lessons to learn. You have to understand that.

P: So her heart is healed now?

S: We are healing it. We are improving it. We are removing anything that is causing her pain. And she's going to see the reflection of that healing in her dog as well.

P: She's very connected with her dog, Kiki, isn't she?

S: Yes. Kiki is observing her.

P: How can she cut off that link so she doesn't send negativity to her?

S: She cannot. It's their soul contract. Kiki signed up to be both a neutralizer and an observer.

P: She's helped out a lot, hasn't she?

S: Yes, too much even.

P: It's amazing that they have a soul contract and live together in such a loving way...

S: They're soulmates. They're from the same soul group. She knows that. But she didn't know that Kiki was absorbing her troubles and her negative energy. Otherwise, Volha would get the same things Kiki experienced.

A few months ago, Kiki was diagnosed with heart failure, a heart tumor, and an excess buildup of fluid in her abdomen.

P: Any problems with her legs at all?

S: No. She thought she had. She's walking toward her future, so she's not refusing anymore.

P: She's so connected with her soul sister, Kiki. She's so worried about her.

S: Kiki is fulfilling her soul contract. She knew what she was doing, what she was getting herself into.

P: So can you help Volha understand that better? It's really tough to watch.

S: What Volha went through—she could not do that on her own. She needed support. And she needed someone to observe it. She went into darkness. The project of bringing light into darkness (in New Orleans)...Yes. We were not kidding about it. That was her project. She signed up for it. It was one of the hardest ones in this lifetime. But she just finished it. She could not have done that without help from a physical observer who could hold the negative energy. Otherwise, it would have disturbed and damaged Volha's body even more.

Bringing Light into Darkness

To explain this part of my session - Right after Mount Shasta, I returned to LA, but nothing felt aligned. I felt a strong pull to go somewhere else. When I asked my Spirit Guides where to go, I received a clear sign: New Orleans. It felt perfectly right.

I had been to New Orleans many times before, and it held both positive and negative memories for me. Still, I packed my carry-on, brought Kiki, bought a one-way ticket, and left—planning to stay only a few weeks. I ended up spending two months there. After a brief return to Los Angeles, I went back to New Orleans again, and that's when Kiki was diagnosed with heart failure.

During that period, everything seemed challenging. Negative events unfolded one after another, creating tension in my body. When I asked my Spirit Guides about my purpose there, they explained that I had signed up for a project: to bring light into the darkness of New Orleans. The city attracts people from around the world, and when traumatic or negative events occur, the energy remains in the space. My task was to maintain a high vibration and, when possible, visit these places to bless the land and transform the energy, so others would absorb positivity instead of pain.

It was overwhelming. The work drained me physically and emotionally, and I needed support to complete it without harming my body. By the end of my time there, I fully understood my role. Leaving New Orleans, I felt like a wounded soldier returning from war—but proud of the light I had brought into the darkness.

P: Is there anything else left in the body scan that needs to be completed?

S: Hips.

P: What's wrong with the hips?

S: They're too tight.

P: Why?

S: Tension.

P: Where does this tension come from?

S: From her living situation. Always being on alert.

P: But she's not going to have that anymore, right?

S: No. She left that behind.

P: So what can we do with her hips?

S: Release the tension from her hips. Let it go. That's it—call it done.

P: Is there anything else left?

S: Shoulders.

P: Let's check her shoulders. What's wrong with them?

S: Too much weight.

P: Whose weight is she carrying?

S: Her parents.

P: Why?

S: She talks to them too much.

P: But we cleared all the karmic debt with them.

S: Yes, but she needs to reduce phone calls to a minimum. She's spending too much time talking to her parents. They don't understand her. She's just losing her energy.

I was told that I didn't have to completely cut my parents off, but I had been calling them almost every day. Reducing that communication to once or twice a week was enough to be a caring daughter without expending so much energy. By cutting back, I could preserve my energy for my own projects and move forward faster.

P: Allow her to feel what it's like without that weight.

S: Yes.

P: Why has she been so low on energy lately?

S: The people surrounding her personal space were living off her life energy. They were sucking it like vampires. In the end, she started to protect herself with a pyramid of light, but still they were too close to her physical body. The roommates, the building—it's all dark. There are dark energies. In the beginning, she didn't protect her energy at all. She thought she was protected, but she had to set intentions every day to protect her physical and energetic bodies.

P: And now she does that?

S: Yes, she does.

P: Can we give her a moment to fully breathe in, through her whole soul and physical body? To take in that pure energy from Source, to help cleanse any negative energy she's been carrying?

S: Yes.

P: New Orleans is in the past. She doesn't need to carry that energy anymore. Let her really breathe it in.

S: She did a really great job there.

P: Yes. She did.

S: We are also working on Kiki now. She did a great job too. We're sending light energy to her abdomen to reduce and eliminate the excess fluid and to shrink the tumor on her heart. Her heart is strong enough for another mile or two—she has another long journey ahead. She will make it. She will make it all the way to Mount Shasta.

P: Speaking of that one trip that's coming up so soon... Why is Volha so drawn to Sedona?

S: It's her home.

P: Where is her home?

S: In the mountains. Red Rock.

P: I thought it was actually part of Lemuria.

S: It was. Close enough. That's her connection. The energy is the same. She felt the same energy in Pluto's Cave in Mount Shasta. That's the same energy. The same energy as Lemuria. When she feels that energy in different spots, she feels like she's home. And the entire area of Sedona is filled with that energy.

P: And why is she in Asheville, North Carolina, right now?

S: To activate this spot and get activated. It's an exchange of energy.

P: She remembered, from the past, the story of what happened to her at the end of Lemuria.

S: She went "home" and decided to incarnate over and over again.

P: Yeah, but she left somebody behind.

S: Her family.

P: How does she know they're still there?

S: He's waiting for her. He's helping her.

P: Can you bring him here now and let him say something to her?

S: Yes.

P: Allow them to connect so she can get that reassurance that it's still there.

S: Everything she's experiencing is true. It's actually happening. She's not making it up. She's not creating it. It's already created.

P: And what about her daughter?

S: She's coming at the right time—when she raises her frequency to the point that she's ready to bring another soul into physical form.

S: It's funny, because she tells me that she screams at you all the time that she's ready.

S: She's not. She is ready for Los Angeles... Yes, it's a big project, and she knows what she's putting herself into. She's ready for that. She's tough now, and she has to be tough. Just being nice in that area wouldn't do anything. She would give up and end up losing. That's why we brought all that hustle and bustle in New Orleans, opening up her heart and throat chakras, so she'd be ready for the challenges—the wolves. But she has to work in that area too. She signed up for that. That was the second project. She wasn't ready for Los Angeles at first. She had to go through New Orleans first to get that rough, tough ex- perience, to be able to work in Los Angeles.

P: Speaking of the upcoming Los Angeles project, part of her un- dercover work requires her to be... what we call... pretty. She's under this crazy assumption that she has bags under her eyes, but I don't see anything.

S: It's a little bit of swelling from her kidneys. She's had late nights and had to carry Kiki to the dog park at night, so her kidneys didn't have a chance to fully cleanse as they should during sleep.

P: So the puffiness and swelling in her body will go away once she restores her sleep?

S: Yes. We are fixing and detoxifying her kidneys now, but once she gets normal sleep, everything will return to normal.

P: You keep helping her heal every time she sleeps, correct?

S: Yes. And she hasn't had a normal sleep pattern for the past six months. She really needs to focus on that.

P: I think there's only one thing left, and that is to let her and Kiki take a moment to be fully engulfed by that white pyramid we know as Source. Allow her to breathe it in, allow Kiki to breathe it in, and really cleanse anything left that we might have overlooked.

S: Kiki has too many toxins.

P: How can we clean those out?

S: We are doing it now. She's a dog, so she's really close to the ground, and she was sniffing those toxins. We need to clear Kiki's kidneys as well.

P: Yes. What else does Volha need to know?

S: She is exactly where she needs to be. She is at that point in life where the next level is around the corner. She is not quite ready yet — but we are guiding her, pushing her gently forward. She will have to take that step and cross the river of fear. And when the moment comes, she will know it without doubt. She cannot play small — because she didn't come here to play small. This lifetime is not about hiding. Yes, she is scared. But we are here to help her — even with the financial aspect. Support will be there when she chooses to step fully into her purpose.

Kiki still has adventures to continue. They are not done yet. Kiki will return, yes — in a different form. And she will remember everything. The children being born now — they remember.

P: Though at times it also feels confusing.

S: Much of that confusion comes from their unhealed parents. Yet children, at a young age, they remember. Some will remember forever. Some will be harmed by society, by the systems of Earth. But more and more of them will stay awake. They are born awake, and they will stay awake. And they are the ones who will break the system.

P: What else does she have to do? What other projects must be completed before her daughter comes?

S: She needs to activate the Divine Feminine Energy.

P: She is trying, isn't she?

S: She must do it on Mount Shasta. That will be the final step. It is also the place where she will finish writing her second book. And the second project will be completed there as well. It will look like magic — but by then, she will already believe in magic.

P: Yes. We are here this week in beautiful Asheville, North Carolina, for a Quantum Healing Hypnosis reunion. What else is Dolores pushing her to learn?

S: It is a Gridwork. People from all around bring their energy here, get recharged, and then carry that energy back home. That is called grid work. Yes — that is one of the projects, one of the missions. It is what everybody is doing, even without knowing it.

The second one is the exchange of energy. It is collective work. Like bringing cars to a charging station — they get charged, and then drive in different directions. The same concept. People come to this place to recharge, then go back where they are needed, to do the work.

P: There were other questions she had. She came with a whole list of them. But she lost them. Why did she lose the questions?

S: We hid them. She will find them weeks later.

Both laughed. I had prepared a long list of questions, carefully choosing each one and making sure all the main things on my mind were included. But somehow, I lost the list. And I'm usually so organized; I always know exactly where I put my things. I searched and searched, and eventually, I gave up. When we started the session, we created a new list of questions on the spot, and the conversation took a completely different direction than I had planned. Looking back, I realize now that the Subconscious (collective energy) was redirecting my focus to something far more important than what I had originally written.

P: She has a lot of contact with her Spirit Guides. We spent so much time talking about past lives, Ascended Masters, St. Germain, Archangel Michael, even Lady Magdalene and Jesus. Yet today, you showed her such a strange, different world in a past life. Why did she see that? Yes, we've covered this before, but it's important. She's done many past life regressions and never mentioned being on a ship, out in space, failing a mission because she was distracted by beauty. How is that so disconnected from everything else she's seen before?

S: Everything else she has seen before, she has already cleared. We bring things up step by step to clear, to heal, and to move forward. The hardest lessons and karmic debts have been paid — mostly connected to her parents. Now she is clear. There is no need for her to return to those past lives because the work is done. It was hard, but she did it. There are so many more parallel realities she is not aware of. We chose this one — where she failed her mission — because she had responsibilities she neglected due to distractions on Earth. And even now, on Earth, she still gets distracted by earthly things. We want to make sure... she has a big project ahead. She cannot allow herself any little earthly distractions to prevent her from achieving what she came here to do. Focus the energy on the main thing. Don't lose the energy on distractions.

P: Is there any final message for Volha?

S: Be mindful of your surroundings. Keep protection. Set healthy boundaries. Sometimes you will live like a wealthy woman, sometimes like a homeless one — but that is all part of the game. Keep going. And she understands the game now. She spent two years without a car, and she was fine. She was able to complete such a heavy project in New Orleans. All energies, soul contracts, and attachments from New Orleans have already been released.

But there is a positive part, too. She had to meet certain people for their own activation. So that project is not only about darkness; it is also about moving forward in a different form. Just continue.

Group ET Contact Meditation

During a group ET contact meditation in Asheville, held with sacred intention and cosmic openness, I slipped into a deep ceremonial trance. The edges of the physical world dissolved. I was no longer just myself—I was vast, eternal, multidimensional.

In that still, shimmering space, I reconnected with my star lineage. I am Electra, one of the Seven Sisters of the Pleiades.

All around me, my radiant Pleiadian sisters danced—divine, mesmerizing goddesses spiraling in waves of light and love. Their movement wasn't just visual; it was felt in every cell of my being. Their presence was healing, electric, familiar. A spiral of remembrance.

I remembered the moment my soul chose to come to Earth ‑ to heal and open hearts, expand consciousness, and fulfill my mission. I saw myself volunteering—stepping forward to fulfill a mission of the awakening. I had come to help humanity remember. At that moment, my sisters vowed to support me across time and space. They whispered, "You will never be alone."

I was also told that my cosmic mother, Pleione, has incarnated on Earth—and that I would meet her once I get married. I was then shown my descent from Source. I saw the joy, the willingness, the excitement I carried as I left the higher realms. But the moment I entered 3D density, everything changed. The joy gave way to sorrow, and I felt very uncomfortable. I remembered what had been lost—the lightness, the love, the unity. Still, even in that ache, I was gently reminded:

"The Pleiadians are here. Around you. Within you. You are one of them."

I was shown that I would soon begin visiting the ships during sacred windows—during high-energy gatherings and celestial alignments. And that during great meetings of consciousness on Earth, my awareness would be fully present, interconnected with the galactic field, participating beyond the body.

In another vision, Saint-Germain appeared before me with profound gentleness, his presence cloaked in light and deep familiarity. When he saw my surprise at seeing him, he smiled with that big, radiant smile I've come to recognize from my visions. Without speaking, he poured an Ascension Elixir into a uniquely shaped vessel—something like a curved wooden spoon, almost spiral in design—and handed it to me with great care. For a long time, I believed this sacred moment would take place on Mount Shasta, but instead, it found me in Asheville. That was the deeper teaching: the sacred doesn't always arrive where we expect it—it arrives where we are truly ready.

Then came Mary Magdalene. Her presence was soft, yet deeply powerful. She approached me with grace, placed her hands upon my womb, and transmitted healing—pure, divine feminine essence. Through her, I received a sacred blessing... a remembrance of my creative force, my womb's intelligence, and my divine power.

At the culmination of the vision, a clear message streamed through: "You have been asleep. Now, you are awake."

And I was.

My consciousness was returning—layer by layer—streaming from the Source like a beam of crystalline light. I saw multidimensional fields: auras, frequencies, rainbow bands of energy wrapping around all life. I witnessed a radiant pillar connecting me directly to the Source, and felt my own light body being activated for the next phase of my mission.

I remembered that many Pleiadians who walk this Earth are here as healers. Gentle, radiant, loyal beings—teaching through love, presence, and resonance. They are hidden in plain sight. They are among us.

33

Aligned by Destiny

The time was drawing near for my journey to Mt. Shasta—as promised, as agreed. Not with anyone in particular, not in a traditional sense, but with the Universe itself. A sacred contract had been signed somewhere beyond time, and my soul remembered. I was coming back.

Before the physical journey began, I started looking for housing. My favorite home from the previous summer—the one that held such sweet memories—was, of course, already booked for the entire season. Everything else was either wildly overpriced or simply not aligned. It felt like a game of hide-and-seek with destiny.

The only house available was the same one I had considered last year. Back then, I was negotiating to rent it for a full month, but someone else swooped in before I could gather my thoughts. This year, that very same house was the only one within reach again. As if the Universe had put it on hold.

I reached out to the management company. They responded warmly: "Yes, we're moving forward with you." A flicker of hope. A whisper from the mountain.

But then—delays.

Day one passed.

Then day two brought only a brief "Stay tuned."

By day three, they requested my address.

By day four... silence.

Doubt crept in like a slow fog.

Maybe I wasn't supposed to go to Mt. Shasta this year.

Maybe it was time to root myself in Los Angeles—roll up my sleeves, get serious, and "build a foundation." That's what the rational mind said. The one that speaks in bullet points and deadlines. It tried to quiet my heart's desire, which still softly whispered, "Go. Finish what you started."

But the voice of logic grew louder, demanding structure, commitment, grounding. And so, with a heavy heart, I typed the message to the property manager:

"My plans have changed. I'm no longer coming to Mount Shasta."

I sent it.

No reply. Not even a read receipt. The silence felt like a door closing. And then, five hours later, I got the email:

"Please sign the lease agreement."

Wait, what?

I had just said no. I had just let it go.

Without hesitation, I signed. I emailed it back. Then I sent another message to the manager: "Please disregard my earlier message. I'm coming."

To this day, I'm not sure if they ever received the cancellation. Maybe they didn't see it in time. Maybe Spirit made sure it was lost in the void. Whatever the case, I was going. I was finally going back to Mount Shasta.

The moment I hit "send," a surge of energy moved through my entire body like lightning in the bloodstream. I felt alive. I felt like a feather—light, unburdened, floating in harmony with the wind of divine timing. All the heavy options I had considered in Los Angeles suddenly felt gray, misaligned, flat.

This was the only path that made sense.

I began to pack—not just clothes and essentials, but intentions, dreams, and prayers. I packed my journal, my crystals, my sacred tools. I packed for transformation. Because I could feel it: this summer would be different. This summer would be life-changing.

When it's meant to be, it will be.

Even when you try to walk away. Even when your doubt whispers louder than your faith.

Mount Shasta calls who she needs.

And this time, she was calling me home.

That night, I had a dream. I saw my light body—radiant, translucent, shimmering with divine geometry. I wasn't dreaming of light... I was light.

And there was a voice: "Six days after arrival in Mount Shasta."

That was it. No more, no less. A cryptic message, delivered with cosmic certainty.

I woke with my heart racing, not in fear, but with the quiet thrill of destiny unfolding. What would happen six days after I arrived? A meeting? A memory? An activation?

I didn't need the answer. I just needed to trust.

And keep packing.

34

Return to Mount Shasta

"When the student is strong enough to stand against the opinions of the world of ignorance then he or she is ready to bear witness to the Marvels of the Individual Activities of God manifested by the Ascended Masters."

—Godfre Ray King

It was the 4th of July, and I found myself deep in thought. One year ago—almost to the day—I was in Mount Shasta, preparing to leave. Technically, I left on July 5th, but the 4th still felt like my last real day there. That afternoon, I was picked up by a friend, and we made our way north toward Washington. But on the journey back to Los Angeles, we stopped for one final night around Mt. Shasta.

Now, exactly a year later, I had just booked a house in Mt. Shasta again. The start date? July 10th. Just five days off from the previous year's departure. It felt like time was folding over itself. A subtle overlap. A gentle echo.

I sat with that thought, marveling at how strangely aligned it all seemed. What were the chances? What did it mean?

The next day the same thought returned: What if I didn't wait five more days? What if I could manipulate time and go to Mt. Shasta now? The pull was strong.

At the same time, I found myself surrounded by my relatives who were busy preparing for a party—one I hadn't even known about. It quickly became clear that there would be little peace, and plenty of alcohol. That alone was enough to disturb my inner balance. I wasn't drawn to the gathering at all.

I considered escaping to the beach and coming back later that evening. But I knew these gatherings never ended early. I could feel my energy slipping. Something inside me, quiet but firm, whispered: No. It's time. Go now.

There was no overthinking, no hesitation. Within an hour, I was on the freeway. It was 4 PM in the afternoon. I hadn't booked a hotel or packed with a plan. I didn't even fill the gas tank until I was already on the road. I grabbed coffee, and that was enough. Kiki, as always, was thrilled. She loves road trips—tail wagging, nose pressed to the window, soaking up the freedom.

We drove for nearly nine hours, stopping here and there, but I didn't make it all the way to Mt. Shasta that night. Instead, we pulled off near the lakes, about an hour south of town. It was quiet, wrapped in trees and starlight. I had never slept in the car before, but I had a soft, warm blanket and Kiki curled up beside me. It felt safe. It felt like exactly where I needed to be.

I slept for just four hours, but it was enough. At 6 AM I was up, heart open, ready for the mountain.

The first stop was Seven Suns, my favorite little spot in Mt. Shasta. Coffee and a breakfast burrito, shared with Kiki outdoors.

The place was already buzzing—early risers, travelers, locals. But I was in no rush. We soaked in the morning light, letting the stillness settle around us.

After breakfast, we headed to the park to fill up on healing spring water. Real, living water. Kiki drank deeply, and I followed. Then we walked, slowly, through the cool morning air. The sun had started to rise in golden threads, warming our faces. We sat, we breathed, we just were.

Then, as if guided, I felt the unmistakable urge: Drive up the mountain.

It reminded me of the decision I almost made on the drive up—the one where I nearly changed course and went through San Francisco to visit the Redwoods instead. I was pulled to that idea, tempted to take a different path. But something stronger kept nudging me toward Mt. Shasta. Only later would I find out why.

An Unexpected Encounter on a Mountain

The sun was climbing higher and higher when Kiki and I began the familiar ascent up the mountain. We made a few stops along the way—stretching our legs, taking pictures, soaking in the views that always seemed to shift with the seasons and my own inner state.

But something felt... different.

As we drove higher, the air grew sharper, crisper. Not cold in temperature, but cold in energy—clean, distant, like a crystalline veil had descended over the mountain. I had been here around the same time the year before, and yes, there had been snow then too. But it hadn't felt like this. This time, it felt like winter was still lingering in the bones of the land. Mystical. Magical. But also remote—like the mountain had pulled back just a little, watching quietly from a distance.

Still, I felt the pull.

We finally found a parking spot and stepped out into the quiet. The first thing I wanted to do was show Kiki one of my favorite sacred places—what I call the Twin Flame Tree. I wrote about it in my first book. It's actually two trees, grown from the same root, merging upward together. You can feel it—one tree carries strong, masculine energy; the other, gentle and feminine. They seem like they've been in love for centuries.

As we started walking toward it, I barely made five steps when Kiki simply lay down in the middle of the trail. She refused to go any farther. I laughed to myself—Well, I guess we're not rushing today.

And that's when I saw her.

Sitting under the tree nearby was a woman. She looked radiant, completely at peace in the silence of the mountain. Our eyes met, and in that moment, there was instant recognition—soul to soul. She smiled and made a gentle joke about Kiki giving up so quickly. I laughed and responded without even thinking. It all unfolded so naturally.

We started talking—just talking. No introductions, no names, just two women sharing stories like childhood friends reunited after years apart. It was as if we picked up a conversation we had left unfinished lifetimes ago. We spoke for thirty minutes, maybe more—I lost track of time completely. Everything else around us faded, and the connection felt pure and effortless.

Eventually, she told me she was there with a friend and wanted to introduce me. So we walked together across the road where her friend was resting. While she slept, the two of us kept chatting. Her energy was soft but grounded. She told me about her life, her spiritual path, and the healing work she does.

Her friend eventually woke up, and we all started talking. I learned that both of them were energy healers, camping on the mountain for a few days. They had been called there too. And then something happened that made everything click into place.

She told me they were leaving on the 10th.

The exact day I was originally supposed to arrive.

If I hadn't left early—if I had waited just five more days as planned—I never would've met them. Our timelines would never have intersected. But because of the party, the noise, the uncomfortable feeling, and the sudden knowing that I had to go now, the connection happened. The mountain orchestrated it.

She told me she felt my energy when I first approached and instantly opened herself to receive it. That's why we started talking. That's why we trusted one another without even knowing names.

Sometimes we don't understand the detours, the sudden urges, the discomfort that pushes us away from where we thought we were supposed to be. But when the story starts to unfold... It all makes perfect sense.

Everything happens for a reason. Every soul we meet, every turn we take, every whisper we follow.

The Redwoods Calling

After our magical conversation on the mountain, I didn't even make it to the Twin Flame Tree. I felt complete. The mountain had already given me what I came for. I looked up at her, that majestic, snow-tipped peak watching silently over us all, and I whispered a quiet thank you. I knew I'd be back in just a few days, and somehow, that felt just right.

The move-in was planned for the 10th, so I had a few open days. As I stood there, breathing in the crisp mountain air, I suddenly felt something shift inside me. I was free to go now. The Redwoods were calling.

And the trees were waiting.

We entered the land of ancient sentinels—giant Redwoods standing like timeless guardians. At first, I didn't stop. I just drove, letting the trees speak. They didn't speak with words, but their presence was a vibration. I could feel it in my bones, in my chest. As I drove, I began to speak to them—not out loud, but through thought. From my heart.

"May you be protected. May you be honored. May no harm ever come to you—not mentally, not physically, not spiritually. May this land remain sacred. We are one. You are me. I am you."

With every thought, I felt waves of goosebumps surge through my body, like electricity dancing across my skin. Up and down. Again and again. It felt like they were responding. They heard me.

By the time we reached the coastline, the sun was lowering and the ocean was wild. We stopped in Crescent City to eat a simple sandwich and watch the waves. It was too cold for a walk, and Kiki once again refused to leave the car. So we stayed, cozy inside, watching the water crash against the rocks.

And that's when I saw it.

On the horizon, there was a rock rising from the sea like an island. It stood quietly in the distance, draped in mist and sunlight. There was something ancient about it—something familiar. My heart stirred. What does this remind me of?

And then, like lightning, the memory came rushing back.

Lemuria.

That silhouette... the crashing waves... the energy in the air—it all mirrored a place I knew deep within my soul. A place I had seen in dreams. A place I remembered before I ever knew what remembering meant. I had felt Lemurian energy in the Los Angeles area before, but this—this was different. This wasn't just energy. This was home.

As I continued driving along the coast, more shapes appeared—cliffs and outcroppings that looked just like the ones I'd seen in visions. It felt like Lemuria was there, just beneath the surface. Like the land was still alive, still breathing beneath the ocean, whispering from beneath the waves.

And I found myself asking a question:

Could we bring Lemuria back?

Not just in memory. Not just in energy. But physically. Could we raise the lost continent—not with force or disruption—but gently, with intention, with love? Could we become powerful enough, aligned enough, to bring back what was lost?

To cross that land again. To step on Lemurian soil in this physical body.

To remember everything. To rebuild something sacred, something real.

And in that moment, looking out at the waves and the ancient mountain in the sea, I knew it wasn't just a dream.

The trip was only a five-and-a-half-hour drive, but something strange happened. By the time we pulled up to the little hotel near the forest, I felt like I had been gone for an entire week. It was the strangest sensation. Time didn't feel real.

I even looked at the clock again to make sure. Five and a half hours? That couldn't be right. The shift in energy was too big. It felt like I had driven through a portal—like something opened between Mt. Shasta and the Redwoods that swallowed time and rearranged space.

35

My Mystical Detour

I had booked a hotel for two nights. After the night Kiki and I spent sleeping in the car, the room felt like a cloud in heaven. The bed was soft, wide, and forgiving. I couldn't get up the next morning. My body had other plans. It wanted stillness.

Kiki refused to leave the bed too. She was curled up like a little guardian angel, blissfully surrendered. It was so peaceful. After all the movement, it was a rare pleasure to stretch my legs, sip my coffee in bed, and do some light work - I had my laptop, full internet, and a whole list of people scheduled for consultations. I had full permission—from the Universe and from myself—not to push. Not to explore. Not to be "on." Just to be.

That hotel room became a sacred pause. Maybe I had already received what I came for on this journey. Maybe there was nothing else to seek. The energy, especially between Mount Shasta and the edge of the Redwoods along the West Coast line heading north, had already spoken to me in powerful, invisible ways. That was the area I felt it the most—like a pulse coming from the Earth herself.

But in the hotel? The energy was noticeably softer. Dimmed. As if the Spirit said, Rest now. So I did.

The next day, it was time to return to Mount Shasta. I thought two nights would be enough, and I still felt no urge to wander further.

Instead of retracing my steps north, I decided to complete the loop. I chose a different route—one that crossed the mountains and led through Redding. The GPS showed about four hours, a smooth, shorter drive. A perfect circle. From where it began... back to the mountain.

But as always, the road had its own soul. Somewhere along the winding mountain path, traffic came to a dead stop. Road construction. We sat there for what felt like forever—at least 30 or 40 minutes. And of course, right at that moment, nature decided to remind me I wasn't entirely in control.

When the traffic finally began to move, I drove quickly. Then, just ahead, I spotted a small turnout near the river—a simple rest stop tucked into the landscape. Without hesitation, I pulled over and stepped out.

The air was warm, the river inviting. It felt like a moment meant for healing. Kiki and I made our way down to the riverbank. I kicked off my shoes and stepped into the icy water. A sudden release shot through my body—powerful, grounding, electric.

I remembered what the woman on the mountain had told me just days before: "You need to walk barefoot. There are blocks in your legs. In your feet. Let the Earth pull them out." And in that moment, she was right. As the water touched my skin, I felt it: A letting go. A release. A weight I was carrying lifted from my legs and feet.

Kiki waded nearby. I splashed cool water over her fur to ease the heat, and we stood there in silence. Time paused. My feet were on fire—not with pain, but with energy. Something had been blocked... and now it flowed.

That stop—unplanned, inconvenient, even frustrating—turned out to be a moment of divine design. If not for the construction, I would've just driven by. I would've admired the river from the car window, thinking it was beautiful... but never stopping. Never stepping in. Never releasing. It reminded me, once again: Everything happens for a reason. Even delays. Even detours. Especially those.

We hit the road again, feeling refreshed from our time at the river. The GPS suggested—"Save 22 minutes? Reroute to avoid road construction?" Sure, I thought. Twenty-two minutes sounded reasonable. I tapped OK without hesitation. I didn't know that saving 22 minutes would add two hours to my trip.

At first, it seemed fine. Then the road narrowed. We were climbing, climbing, and climbing again. The air got thinner. The trees grew wilder. My car struggled to keep speed. It was steep—so steep. And suddenly, there were no cars. No one in sight. For 30... maybe 40 minutes... nothing. Just me, Kiki, the humming engine, and the sound of mountain silence. It got surreal fast. "Are you guys (my Spirit Guides) driving me into another dimension?" I laughed out loud. It felt exactly like that—like I'd been plucked from one reality and placed into a parallel one without even realizing it. I saw one car. Then nothing for another half hour. "This can't be real," I whispered. "Where is everyone?"

The more I drove, the stranger it felt. Beautiful, yes. But strange. Like the trees were watching. Like the road itself had a secret. I couldn't shake the feeling that I was driving through a fold in time. We were somewhere deep in the Shasta-Trinity Forest. But the GPS... had nothing. It showed a blank screen. No lakes, no roads, no names. Just a blue line floating through white nothingness. It was like driving through a dream.

We were so high in the mountains. There was no way this saved me 22 minutes. It added up to at least two extra hours. But I knew—again—everything happens for a reason. And so I surrendered to the detour. I pulled over by the lakes. I took photos. Let the forest fill my lungs. Let the water reflect my own stillness. Every time I thought, This is so surreal. There are no cars,—a car would drive by. Just one. And then nothing again for 40 minutes. I started laughing again. "Are you guys listening to my thoughts? Throwing in a hologram car so I don't freak out?" It was hilarious and a little spooky. But the beauty—oh, the beauty—was mesmerizing. And that's when I thanked my Spirit Guides out loud. "Thank you for this sightseeing trip. Thank you for this detour. I had nowhere to be. No one to rush to. And not many people get to just wander through ancient forests like this, on roads where time doesn't apply." It felt like a luxury of the soul.

Then... the forest changed. Suddenly, we were driving through blackened trees. A ghost forest. An entire stretch of mountain that had burned—miles and miles of charred trunks, branches turned to ash, and silence that held pain. I could feel it in my chest. In my bones. I slowed the car. The land was grieving. It wasn't just what I saw—it was what I felt. A deep ache. A scorched silence.

Without thinking, I rolled down the window. I extended my hand. I began to channel. Words flowed from me—not rehearsed, not planned—just pure intention from Source. "May this land be protected. May all living beings here be restored and healed. May rain come to satisfy your thirst. May you never feel thirst again. I call upon Angels, Archangels, and Spirit Guides— Bring rejuvenation to this sacred land. Bring peace, light, and life back to this place."

It was more than a prayer. It was a transmission. Suddenly, the detour made sense. That route was chosen not for time, not for efficiency—but for purpose. I was sent there to witness... to feel... to bless.

Eventually, the road led me back into town. The energy shifted. I stopped for gas and grabbed a small bag of nuts from the gas station. Filled up a big bottle of spring water from the park. Then, Kiki and I were back on the road—heading up the mountain to spend the night on Mt. Shasta. I felt the weight of something sacred had just moved through me. And yet... part of me was hesitating.

The Preparation Room

I always receive the same message from the mountain: Whenever you have no place to go, you can come to me. She feels like a mother—always there for me, always loving. She would welcome me like home—where I'd feel cherished, seen, and refreshed.

But until now, I had never spent a night actually camping here. Sleeping in a car or in a campground was something I had never considered. I've always been so used to the comfort of daily life—hot showers, clean beds, being able to brush my teeth and use the powder room without effort. So when I realized I had a few nights before moving into my next place, I had a choice: book another hotel... or try something completely different. I hesitated. But I kept hearing: Whatever happens, happens for a reason. So I said yes to the experience—and we drove up the mountain.

There were people around. Cars parked. The sun was going down quickly, and it was getting colder by the minute. I wasn't prepared for the drop in temperature. I had Kiki's little jacket in the car, but she wasn't wearing it, and soon she started to shake. I carried her close as we walked, trying to warm her up. We headed slowly toward the mountain—and that's when the tears came. It hit me so deeply. I could feel them. Everyone I love was there. My soul family, beings I've known in lifetimes beyond memory—they were all there, waiting for me. But I couldn't see them. I had forgotten. I had lost my memory. I was here, walking this Earth in a heavier vibration, while they stood in a higher frequency, watching, holding space.

On the way back to the car, I met a beautiful couple who had been camping there for days, sleeping in a tent. We exchanged names, energy, stories—beautiful humans spending time in a beautiful place. I realized I wasn't alone.

There were facilities, though they had no running water. Everyone brought their own. I had mine. I asked them about showers, and they smiled. "We're just jumping into the lake."

"Oh, the lake is warm?" I asked.

They laughed. "No, it's freezing."

Ohhh. Something completely new to me. But I had made a decision: to become comfortable being uncomfortable. So Kiki and I climbed into the backseat, wrapped ourselves in my goose blanket, and settled in for the night.

I fell asleep quickly, excited to see the stars later. I woke a few times—checking if anything magical was happening outside the windows. The mountain was still, the air cold, the sky brilliant. Dozens of others were sleeping in their cars too. Some left before midnight, but many stayed. Around 1:30 a.m., Kiki needed to go outside. It wasn't scary. Just uncomfortable. Still, she couldn't hold it, so I gathered my courage and stepped into the night.

It was the stillest night I've ever experienced. No sound. No motion. Just crisp mountain air, the snow-covered peak in the distance, a sky full of stars, and the soft radiance of the almost-full moon. The moon was so bright it illuminated the parking lot—it wasn't pitch black; it was silver and sacred.

When we returned to the car, I glanced up at the mountain one more time. Then I fell asleep. And that's when I had the dream. Only, it wasn't a dream. It was real—so vivid, so clear. It was an experience, a visitation. I saw all of us—the people sleeping on the mountain that night—gathered underground, in a large room. We were preparing, getting ready. It was a cleansing space, a sacred space. Everyone was showering, rinsing off the day, the density. It wasn't physical; it was aetheric/energetic. I was shown to a private curtain where I could undress and step into a cleansing shower. Someone came to me and said, "It's good you're wearing cotton."

Everything was symbolic, intentional. Everyone moved around quickly but with care, helping each other prepare. It was clear: this was the room before the Light City. The preparation room. You had to cleanse before entering. You had to let go.

And I understood: this is what the mountain had called me here for.

The Morning After

I woke up several times throughout the night. It was cold—truly cold—and I kept trying to turn on the car's heater to warm us up, but the warmth would vanish quickly. The temperature had dropped to 43°F, and the chill crept into my bones.

By 6:30 a.m., Kiki and I were both awake—and freezing. She was breathing heavily, and I could tell immediately something was wrong. Her little body was bloated, uncomfortable, and she wasn't herself. My heart sank. She's my soulmate, my best friend, and her well-being is always my top priority.

My own body ached from the night spent curled up in the back seat. My voice was fading from the cold, and everything in me just wanted warmth. We stepped out for a short walk—it couldn't be long; it was far too cold.

But the sunrise... the sunrise was breathtaking. Despite the discomfort, it was magical. A moment of quiet beauty.

Still, the experience left me with mixed feelings. The freezing night, the aching body, Kiki not feeling well—it was too much all at once. I decided to drive down into town for some warmth, a cup of coffee, and maybe breakfast. I also wanted to find a local vet as soon as possible.

While sipping hot coffee, I started calling veterinary clinics in the area. But it wasn't promising. The closest clinics were booked out for a month. My heart dropped again. My stay here was only for a month.

I paused. Breathed. Kiki was stable—just uncomfortable. I remembered that the mountain water here has powerful properties. It detoxifies, it heals, it clears both body and spirit. I had brought this water for both of us. I trusted it. I decided to give it a little time. Deep inside, I knew: We're going to be okay. We just need a few days to reset. So even though I was looking for help from a vet, I also knew we were already receiving the healing we needed, in a different way.

A Day Guided by Spirit

After breakfast, we went to the city park. The air welcomed us as we filled our bottles with fresh, cold spring water. We sat on a bench, soaking in the warmth of the morning sun after a freezing night on the mountain. The light felt healing—soft golden rays kissing our skin.

Then my sister called. She shared that she, too, was going through a huge life shift. We talked for over an hour, hearts open, souls realigning. After the call, I suddenly felt that instead of spending another night on Mt. Shasta, I needed rest, stillness—a real bed, a hot shower, and time to write. After five days of constant driving and extreme temperatures, I could feel in my heart that Kiki needed to rest too.

I tried booking a hotel from the park, but reception was bad. So I trusted my intuition, started driving, and let Spirit guide me.

I passed by the hotel I had stayed at on my first trip to Mount Shasta—familiar and central—but something told me, "Keep going."

That's when I saw it: a hotel nestled in the trees, a little further from downtown. Quiet. Peaceful. Surrounded by green. I didn't have a reservation, and check-in wasn't until 3 p.m., but I walked in, holding Kiki, and asked anyway. At first, the woman said check-in wasn't until 2 p.m. But something softened. I asked again—kindly, patiently—and she smiled and offered us an affordable room right away.

It was perfect.

I took a hot shower. Kiki curled up in bed and finally relaxed. We opened the window, and there She was: the majestic Mt. Shasta right in front of us. I didn't want to go anywhere. The view, the calm, the sense of being held—it was enough.

That evening, we explored the property. It was set on a slight hill, with views of the forest and mountains in every direction. Five or six hammocks swayed gently between tall pine trees. The energy was sacred. I knew I had been guided here.

36

The Open Gate

And finally, I found out—the gate to the Old Ski Bowl Road was open.

It had been closed for as long as I could remember. No matter how many times I visited Mount Shasta, that gate had always blocked the path. I knew of the road behind it only through maps and other people's stories, but never through my own feet, my own breath. Yet yesterday, for the first time, I felt the urge pulling me toward it—strong, persistent, undeniable.

It was hot—over 90 degrees—and I reasoned with myself: No, not today. Not in this heat. And yet, beneath the logic, something in me ached to go. Something ancient. Something stubborn.

Today, it was even hotter—95 degrees—but the feeling hadn't faded. In fact, it had grown stronger. By the late afternoon, I couldn't resist anymore. I got into my car and drove up the familiar winding road to Bunny Flats. The path was familiar, almost ritualistic, but as I approached the gate—something shifted.

It was open.

I drove further up, higher than I had ever gone before in this body. Higher toward something unknown, yet somehow remembered. I reached the very last point where the road ends and vehicles must surrender to the mountain's will. I stepped out of the car and began to walk.

Not far up the trail, I met an older man making his way down. His energy was light, almost playful. I asked him, "Where does the fun stuff happen?" He smiled, amused, and pointed the way. "See that tree up ahead? There's a piece of metal on it. That's where the magic starts."

Magic. Yes, that's exactly why I had come.

Further up the path, I encountered two women. They spoke easily of Saint-Germain, of messages they had received from the Ascended Master.

I continued walking.

The sun hung high but softened now, losing its fierce grip on the afternoon. Still, the heat clung to the rocks and boulders scattered like ancient bones across the landscape. The trees stood sentinel, silent witnesses to my slow ascent. When I turned to look behind me, the view stopped my breath: mountain upon mountain, veiled in soft, ethereal mist—not fog exactly, not smoke either, but something otherworldly. As if a painter's hand had blurred the lines on purpose to remind me this place belonged to dreams as much as to the earth.

Ahead of me, the mountain rose steadily, beautifully, unapologetically.

I remembered a message I once received in a regression session:

"When you reach the top of the mountain, you will meet Him. You will recognize Him immediately."

My Lemurian husband. My beloved from another age.

I looked to my left — one peak. Then ahead — another. Both seemed within reach.

Snow still clung stubbornly to their slopes, but in a few days, the sun would clear the way.

A thought crossed my mind:

Could you guys be more specific? Which top of the mountain is the one?

Here they are — two of them.

But deep down, I knew.

By the time I return, I won't need anyone to tell me.

I'll follow my heart.

And whichever peak I choose in that moment — that will be the right one.

That will be enough.

But then something else pulled my gaze sideways—to the darker mountain on the left side, half-formed as though sliced by some invisible force. No snow there. A strange, incomplete shape. I had seen this mountain before—in meditation.

And when I saw this halved mountain, memory rushed back through me like a current. I remembered myself—not in this body—flying straight toward the center of this mountain. And then, without resistance, I moved through it—into the mountain, into something beyond stone and matter. I disappeared.

At the time of that vision, I didn't understand. But now, standing here in this body with my feet on the Earth, seeing this exact shape—I knew I have been here before.

Not as human. But I have been here.

I remembered something else, too—something my subconscious had once told me during a session:

"Some things will not make sense right away. But when the story unfolds, and when all the pieces fall into place, everything will become clear."

My whole body hummed, vibrating with a quiet, high frequency—almost imperceptible, but undeniably real.

Before turning back, I stood still and spoke inwardly to the mountain:

"Do you have a message for me?"

The answer came gentlY:

"Do not grow frustrated if you do not see or experience something extraordinary right away. This is preparation. Step by step. Trust the unfolding. Patience is part of the path. Return when you are ready. What is meant for you will not miss you."

With a soft heart, I thanked the mountain.

As I began my descent down the hill, something whispered to me—soft and clear:

"Sunday. 8 a.m."

It landed in my mind like a gentle echo, stirring a memory from a year ago. Back then, I had stayed in a little guesthouse on the west side of I-5. Every Sunday morning, without fail, I would look out toward the mountain and see it—a huge lenticular hovering above Mt. Shasta like a ship, like a sign, like a gathering waiting just beyond the veil. I used to laugh and tell myself, "The friends are visiting again!".

But now, as I walked down the rocky path, hearing "Sunday, 8 a.m.", it felt different. It felt like an invitation.

I thought practically: If I come here early, park by 6 a.m., it will probably take me about two hours to make my way up to that place. That would bring me right to the top around 8 a.m.—just in time for whatever is meant to happen.

Still, there was preparation to do. I needed to walk the path again, to find the safest and clearest route, to ensure I could reach the top in time. This wasn't a climb to take lightly. Not just physically, but energetically.

37

When Two Souls Remember

The day finally came when I scheduled my meeting with Peter Mt. Shasta. It was at his house, tucked away outside of Mount Shasta. Driving there, the scenery reminded me of my visit to Pluto's Cave last year — the memories of that place, the experiences, and the connection with Sedona and the Lemurian energy. It felt so familiar, so good.

At some point during the drive, something awakened deep within me. I felt the Earth herself calling me to roll down the windows, breathe deeply, and let something out. And I did — I began to hum, a long, deep "aaaaa" sound. I let it flow without pausing, letting it carry whatever needed to be released. I don't know where it came from. But it felt incredible. Out there in the wilderness, with no one around, not even passing cars — it was safe to release it all. I hummed four times, and with each hum, something shifted. I felt lighter. I felt freer.

Then, I noticed the energy changing within me. Before this trip, I had asked the Ascended Masters: What is it you wish me to receive from this meeting with Peter? The answer was clear: Being close to Peter will help prepare you for the energy you're stepping into. You've been surrounded by lower vibrational influences lately. Right now, Saint-Germain's energy might feel too intense for you directly. But Peter — Peter can hold that frequency perfectly. Through him, you can adjust.

When I arrived, Peter opened the door. He looked radiant, vibrant. His home carried a beautiful energy — calm, alive, balanced. We sat down together, two chairs facing each other in the center of the room.

As we began talking, I remembered what my guides had told me on the drive: Life is a game. It's like a puzzle. Today, you will receive another piece. Listen carefully. I know I can talk a lot — about my past lives, my experiences, all the layers of my journey — but this time, I allowed myself to listen more. I let Peter speak, and slowly, the energy between us began to unfold.

At one point during our conversation, he gently asked me to be silent for a few minutes. Without speaking, we simply gazed into each other's eyes. I looked at him, mesmerized, and felt waves of love moving from my heart to his, as he sent love from his heart to mine. He told me he had done this before with his mentor, Pearl — the same Pearl who had once been the assistant to Godfre Ray King, the author and spiritual teacher.

As we sat there in silence, something extraordinary began to happen. My gaze settled on Peter's third eye, and suddenly his face began to blur. Slowly, it shifted into the face of someone entirely different — a younger man, but not Peter himself, and not even a younger version of him. I have seen pictures of Peter in his youth, but this face was not familiar. Then, his face transformed again — this time into that of a bearded man with a round, full face. His hair was salt-and-pepper, and his eyes seemed to twitch slightly, as if making small, involuntary movements. His facial expression shifted subtly, full of tiny, almost imperceptible movements. Finally, it dissolved into pure light — a luminous presence without any recognizable human form.

At that very moment, Peter said softly, "You are almost disappearing. Your body is hardly here anymore." I realized I was witnessing the same with him. His body, too, seemed to dissolve, becoming less and less solid. It was a remarkable and humbling experience.

Afterward, we resumed our conversation. I asked him to sign a book for me, and we began speaking about past lives. I shared with him my memories of my incarnations as Queen Elizabeth I and Madame de Pompadour. After hearing that, he simply nodded. We both knew the story: Elizabeth I, the mother of Francis Bacon (Saint-Germain), had given her son away to be raised by another family. I hesitated to share this before because I thought he might not like knowing that I was that exact woman. To my surprise, we discovered that we had shared that lifetime together. Peter asked me not to reveal who he was during the Elizabethan era, and I will honor his wish. Yet, it made so much sense why we had been drawn to one another in this life. We knew each other then, and now, once again, we find ourselves reunited. Saint-Germain often brings people together across incarnations — those who share a soul bond through time.

Sitting in Peter's house, in this life, silently honoring each other's presence, felt sacred. We spoke, too, about Inner Earth, and I was thrilled when he confirmed what I had already seen in my visions. I nearly leapt from my seat with excitement, exclaiming, "I've been there too! It's so beautiful!" How rare and precious it is to share such experiences with someone who truly understands, someone who walks in the same consciousness.

Before I left, I mentioned my upcoming meeting on Mt. Shasta at 8 a.m. Peter smiled and asked, "This Sunday?" I said, "Yes, I am preparing and planning to go this Sunday." He smiled again and said, "Sunday is a special day."

I left feeling both eager and uncertain about my early morning journey, wondering if I would oversleep, yet knowing I was preparing for something important.

As we were saying goodbye, I felt myself drifting, as though part of me was already in another dimension. Without intending to, words slipped from my mouth:

"The Ascended Masters told me you will become an Ascended Master. I would like you to stay around me — it doesn't matter in what form, physical or etheric. I would like to feel your presence."

He smiled again. "Of course," he said.

I also told him, "If we don't see each other again in the physical, I would like us to keep this connection alive beyond the veil, as we have done across lifetimes and centuries."

He lives simply, quietly, and humbly, continuing to offer light, clarity, and encouragement to those who are ready to walk the path of mastery and self-realization.

His presence carries the qualities of calm wisdom, purity, and gentle authority—reminding us that the true Master does not impose, but rather illuminates what we already hold within.

38

Trusting the Divine Time

During the night, I woke up a couple of times to take Kiki outside. The night air was crisp, still, and full of quiet beauty. The sky stretched out, crystal clear, with countless stars twinkling above me like silent watchers. I felt wrapped in a calmness I couldn't explain — only experience.

The second time I woke up, it was around 4:00 in the morning. I noticed how cold it had gotten. As I returned indoors, I switched off my alarm. I made the decision: I wasn't going up the mountain today. Not this Sunday. Not this time.

When I woke up later, I felt no guilt. Instead, I felt a soft release. A knowing. There was a reason I hadn't gone. Perhaps it simply wasn't the right time yet.

Earlier, I'd received a message: "Sunday, 8 a.m." But Spirit never gives details in the way our minds crave. I didn't know whether it meant this Sunday, next Sunday, or some symbolic "Sunday" beyond linear time. I've come to understand — as my guides often remind me — there is no time. Only vibrational alignment. Things unfold not by dates on a calendar but by resonance. This morning, the resonance wasn't there.

Instead, I felt guided to stay home. To keep working on my book, to finalize my cover, and to let yesterday's conversations settle within me. My neighbor's words echoed in my mind from our recent conversation. I had told her I planned to hike up the mountain, and she had asked with concern, "Is it safe yet?"

"What do you mean?" I'd asked.

She explained about the heavy snow this year, the accidents, the risks still lingering on the summit.

"Maybe check with the fire department before you go."

Perhaps that's why I didn't go. Just divine timing. I didn't feel like I had failed to fulfill some promise to myself or the mountain. It felt organic. Natural. As though things were simply aligning as they should.

After spending the afternoon working on my book, something inside me stirred. Almost on impulse, I decided to take Kiki up to Bunny Flat. I grabbed a warm jacket for myself and one for Kiki, and we set off. I felt this light, bubbling excitement in my chest as I drove — as though something meaningful was waiting for me up there. As I climbed the familiar winding road, my thoughts turned to how this visit, this time on Mount Shasta, had already shifted me. It felt like living between worlds — somewhere beyond my usual life in Los Angeles. I didn't want to return to the so-called "real world." I wanted to remain in this high vibration, this expanded state. But I also knew, deep down, my purpose wasn't to stay here indefinitely. My work was to experience, to receive, and then to return — to carry it forward.

When we arrived at Bunny Flat, I was suddenly flooded with the memory of the night I once spent on the mountain. It felt good to be back now. Right. Necessary. I was grateful I had come.

We started walking toward the Twin Flame Tree. The cold settled in quickly the moment we stepped onto the trail. I realized then how unprepared I would've been had I attempted the sunrise hike I'd considered that morning. My clothes were too light, my layers too thin — and this was already 7 p.m. Can you imagine how cold it would have been at 6 a.m.? Probably unbearable. I understood then: my guides must have seen this coming. They must have whispered, "Not like this, girl. Not today. Not in that outfit."

It all made sense.

Kiki and I continued toward the tree. We found a quiet spot, sat on a rock, and simply listened. I played a podcast where people shared their own Mt. Shasta experiences — their stories echoed my own. They spoke of humming to shift energy, and I smiled, remembering my own spontaneous humming while driving the day before. Without realizing it, I had been raising my own vibration in simple, natural ways.

Feeling renewed, I decided to drive higher. I wanted to watch the sunset from the Old Ski Bowl trailhead, the highest point accessible by car on the mountain. As I ascended, an unusual excitement grew within me once again — like I was going to meet someone important to me.

I parked, stepped out into the cool, thin air, and admired the stunning panorama. The sky blazed with soft colors as the sun dipped behind the distant forest. I didn't hike far. Instead, I sat on a massive boulder with Kiki, ate a light snack, and watched the light shift over the peaks. I thought about the trails, the paths I might have taken. And again, I heard my guides say: "The best GPS is your heart. Trust your heart. You'll know where to go."

As we began to head back down toward the car, a tall man appeared on the path, carrying a drum. He was preparing to play at sunset. Our eyes met. At that moment, it struck me: I know this man.

His energy was clear. Pure. Unburdened. Like someone who had processed it all, or someone who had never carried trauma to begin with. I could see it in his face, in his aura.

We spoke effortlessly, naturally. He had moved here from Georgia. Bought his house sight unseen — just knew it was his. On his land, he discovered lava tubes carrying ancient Lemurian energies. We exchanged stories easily, like old friends catching up. When I really looked at him, recognition surfaced. His was the face I had seen yesterday during my exercise with Peter. The second face, so clear now. Especially in the way he moved, his expressions — it matched exactly what I'd been shown.

He told me there had been distractions trying to keep him from coming up the mountain that evening — people inviting him to gatherings, pulling him in different directions. But he'd said no. He felt called to the mountain. And not through his usual route either — he'd been guided to this very spot.

Of course. These meetings aren't coincidences.

We exchanged information. He mentioned he works with Ascended Master Hilarion, the Lord of the Fifth Ray of Truth, Science, and Healing, associated with the green ray of healing energy. His teachings focus on the power of thought and intention, the healing of the body and mind, and the integration of higher frequencies into the cells to support the process of soul ascension.

I shared that my guide is Saint-Germain, the Master of Transformation, Alchemy, and the Violet Flame of Transmutation. He is the Lord of the Seventh Ray, representing freedom, spiritual alchemy, forgiveness, and purification. Saint-Germain guides humanity in mastering personal and collective transformation, helping to transmute negative energy and karma into higher consciousness through the power of the Violet Flame. He is also associated with spiritual sovereignty, manifestation, and the Age of Aquarius.

As we spoke, a memory returned — something my Subconscious once said during a regression session:

"You need to be physically present in Mount Shasta. You will meet people essential to your evolution. Not online. In person."

We planned to meet again. He keeps his work quiet, staying under the radar. He works with the land, raising Shasta's frequency in his own way. My path, by contrast, is meant to be visible. My guides are clear: "You didn't come here to play small. You promised to teach. To serve. To participate in the ascension of others."

Driving home, I felt an inner release. A deeper understanding settled in:

Timing isn't linear.

Meetings aren't accidents.

Everything unfolds by vibrational alignment.

This was one of those moments.

39

The Lemurian Pond

The other day, I stepped outside just to take Kiki for a quick walk. I wasn't planning to talk to anyone—but the universe had other plans. As we walked, I ran into a visitor at a neighbor's house. We exchanged smiles, struck up a conversation, and instantly connected. It turned out that we both worked in Beverly Hills—me as a real estate agent, and she as a title insurance rep. Small world.

She leaned in like she was about to tell me a secret.

"You have to check out this hidden spot nearby," she said. "Locals know it, but it's not touristy. It'll feel like you're in a different dimension. Like time doesn't exist."

The next day, I followed her directions.

As I drove toward the location, the road began to narrow. It eventually turned into dirt, the kind of road that makes you question whether you're lost—or just about to find something important. I caught myself thinking, What am I even doing here?

But then I saw a couple of parked cars and felt reassured. I wasn't alone.

I parked, took a breath, and started walking.

The path was rocky and wild. Untamed. The land around me opened like a secret unfolding—giant boulders scattered like ancient bones, and a vibrant river rushing alongside them. The rocks rose tall, like natural temples. Trees grew out of the stones, twisted around each other as if dancing through dimensions.

The deeper I walked, the louder the river roared—like it was speaking in an ancient tongue only the soul could understand.

Time began to stretch. Or disappear altogether.

Near the river's edge, I saw what looked like a piece of an ancient wall — raw and cracked stone, resting quietly as if it had always belonged there. But from a distance, it looked like a symbol. Like something sacred had been etched into it long ago. I walked toward it, placed my back against the stone, and closed my eyes.

The sun was kissing my skin. Warming me from the outside in.

Leaning against the stone, I felt a wave of emotion rise. A deep, ancient ache. I felt fear—irrational but real—of the water rushing in front of me.

Memories of Lemuria stirred within me.

I had lived through its fall. Here, by this river, I allowed myself to release it. All of it. The fear. The mourning of a world long gone. I let it go into the rocks, into the current, into the trees that had seen it all.

And then I looked around.

That's when I saw them.

Faces in the rocky cliff across the river. Not carved, not sculpted—but revealed. By time, by wind, by something more. They emerged as I looked:

A native elder, wearing sacred color on his forehead.

A fierce woman who looked like Queen Elizabeth I.

A smiling face, light and playful.

A bearded king, touching his chin in deep thought.

Wherever I turned my gaze, more faces appeared—like the land was remembering for me. Or through me. Like the rocks themselves carried stories, waiting to be seen again.

Each face held a presence. A message. A trace of a civilization that once breathed deeply here, and perhaps still does, just beyond our perception.

The longer I stayed, the more I could feel: these weren't hallucinations. They were activations.

I looked up.

The trees on the ledge ahead stood unnaturally still—motionless, timeless. Like beings holding space, watching quietly. They didn't seem quite real. And yet they were deeply alive.

The entire forest radiated a mystical calm. Not flashy. Not loud. But vast. Like it was cradling the energy of a thousand stories.

The river's sound shifted. It stopped being "noise" and became vibration. Soothing. Forgiving.

It didn't feel like I was simply visiting this place.

It felt like I was returning.

Just as I was preparing to leave, a man appeared on a float, gently drifting across the water right in front of me, as if carried in by the moment itself.

We exchanged a few words, and then he casually said,

"A couple days ago, I saw a bear here—bigger than me—just walking around."

That was my sign. It was time to go.

But as I walked back to my car, something shifted inside me again. I felt like a patient stirring from deep primal slumber—emerging slowly, seeing familiar places, feeling the energy of recognition... but not yet remembering the full story.

And I want to remember.

Not just fragments. Not just pieces.

I want to remember where I came from. Why do I feel the way I do? Why certain landscapes awaken grief and joy I can't explain? I want to know what the rocks are trying to show me. Why are the faces so familiar?

Of course, I understand this is the soul's agreement—this forgetfulness. This cosmic game. We come to Earth and wipe our memory, like starting a story from blank pages.

But I'm asking now. I'm asking the Source... and I'm asking this mountain to help me remember.

Because I know everything you ask for on Mount Shasta is amplified.

Prayers here don't echo—they manifest.

So I ask carefully. I ask with reverence.

That what I'm ready to remember... will return to me.

And perhaps, by the time I leave this mountain, more of me will have come home.

40

The Temple of Love or Ascension Rock?

On the to-do list for next time—Ascension Rock, a portal to spiritual connection. People believe that rock sits right above Telos. It's not just a spot on the map. It's something sacred. People go there, climb the rock, sit, meditate, observe, connect with their Higher Selves, restore energy, release pain, let go of trauma.

Just with a little careful preparation—how to get there. You make one step, you get sightseeing, you get an activation. You restore your energy. You restore your aura. And then the Source is giving you the next upgrade. The next beautiful spot to discover.

And what I realize—it's really hard to stay at home all day.

Why would I do that while I'm here for just one month? Why would I stay home?

I do a few hours of writing and preparation and work. And everything else—I'm exploring. I'm letting this land teach me. Every day is a different part of this magical mystical area. A different discovery. And I think I read somewhere that Telosians work only four hours a day. And everything else, they spend time in nature.

And I do understand why.

It feels so good. And it feels like a luxury to me—to drive the roads. They're not packed with cars. There's no traffic. There aren't many people. The air is fresh. I cleaned my car a week ago—it's still clean. That means we're breathing clean air.

Another day, I got spring water from Panther Meadow. And I can tell—it's not just water. It's saturated with herbs. Saturated with life. Nature here is really like a masterpiece. Like a healer that gives you natural medicine to recover.

And I can see improvement. In Kiki. In myself. After just two weeks of being here.

And I see that my schedule—my sleeping pattern—is shifting.

I used to go to bed really late. Midnight. Sometimes even later. I'd sleep until 7:30, 8:00, or even 9:00 in the morning. But now? Around 8:30, 9:00 p.m.—I feel tired. I want to go to bed. I want to rest.

And I remember last year, when I was here—my sleeping shifted completely. I would go to bed right after sunset. And I would wake up, naturally, without any alarm, a few minutes before sunrise. I would lie in bed and just watch the light change. Watch the sun slowly rise above the mountain.

Such a beautiful thing.

Like syncing in with nature. With the natural pattern. With something bigger than me, but also part of me.

And I'm looking forward to returning to that rhythm again.

Because I know... this mountain... this place... it's not just where I am... It's who I am becoming.

The Day the Sky Cried With Me

I was ready.

Backpack packed. Water from Panther Meadow tucked inside. I stepped into the car and began my drive with soft humming, letting the sound rise from within. The humming turned to chanting, and the chanting turned to something ancient and wild—funny, rhythmic mouth movements that made sounds I couldn't explain, like something Native or tribal. As if another part of me was waking up. Remembering.

By the time I reached the parking area, I was in a trance-like state. Deeply relaxed. Buzzing. Tingly. Present.

I got out and began to walk.

The area was open and scattered with large stones—many of them. I started running around like a child, scanning them with my eyes, trying to feel where I was being pulled. Where is Ascension Rock? I asked aloud, not really expecting an answer from anyone nearby, but hoping the land would speak. I checked my phone again. Some descriptions online mentioned it's not an easy path, that the climb is rough, the directions unclear. I looked around—nothing labeled, nothing obvious

But then something inside nudged me:

Go around the stones. Don't think. Just feel.

I paused, turned around, and looked up. The way forward was steep, uneven, and somewhat intimidating. But a soft voice within said something:

"Wherever you go, the path is easy. Choose the way of least resistance. You'll be on top quicker than you think."

So I did.

One step. Then another. No rush. No effort. Just trust.

And within seconds, I was standing at the top of the rock.

It was massive. Warm to the touch. Solid beneath my feet. From up there, I could see far—at least the height of a two- or three-story building. And then, when I turned around, She appeared: Mount Shasta, right in front of me. Majestic. Silent. Powerful. A small, delicate cloud hovered above her peak. The air was crisp and cool, brushing across my face and through my hair like a sacred breath.

I began to speak.

To whisper.

To release.

I opened my heart and let go of anything heavy that I'd been holding. Any sadness, confusion, or resistance. And then—suddenly—out of nowhere, thunder.

A deep rumble across a clear blue sky.

There wasn't a single dark cloud in sight. The sun was bright and bold above me. But the thunder came anyway, and it felt like a message:

Welcome home.

I closed my eyes and whispered, Thank you. Thank you for having me here. Thank you for supporting me. Thank you for everything you do for me on this path. For healing. For guidance. For holding this space.

And then I cried. Tears poured down my cheeks. And at that very moment, the rain began. A single drop landed on my face, almost right next to my tear. Then another. Gentle. Like the sky was crying with me.

And I knew—deep in my soul—I wasn't alone. I was seen. I was supported. I was being held by something far greater than I could name.

I placed my hands on my body and began giving myself Reiki. Energy moved through my palms, through my chest, down into the Earth. The thunder came again—softer this time—then faded. The air around me shifted. It was fresh. Clean. Silent. Sacred.

And I felt something lift.

I remembered a different day on this land—when I had Kiki with me and a full gallon of spring water strapped to my back. It was heavy. My body felt it. And then a quiet voice said:

"You're still carrying too much. Let it go. You don't need to bring everything with you."

It wasn't about the water. Or the weight. It was about emotions. The stories. The expectations I was still lugging uphill.

That day, I listened. And today, I finally felt the shift.

Now I go to the mountain almost every day. I crave it. After a few hours of work on the computer, I need the forest. I need to breathe the mountain air, feel the Earth beneath my feet, see the way the pine trees move with the wind.

I'm not sure how I'll go back to the city. To the noise. The density. The distractions.

But I'm not thinking about that right now.

Right now, I'm here.

Eye-level with the tops of the pine trees.

In silence. In stillness. In grace.

When I got home, I posted a few pictures with the location tag on Instagram. I didn't think too much about it—just felt called to share that magical place. But then, someone who knew the area left a comment that surprised me. "That's actually not Ascension Rock," they said. "That's the Temple of Love." Or maybe they called it the Tower of Love.

It made me pause. How did I end up there, if it wasn't Ascension Rock? It truly felt like some invisible force brought me there on purpose—took me gently by the hand, showed me exactly where I needed to be. That place—whatever name it carries—was the place where I needed to release. To grieve. To let go. To open my heart even more.

Now I know: I still need to go to Ascension Rock. It's still on the list. It's still calling. I can feel that the next energetic upgrade will happen there. But if I had gone to Ascension Rock first, I would've never wandered or even searched for this Temple of Love. I would have missed this entirely. And I can see now—it had to be this way. There was a divine intelligence guiding the order of things.

It wasn't a mistake. It was preparation.

So maybe that's how it works sometimes—you're brought exactly where your heart needs to soften before it can rise. That Temple of Love wasn't just a detour. It was a sacred initiation in its own right. And I know, without a doubt, that I received a download there—something deep, subtle, and true. And now... Ascension Rock awaits.

41

The Body as a Portal

By the third week in Mount Shasta, something within me shifted even more. I could feel it in my body—subtle, yet undeniable. The energy was moving, flowing differently than before. But I also noticed stiffness clinging to certain parts of me, perhaps from long drives, or maybe from the weight of recent life events that had imprinted themselves into my muscles. My body had been holding on—guarding, resisting. Despite the spiritual awakenings and activations that Mount Shasta so generously offers, I realized there was still one layer I hadn't addressed: the physical.

During meditation one night, a clear message came through:

"Go get a massage. A beautiful, real one. Don't hold back on the money. You need this. Your body will thank you."

There was no doubt. I listened.

Unlike Los Angeles, where massage options are abundant, Mount Shasta offered a few choices. But as soon as I began my search, one listing called to me with quiet certainty. I booked a 90-minute session immediately—no hesitation. I knew this was guided.

When I arrived, I found myself at a cozy wooden cabin nestled in the heart of downtown. The energy was grounding the moment I stepped inside. The space whispered peace. The massage therapist—a young-looking man with a calm, steady presence—greeted me.

As his hands began working through the layers of tension in my body, something extraordinary started happening. I began seeing my own skeleton—not metaphorically, but visually, vividly, through my third eye. It was as if I were looking at a medical screen in a clinic, but instead of a doctor, it was some unseen force showing me the inner map of my body. I could see black spots of energy—dark patches where trauma or stress had been stored. When he massaged a specific area, I pointed to it and said, "There's something there."

He confirmed, "Yes, there's a lot of tension in that spot."

Then, I saw another black spot—about two inches higher. I asked him to move upward. Again, he found another pocket of tightness, exactly where I had seen it in the vision. It was as though we were co-navigating a healing map of my body, guided by something beyond both of us.

When he began working on my jaw, I immediately tuned in even deeper. I've known for a long time that the jaw holds trauma—years of clenching, swallowing emotions, bracing against life. And although I've done deep trauma work, I wanted to make sure nothing remained trapped there. As he massaged both sides of my jaw simultaneously, I saw the image of teeth and jaw like you would see at a dentist's office. A light moved back and forth along the left side, from the back of the jaw to the front, almost like a scanner highlighting something that needed attention.

I placed my hand near the left side of my face and said, "There's something on the left side."

He responded, "Yes, I feel more tension on the left side of your jaw."

And when he began gently pulling at my scalp and stretching my neck, another vision emerged—I saw my full skeletal structure. No skin, no tissue. Just bones illuminated on a screen, like a glowing blueprint of my physical form. Every area he touched would light up or shift, and I was able to tell him in real-time what I was seeing. I had never experienced anything like it.

He found it fascinating. I could tell he was open but also respectfully grounded. We both understood: this wasn't just a massage.

There were other forces in the room. Beings, guides, energies—whatever name we choose to give them. This healing was collaborative. There was help from beyond. I wasn't just receiving a massage from a skilled practitioner—I was part of an orchestrated multidimensional healing session. We spoke softly during parts of the session. I asked if he was local. He said he had spent most of his life in the area. I felt called to ask, "Do you believe in Inner Earth?"

He paused for a moment, then said carefully, "I believe in awareness... and I do believe there are beings." His response was measured, cautious—like someone who knows more than they say. I could feel it. So I gently asked if he had ever experienced anything... unusual.

He nodded, without hesitation this time. "I've been visited by Grays," he said quietly.

I knew it—I was meant to meet him. This wasn't random. Whether it was a soul agreement, a vibrational alignment, or divine orchestration, I had found someone attuned to the frequency I was moving into. Someone I could trust to work on my body, to move energy through touch and presence.

At one point, my stomach began to gargle.

He smiled knowingly and said, "That's your nervous system shifting out of fight-or-flight. You're finally relaxing."

Yes. That was exactly it. I had normalized tension. I had made it my baseline. And now my body was learning what it felt like to let go.

Time melted. When I came back into full awareness, we had gone beyond our scheduled time. But it didn't matter. Something had shifted. I left that cabin lighter—spiritually, emotionally, and physically.

Later that day, I wandered into the I AM Reading Room. Drawn to a random book, I opened it to a page that read something like:

"You must learn to relax the muscles. Tension is not your natural state. You've simply gotten used to it."

It hit straight to the heart. I felt seen, guided, reassured.

When the Past No Longer Fits

That afternoon, I cooked a light meal—fish and greens. No bread. No heaviness. Just simplicity. After a meal, I opened my closet and suddenly had the strange sensation that I was staring into someone else's wardrobe. The clothes belonged to an old version of me—one I had already outgrown. I knew what I had to do.

It was time to donate.

As if the massage had triggered not just physical release but also an energetic one, I saw clearly: This doesn't represent who I am anymore. These clothes were part of a timeline that no longer matched my vibration. They had served me well, but I was becoming someone new.

Interestingly, before I left Los Angeles, something nudged me to pack a lot of clothing—more than I needed. Now I understand why. I needed to see them. To say goodbye. To release them.

I was standing in front of my closet, hands moving through fabric and memory, sorting what no longer felt like "me." Piles were forming—some to keep, most to release. I wasn't just clearing out clothes. I was clearing energy. Timelines. Versions of myself that no longer fit.

While I was packing, I started wondering where to bring these clothes. Who might need them? Who might want them? Could I ask someone local if they knew of a place that would accept donations?

And then—a knock on the door.

It was my neighbor, holding her phone up with a map on the screen. "Here," she said, smiling. "This is the exact location of Ascension Rock you asked me about earlier when you were walking Kiki."

I had almost forgotten I asked her. But here she was, standing at my door, answering the very question I had carried into the morning. The synchronicity was so perfect, it made me pause. There was magic unfolding in real-time.

I invited her in.

As we began chatting, she mentioned she had a daughter. I asked what size she wore. "Small," she said, "about your size. Similar shape." So I asked if she'd like to take a look at some of the pieces I had just packed. Maybe her daughter would love them?

She agreed.

And as we sifted through the clothes together, she said that not everything would fit her daughter, but there was a spot in downtown Mount Shasta where donations were always welcomed. She added:

"The community here is very poor. There are a lot of people who would love to wear clothes like these. They'd be so happy."

So we made an agreement: she would take anything her daughter liked and bring the rest to the donation center herself.

When she left, I felt it—a wave of energy just lifted off me.

Something shifted in a real, tangible way. I felt... lighter. Like space had been created in both the closet and the soul.

A lot of those clothes held memories. Some of them carried old energy, emotions from chapters I've since closed. Just seeing them again would sometimes bring a pang to my chest—reminders of past lives I no longer needed to revisit.

For a long time, I used to believe you shouldn't give away clothes you once wore. Maybe someone could "step into your energy." That belief lived deep inside me, almost like a protective charm.

But standing there in the stillness after she left, I realized something:

It's much worse to hold onto things that anchor you to a life you no longer live.

Those clothes weren't just fabric. They were holding stories, patterns, identities that I've outgrown. And the more they sat there in the closet, the more they created stagnant energy.

Why not give them to someone who will feel joy? Who will feel beautiful? Who will give them new life and, in return, send out appreciation energy?

So I rewrote the belief.

And with that, another veil lifted. Another portal opened—not in the sky or on a mountain—but right there... in my closet.

Mt. Shasta doesn't just work with your spirit. It works with your whole Being.

42

The Second Activation — Adama Temple

It was my second attempt to find Ascension Rock. I parked in the same spot as before, walked the familiar path, and let my GPS guide me. Once again, it pointed me back to the same place I had already been. Still unsure if I had truly reached Ascension Rock the first time, I hesitated at the second turn that might have led me there.

So instead of insisting, I turned around and decided to drive up the mountain instead.

But something shifted. The engine started, but it didn't feel right. There were no warning lights, no obvious signs of trouble — just a strong, quiet knowing that something was off. It felt almost as if the car was overheated, yet everything appeared normal. A soft unease crept in. I didn't feel safe heading up the mountain, not with this strange sensation lingering. Still, I had already pulled out of the parking lot.

What made it even more puzzling was that just before this trip, I had taken my car to the dealership for a full checkup. I never leave for long trips without making sure everything is in perfect condition — I had the fluids topped off, the tires checked, every system looked at.

Everything had been working flawlessly. There was no logical reason for the car to act strangely now.

I was stuck between two options: drive back home,

or quickly cross the road and park in another lot nearby. I chose the latter. I parked and sat for a moment in silence, as if listening for instructions. Then I popped the hood. It took me longer than usual — I hadn't done this in a while. The engine was hot, but not alarmingly so. No signals. No damage. Nothing out of place. Just heat, and a lingering mystery. I turned the engine off and decided to walk, letting the car — and myself — cool down.

As I crossed the road, I noticed three people nearby. Something nudged me to approach them.

"Do you know where Ascension Rock is?" I asked.

They pointed in the direction I had already been — confirming that I had, in fact, found it. Perhaps the confusion was only in the naming, the expectation of what the path would look like. But then one of them said something unexpected:

"There's also a place called the Adama Temple nearby. We're going there now. Do you want to come?"

Without hesitation, I said yes.

I jumped into the car with three kind strangers, and we drove a short distance to a quiet, hidden place. As I stepped out, I felt a strange joy rise within me — the kind you feel when life's script flips without warning and places you exactly where you're supposed to be.

Before they left, I told them how surreal it all felt. "The other day, strangers jumped into my car and I gave them a ride to another parking lot," I laughed. "Now here I am, jumping into a stranger's car and being driven somewhere sacred." We all laughed together.

One of them said, "You can't do that in Los Angeles."

We stood before the Adama Temple — not a formal structure, not something built with concrete and steel, but a quiet sanctuary created by nature herself. A few massive boulders, stacked together like an ancient altar. You could climb them, sit there, and simply be. It wasn't as high as Ascension Rock, but the energy was peaceful, loving, still. A perfect contrast to the striving that often surrounds the "known" sacred sites.

And then the realization struck me.

If I had driven away — if I had ignored the quiet message from my car, if I had brushed off the unease and kept going — I never would have found this place. I never would have met those people. I never would have received this unexpected invitation.

I don't believe in accidents. I don't believe in coincidences. Only divine orchestration.

I believe something made my car pause just long enough to keep me there — long enough for these strangers to cross my path, long enough for a doorway to open to this hidden place of activation.

Adama Temple is not far from Ascension Rock, but it's not something you stumble upon unless you're meant to. There are no signs. No arrows. No trail markers. Just intuition, synchronicity, and perfect timing. A whisper from the unseen that says, "This way."

I climbed the rocks and sat in stillness. The breeze moved through the trees like a prayer. Birdsong echoed softly in the distance, like a coded message from another dimension. I placed my hands on the stone — warm from the sun — and closed my eyes.

Time stopped.

I felt a presence, subtle yet unmistakable — like a gentle current beneath still waters. It didn't speak, yet it communicated. It didn't touch, yet it stirred something deep within. It felt like home. Like remembrance. Like something inside me had just clicked back into place.

I let the silence speak to me. I allowed the stillness to settle in my chest.

How did I end up here?

This wasn't part of the plan. This wasn't on any map. And yet, it felt like something — or someone — had been waiting for me.

Eventually, I climbed down from the rocks, feeling complete.

I returned to my car. Curious, I popped the hood again — and this time, I checked the fluids. Everything was perfectly fine. The engine looked calm, balanced, as if nothing had ever been wrong. I turned on the engine. It started smoothly. No sign of the earlier sensation. No hesitation. Just ease.

I drove down the hill — gently, carefully — and everything was normal. I made it home without a single issue. And when I parked, I just smiled to myself.

I knew why.

And I knew exactly what had happened.

Because what I found today wasn't just a hidden grove or a peaceful view.

It was a sacred appointment.

A second activation.

43

One-on-One with the Mountain

It was a bright afternoon. That kind of day where the sky stretches open, quietly humming with invitation. I had no intention of going up the mountain that day—but I felt a pull. Not a thought, not a plan, but a knowing.

You must go to the top.

And yet... I hesitated.

The last time I drove to Ascension Rock, my car acted strangely, making me question whether it was just a test from my Spirit Guides or something more mechanical and real. Unsafe, perhaps.

But this time, I paused long enough to hear the subtle whisper:

"There is nothing wrong with your car. The journey served its purpose. Now you are free to go."

With that, I decided to trust. I slid into the driver's seat and started the climb. Every turn on the road reaffirmed the message—there was absolutely nothing wrong. The car hummed with smooth certainty, like it, too, had been waiting for this moment.

I drove to the highest point accessible by vehicle. There, the asphalt gave way to stone, and I continued on foot. The air was light, clear, and filled with something more than oxygen. It felt like Spirit.

As I walked, I tuned in and began sending love—heart to heart—to the City of Light beneath the mountain.

And then, on the dusty trail, I saw it—a heart made of stones carefully placed on the path. Not random. Not accidental. I stepped inside the shape, placed both hands over my heart, closed my eyes, and spoke aloud:

"I am sending love and light from my heart to all beings underneath Mount Shasta—to their hearts."

I opened my eyes and looked up. The sky was impossibly blue. On this side of the mountain, not a single cloud floated in sight... except one.

One perfect heart-shaped cloud hovering in front of me. The only one in the vast sky.

And my heart melted.

I felt seen. Not by people, not by hikers, but by those watching from beyond the veil—Light Beings, Guides, Telosians. I could feel their gaze—not in judgment, but in support. Like they were watching me walk this trail on a screen from below or beyond, holding space for me as I released the grief, the stories, the scars that no longer served me.

I felt their patience, their presence, and above all—their respect for my free will.

The sun was high—72 degrees and radiant—and though the air was dry, I hadn't brought much water. I knew I wouldn't go all the way up that day. And that was okay. This wasn't about reaching a peak—it was about answering a call.

The landscape around me shifted with every step: fields of jagged rocks, each a different size, shape, and spirit. Some were like silent sentinels, others like whispering companions.

Eventually, I came to the place I had seen before—in meditation, in dreams, in soul memory.

The wall.

The invisible doorway.

The moment I saw it, I remembered how I once entered the rock itself and soared through the mountain—not around it, but within it.

That memory now shimmered with reality. I wasn't just retracing a dream—I was walking back into it. Into myself. Into remembrance.

And the mountain, as always, said nothing.

But it also said everything.

Eventually, I sat down on a large rock. I turned around—and I just gasped.

Wow. Wow. Wow.

If you could rate the view, it would be AAA+. There's no other way to describe it. It was nature's way of outdoing herself—again. A view that didn't just impress your eyes; it rearranged your soul.

The air, the wind, the soil, the energy, the wild stillness of the rocks—it all felt blessed. I said it aloud, almost laughing:

"You guys have it blessed in here."

And they do. Whoever "they" are—the mountain dwellers beneath, the spirits above, or the soul of the mountain itself—it's all blessed, and somehow it welcomes you into that blessing if you just sit still long enough.

And then, I remembered something.

A message I received last year, before my second summer journey to Mt. Shasta. It was from Adama, the High Priest of Telos. He came to me in a meditation and said:

"Bring a recording device. You'll receive messages from different places, and each one carries a frequency that must be recorded at the exact location. Each spot will have its own voice, its own purpose, its own resonance meant for others."

And here I was—at one of those places.

So I pressed record—not to make content, but to capture a vibration, to bottle the sacred air and intention and love from this precise point on the mountain. I spoke softly, clearly, letting the message come through, not from my mind, but from the ground beneath me and the sky above me. This recording wasn't just words—it was frequency, encoded with the energy of now.

I'd tried before to capture a message like this after leaving Shasta. I'd driven down the mountain, thinking I could simply re-tell the experience once I got home.

But by the time I reached the valley...

The energy had changed.

The message had faded. The words could still come, but the vibration—the transmission—was not the same.

And so now, here I was, sitting with the rocks, speaking to the wind, and letting the moment be recorded in truth.

So I continued my journey, climbing a little higher. The trail turned from stone to loose gravel, then back to stone again—testing my footing, testing my breath.

And then, as I reached another small ridge, the landscape shifted again.

A valley opened up before me—quiet, vast, ancient.

It was like the mountain was showing me one more layer of herself. Just when you think you've reached something, you're given another mystery. A new fold in the earth.

And I realized—there are several ups and downs before you actually reach the heart of the mountain.

So close... but not quite there yet.

I paused to rest and turned around to take in the view again—and that's when I saw it.

From this height, looking down at the winding road I had driven up just an hour before, something clicked.

The road makes the shape of an infinity symbol.

Right there, hidden in plain sight, on the same path that thousands of people drive each year just to get to the highest point by car—they unknowingly drive the infinity code.

I stood there, heart thudding with the synchronicity of it. What a message.

And every soul who comes here, even if they don't realize it, is entering that sacred loop—passing through the gateway of forever, even just for a moment.

So I kept walking, and I entered some kind of island on the top. It had a lot of herbs, a lot of greenery. It looked like an oasis.

However, when I entered, when I started walking through this oasis, there were trees, boulders, more trees, some green herbs...It was hot and dry.

And I had this feeling—like I was entering a dry, hot sauna, and somebody had just poured essential oils all around for intense healing.

That's exactly how it felt.

I felt a little bit light-headed, like a sudden boost of relaxation before you enter a different realm.

It was strange and interesting at the same time. Like a transition chamber.

But then the oasis ended, and I came to another trail.

This one didn't have much greenery. Just boulders, dry land, and the sun above.

I was getting very close. I knew it—I could feel it. I was approaching the part of the mountain I saw in my vision...

The part that looked almost like it was cut in half.

I kept walking. I didn't have much water left. It was a hot day, and the sky was still bright blue, clear.

But some kind of power... or energy... or force...

Something was pushing me up.

I don't even know what my destination is.

I don't know what this experience is about.

The Spring That Found Me

I kept walking up.

I had a few sips of cold water from my bottle—the same water I had filled last night from the City Park spring. And now I saw there was just a little bit left.

My common sense said, Turn around. Go to the parking lot. You don't have much water. You're going to get dehydrated pretty quickly.

But something pushed me up.

I kept walking, without even hesitating, without thinking that I might not have enough water.

And then I started feeling dizzy.

It was that dizziness when you're dehydrated and hot, and your body starts to send warning signs—but your spirit just keeps moving. I knew I was entering a zone where I could collapse at any time...

That's when I turned to self-hypnosis.

I began speaking to myself softly, almost like a chant:

"The cold wind is blowing against my face, cooling my body. I am chilled. I am cold. I am feeling cooler. My entire body is colder. The wind is blowing cold."

And yet, in reality, the wind was not cold at all.

But something inside me shifted. My body believed the words, even if the air did not.

And at some point, I saw snow.

That became my emergency plan: If anything goes wrong, I'll go to the first snow patch and get hydration—just enough not to pass out.

I had reached a high level. There were patches of snow laying here and there, reflecting the sun.

There was an inner force guiding me:

"Be calm. You're protected. You're fine. You're safe."

Then... something told me: "Be quiet."

I quieted my mind. I quieted my thoughts. And I heard it. A sound—soft and impossible—like running water.

My heart leapt. Oh my God... is there water somewhere?

I couldn't see it yet, but I could hear it. I started searching, looking, following the sound.

And then—I saw it. A Spring.

Clear, cold water running down from above, slipping between stones and rocks, sparkling under the sunlight and the wide, infinite sky.

I whispered aloud: "Thank you, guys. Thank you."

That feeling of knowing I'm going to be okay... it washed over me.

I sat down to take a break. I cooled off—splashing the cold water on my face, my neck, my arms. I drank plenty. I refilled my bottle. I drank again.

I had crackers with me, just enough to ground me. I sat down to pause. To reflect. And I watched.

There was someone else coming—running from down the hill. But it was strange... I couldn't really see if it was a man or a woman. I watched from afar.

They didn't stop for the water. Didn't even pause.

And I thought—maybe this spring is just for me.

Maybe I had stepped into a different dimension.

I wouldn't be surprised. Because up here, surrounded by snow and stone and open sky... everything feels like a dream.

And now, sitting here beside the water... It's like meditation.

And this time, the wind really was cold. Maybe I hypnotized myself to the point that I created the cold wind... Or maybe the wind truly became colder as I climbed higher.

But it felt like reality was melting. Like the 5th dimension and 3rd dimension were starting to merge.

Sometimes the unreal becomes real.

Sometimes the real becomes unreal.

And then... I saw it. A lenticular cloud formation on the other side of the mountain. It looked like a spaceship.

I could see the top of the mountain now—it was probably another two hours of walking.

But it was only 3:30 p.m. I had my jacket with me. I had plenty of water now. And I knew exactly where to get more on the way back.

It felt like heaven. Something was calling me to that spot. I followed the path of least resistance, just like my guides always say:

"Follow the path of least resistance, and you'll get to the top quicker than you think."

I kept walking, and the path unfolded in front of me like it had been waiting for me all along. I wasn't following a map—I was following my heart. My intuition led me to a rocky slope, and without overthinking, I started to climb.

I've never climbed rocks before. Not like this. As a child, I never had the chance to do this kind of thing. But now, it was as if life said, Here's your moment. So I went for it. No training, no rules—just raw instinct. It felt like a new form of education.

I grabbed onto edges and tree roots. I was moving like a forest climber, blending into the wild terrain. It felt natural and wild and strange and right, all at once. I climbed halfway up before I even noticed what I was doing. I wasn't planning it. I wasn't analyzing it. I was just doing it.

But then resistance started creeping in. It got harder. I was climbing higher and the wind was stronger. My body started to feel the effort. I became dizzy—lightheaded from the altitude, the heat, and maybe the energy of the mountain itself. So I stopped.

I found a spot to sit, caught my breath, and realized... I had no idea how long I'd been there.

Time had dissolved. It didn't feel linear anymore. It felt like I had entered a space outside of time. I don't know what kind of activation I went through sitting on that rock, but something definitely happened. I wasn't knocked out, but I wasn't fully here either. I was in between.

I remember looking up and seeing a massive dragon-shaped cloud floating right above the mountain.

Then, when I turned around, there it was—another heart in the sky. Maybe more than one, merging together. I can't describe it in words, but it was vivid and undeniable. I also saw a shape like an elephant, then two dog-like beings playing, kissing—just pure, playful energy in cloud form.

The mountain was talking to me through the sky.

Then the wind picked up. I looked around. I was surrounded by boulders and a few twisted pine trees clinging to the rocky slope. One of them was giving off the most hypnotic pine scent—it filled the air like essential oil in a diffuser, grounding me in the moment. It was mesmerizing.

And that's when I knew—I had reached the point I needed to reach. I didn't need to climb higher. I didn't need to go further. Something in me said, You've done what you came here to do. Now you're free to go home.

As I stood to head back, I looked down and saw the road below, winding its way back to the highest parking area. And from up here, I could see it clearly—it was shaped like the infinity symbol. The road itself is a sacred design, and the people driving it don't even realize they're moving through a cosmic loop. A reminder of Source. A reminder of forever.

This mountain... it teaches you through your body, through the land, through the air and sky. It's wild and powerful and loving in ways you can't explain. You just have to experience it.

The Message by the Spring

On the way back, I decided to return to the spring. I wanted to drink straight from it—fresh, clear water running from between the rocks, like a gift from the mountain itself. I cupped my hands and drank. I splashed the water on my face, my neck, my arms—letting it wake me up, ground me, refresh every cell of my body. I refilled my bottle, knowing I'd need it for the journey back down, which would probably take another hour.

And then something stopped me. Or rather... something invited me. I felt it—a quiet nudge—to sit on a large boulder right next to the spring. I had grabbed a small Saint-Germain book just before leaving for the mountain, almost as an afterthought. Peter had given it to me a few days earlier, and something told me to bring it along. So I reached into my bag, pulled it out, and started reading right there on that boulder.

The spring was whispering behind me, the wind was cool, the sun softened just enough not to sting. And then the words on the page... It was the last part of the book. A line that stood out like it had been waiting for me:

"O, how We have waited for you, dear students, while you have struggled with the mind; how sometimes you will be so close, so close you will feel the Divine Light beginning to pour Itself through your minds and hearts, and then the human mind jumps up like a jealous little dog to claim the owner that has been ignoring it, and tries to claim the Light for its own. But It is not its own." —Peter Mt. Shasta

I stopped. I re-read that line again.

How often do we do that? Want something with all our heart, but then try to control how it shows up? How does it unfold? As if we know better than the Light itself. As if our mental patterns are more qualified to lead the way than the divine intelligence guiding us through our intuition.

I sat there for a long time, just letting those words sink in. The mountain had already stripped away so much—my ego, my need for control, my sense of time. And now it brought me to stillness, to this spring, to this book, to this message.

I realized: this whole journey was alchemical. The climb, the heat, the thirst, the dizziness, the surrender, the silence, the cloud dragons, the infinity road—all of it was a message. And now this final piece. A reminder to stop interfering. To stop interrupting the Divine with the mind.

44

The Door to Telos

Next stop: Upper McCloud Falls.

I've been here before — exactly one year ago — but I didn't know what I know now. Back then, I overlooked something extraordinary. I walked the path between the Upper and Middle Falls, unaware that nestled quietly along the trail is what many believe to be a doorway to Telos.

A stone. Unmarked to the untrained eye. Hidden in plain sight. Some people know. Others pass by without noticing. Last year, I was one of them.

This time, I came consciously. Intentionally.

The parking lot was full, so I kept driving and eventually parked near the Upper Falls. I made my way down the trail, remembering what I had learned — the doorway is said to lie between the Upper and Middle Falls. And I found it right away.

It's unmistakable once you know. A certain energy gathers there. Dry roses had been tucked gently into the cracks of the stone. The ground in front of it showed signs that many had stood there — in reverence, in prayer, or curiosity. The view was stunning, but my focus was inward.

I put my backpack down. Tucked my phone away.

I leaned against the stone — with my back touching the surface of the doorway — and I began to relax. I've had lower back pain for quite some time now. Persistent, uncomfortable, and concerning. Deep down, I knew it wasn't just physical. It felt like a message from my body — a symbol of resistance, of hesitation to walk fully in my soul's direction. I had been ignoring it.

I closed my eyes. Breathed deeply. Allowed the release.

The energy of the stone was powerful — more powerful than I expected.

As I leaned against it, with my back resting on the smooth, cool surface, I began to feel it move through me. As if someone placed a cool healing pad over my lower back. And then — something even more surprising — a sensation of suction, like a gentle vacuum drawing something out of me. The pain. The resistance. The old energy.

My hands started shaking. Vibration surged down my arms, and I found myself yawning again and again, as though my body was trying to regulate and release something too big to hold all at once.

The sensation was intense and at some point, I heard an inner voice say, "Go take a break. It's too much on your system right now. We'll continue later."

So I listened. I stepped away from the portal and walked down to Middle McCloud Falls.

The day was warm — nearly 87 degrees — and the trail was busy with tourists, cameras, and chatter. The sound of crashing water echoed through the canyon, crashing against the rocks below. It felt like nature's sound therapy, and it helped ground me. Slowly, my awareness returned. The shaking stopped. The yawning eased. But something inside was calling me back.

On my way back up the trail, I knew I needed more time at the doorway. Not just to witness it — but to receive from it. So I returned to the rock.

I leaned against it again. My hands began to tremble almost immediately. A voice inside me guided:

"Breathe deeply. That will help the energy integrate. The shaking comes when the flow is too intense for the body to absorb all at once."

I obeyed. With each breath, the waves of energy settled slightly, just enough to allow more to enter.

I thought about leaving but was told, "Not yet. Stay until we finish."

So I stayed. And then, I saw it. A vision appeared in my mind's eye: my palms pressed against the stone... and on the other side of the stone, a beam of pure light was directed into me — through my hands, into my body.

Then came a second wave: a radiant crown of light hovered above me, entering through my crown chakra, pouring into every cell of my being.

I yawned again. And again. A cascade of yawns.

Each one a sign: the old was leaving, the new was arriving.

I knew the process. Yawning signals energetic release. A recalibration. A clearing to make space for something higher.

There was one more moment of resistance — the pull to walk away — but I was told: "Just a little longer."

So I stayed until it was done.

I looked up. The sunlight streamed between the tops of the tall pines. I felt still. No more shaking. No more yawning. The work was complete. My body knew it. I was ready to go home.

45

The Sense of Community in Mount Shasta

I was born in a place where life felt like a village — people knew each other, spoke to each other, helped one another. There was a rhythm to life, a simplicity, and a natural sense of community. But over time, I moved through large cities — Minsk, Hamburg, Los Angeles, Houston, Miami, New Orleans. Places saturated with people, movement, noise, and opportunities — but often missing one simple thing: heart-level connection.

When I returned to Mount Shasta for my second visit, I found myself living in a cute home. It was part of a newer building — four units on one side, four directly across. Locals told me that new construction like this is rare here. Most homes in Mount Shasta are older, built in earlier decades. But long before I arrived this time, I had already received the message. Over a year ago, while planning my return, my Spirit Guides told me,

"A new construction home is being finalized. It's for you."

At the time, I didn't know it wouldn't happen that summer. I've since learned that things don't manifest by the calendar — they arrive by vibrational match. And this year, that alignment happened.

The moment I stepped into this home, I knew: this was what I was shown. And it came with something unexpected — a deep reawakening of that long-lost village feeling.

The sense of community here isn't something manufactured — it flows naturally. People smile. They say hello. They stop to talk. They invite you in for tea or coffee. They ask where you're from, and they actually want to know. It's as if every soul that arrives here carries a softness, an openness — and a willingness to connect.

One day, while walking Kiki, I noticed a cat sitting in the window across from my unit. An older woman was out front, watering a small garden, and we started chatting. She told me she used to own a big house, that she had farmed, and now — living alone with her cat — she found joy in tending her miniature garden in front of her window. Tomatoes mostly. I'd see her often, quietly caring for her plants.

We started having little conversations now and then. Kiki loved stopping in front of her place, wagging her tail, sitting down politely, as if encouraging me to pause and chat. And I did. It felt easy. Natural. Kind.

Then one day, I opened my door and found a small basket sitting there — filled with cherry tomatoes from her garden. My heart smiled. I couldn't return the basket empty. I had a huge bag of red cherries — one of my favorite summer fruits — so I filled the basket and brought it back to her. She was delighted. That simple gesture, that small exchange, reminded me: this is what life is really about.

We forget how much the little things matter. A smile. A few fresh tomatoes. For one person, it might be a simple act. But for another, it could be the brightest moment in their day — or their week.

Kiki, my golden-light dog, seems to be a magnet for these moments. She walks up to people, wags her tail, and makes it almost impossible not to talk to me. She opens hearts everywhere we go. She makes me pause — and from that pause, conversations begin.

One afternoon, there was a gentle knock on my door. I opened it to find another neighbor standing there, holding a bowl of freshly baked chocolate banana muffins. "Are you allergic to anything?" she asked with a smile. "I just made these and wanted to share." The smell was heavenly. There were three muffins, still warm from the oven.

Something about that gesture touched something deep in me. I hadn't felt that kind of warm, childlike excitement in a while — like being surprised by a loving grandmother's cookies straight from the oven. There's a difference between store-bought food and something made with love — real love — in a high-vibrational home. You can feel it in every bite.

I thanked her with full sincerity. And yes, I ate two of them right away. The sweetness wasn't just in the taste — it was in the unexpected kindness, the shared humanity. That's the kind of joy that stays with you. That's the feeling of being alive.

Another day, as I walked down the street, a man started chatting with me. He shared that he sometimes sleeps in the forest — not in a tent, but in a hammock hung between two trees. I was amazed. "Aren't you scared of animals?" I asked.

"Only mountain lions," he said calmly. "But I've never seen one." He did have an encounter with a bear once, but only because of a dog. "Otherwise, they're just animals," he said, "and we all belong out there."

The way people share here — the way they speak so openly — fascinates me. There's no rush, no hesitation. Just presence. And stories.

One afternoon, I visited a friend at her home and saw her beautiful artwork. As she shared her stories — her travels, her journey — I felt the presence of something larger. Every soul here has taken a different path, come from a different background, and yet somehow, Mount Shasta called them all. We're from all corners of the world, and yet we've converged here... drawn to something sacred.

That's what Mount Shasta does. It gathers us.

Different people, same pull.

Different timelines, same portal.

Different stories, same longing to remember who we really are.

And in this shared space, this mountain town, we begin to remember — through tomatoes, through muffins, through stories, through smiles.

We begin to remember that we were never meant to walk alone.

46

Heart Opening at Heart Lake

I didn't have any big plans for the 8/8 Lion's Gate day. The night before, I went to the opening ceremony of a local event. I met a woman from France. She spoke with such excitement about a place called Heart Lake. Her eyes sparkled as she described slipping into its waters, feeling the vibration ripple through her body, and how, in that instant, her heart had opened wide. The way she spoke—half whisper, half song—made it feel like the lake itself was a living being.

Her story stirred a memory. Last year, a friend and I tried to hike from Castle Lake to Heart Lake, which was supposed to be a short, easy walk. But it was early June, and the snowmelt was still rushing down the mountains. We reached a small creek, but there was way too much water to cross. We wandered up and down its banks, searching for a way. On one side, water; on the other, a fallen tree blocked the path. The forest felt like it had quietly decided: Not today. Eventually, we gave up. Maybe it simply wasn't the right time.

But this year felt different. After hearing that woman's story, and after the ceremony's messages about heart opening, I knew where I needed to be on this Lion's Gate Portal. The idea felt like a calling—one that arrived without effort, as if whispered directly into my ear.

When I woke up that morning, I knew exactly where I was go-ing—Heart Lake. It felt as if it had been calling me for a long time, and now the time was finally right. There was a sense of alignment, a vibrational match between me and that place. Last year, it didn't work out. This year, I could feel the invitation. I was ready.

I packed my backpack, filled my water bottle, and began the drive toward Castle Lake. I've always loved that area—once having a picnic with a friend, another time hiking there in early summer. Something about Castle Lake feels magical, like it carries its own protective fre-quency.

The road up is beautiful in a way that demands your full atten-tion—not just for driving, but for feeling. The air grows clearer, the light shifts, and the mountains seem to lean in closer. It's not a drive you experience every day; it's alive with energy, filled with views that make you breathe deeper.

Parking is usually difficult, and I worried for a moment that I might have to circle endlessly. But when I pulled in, there it was—one single open spot, right near the entrance, waiting for me like a quiet blessing. I smiled. It felt like yet another sign: everything was aligned for this visit.

I checked the GPS for the trail, but my inner voice interrupted:

"The best GPS is your heart. Follow your heart, trust your heart—it knows the way. Unless you don't trust your heart... then, fine, use GPS."

There was a bit of humor in that message, almost a playful tease.

As I walked, I passed a few people coming down from the trail and asked if it was okay to swim in Heart Lake. The answers were wildly different. Some said, "No, it's too dirty." Others replied without hesi-tation, "Of course, it's healing water."

I couldn't help but wonder—how could the same lake inspire such opposite reactions? I asked the Source, my guides, for clarity. The an-swer came quickly:

"Heart Lake holds a high vibration. To some, it will appear as muddy or unclean, and they will hesitate. To others, it will appear inviting, healing, and they will step in without doubt. It's not about the water's physical cleanliness—it's about vibrational match. The water reveals itself to each person according to their frequency."

That made sense. I was curious to see what it would look like to me. From above, as I approached, the water did appear a bit murky. But as I got closer, I began speaking to the lake itself, calling on the fairies of the water to guide me. I dipped my feet in, letting the coolness ground me.

Then something caught my eye—a sunlit reflection on the water's surface. A golden bubble of light floated there, and as I gazed into it, it seemed to split into two luminous eyes staring right back at me. The light shimmered, and I saw energy swirling in circles around the reflection. It pulled me in, almost hypnotic, a gentle trance. I felt completely still inside, mesmerized, as though the water was reading me.

Drawn in deeper, I stepped forward. The lake floor here was rocky, slippery, and dropped off into depth more quickly than I'd expected—perhaps I had chosen an unusual spot, but it felt right to me. The water wasn't perfectly clear, but that didn't bother me at all. In fact, I joked inwardly: Maybe this "dirt" is some kind of natural detox—herbal medicine from the Earth itself.

I eased in further, but when it came time to submerge fully, something inside resisted. I paused and asked my guides, Why am I holding back? The answer was simple:

"You don't fully trust Mother Nature."

That truth hit me. I wanted to trust her completely, so I asked, How do I do that?

"Let go. Just trust."

So I set an intention: When I go under, I want my heart to open fully. I want to give and receive love freely, without conditions.

With that, I lowered myself in. Once, twice, three times, I went under—each time feeling something shift, something release. I didn't swim, but each immersion felt like a small rebirth.

After my water ceremony, I found a flat spot nearby, stretched out in the warm sun, and let my body sink into stillness. For a while, it was just me and the lake—no one else in my space—only the shimmer of the water, the gentle hum of the wind, and the pulse of the mountain all around me. I closed my eyes and drifted, not quite asleep but floating somewhere between worlds, absorbing the vibration and energy of this place.

Eventually, footsteps crunched along the trail. One by one, people began to arrive. Some came quietly, others singing and talking. There were water blessings, small ceremonies, and even a channeler sharing messages. It was, after all, the 8/8 Lion's Gate—what else could you expect but magic? In town, so many retreats and gatherings were happening at once; the whole area felt like it was humming with collective intention.

I chatted with a few people who stopped nearby. We exchanged stories—how we each found our way to Mount Shasta, what drew us here, and what we were seeking. Several told me they had come just for the summer, leaving behind big cities and their noise to rest in the stillness of the mountains. Each story felt like a thread in a greater tapestry, weaving together strangers who had been called to the same place at the same time.

By then, I was certain I'd caught a sun-kissed glow from my lakeside rest. After more than two hours here, I decided it was time to move on and see how the rest of this Lion's Gate day would unfold. The fire ceremony that evening had already sold out—I'd decided too late, and all the tickets were gone. But the night still called to me.

47

Gifts from Lemuria

At the Lemurian Life Expo in Weed that afternoon, the next town up from Mt. Shasta, I attended a workshop led by a well-known channel and spiritual teacher, recognized internationally for transmitting higher-dimensional wisdom. For more than three decades, she has been channeling beings from various star systems and dimensions, most notably the Ninth-Dimensional Pleiadian Collective. Her transmissions are celebrated for their clarity, depth, and their ability to awaken dormant knowledge within those ready to receive. The Pleiadians she channels often speak of the evolution of human consciousness, the remembrance of multidimensional identity, and the integration of higher frequencies into everyday life.

As a Pleiadian myself—Electra, one of the Seven Sisters—I felt an immediate resonance with her energy. My intention for the guided meditation was clear: to revisit my Lemurian lifetime, to remember what it was like, to reclaim my healing gifts from that era, and to continue in this life from where I had left off. I also longed to visit Telos, the Light City beneath Mount Shasta, and to unlock the ability to speak Light Language freely.

The meditation began, and instantly my Spirit lifted, soaring above a snow-covered mountain. From high above, I could twist, turn, zoom in, zoom out — my favorite way to move when I am free from the weight of the body. In these moments, I am pure joy, pure essence, a traveler in time and space. Below, I saw trees dusted with snow, scattered hikers making their way along the slopes, each in their own quiet journey.

Then I noticed a tunnel entrance. From above, I hovered, watching for a moment before melting through the rock wall. The tunnel curved gently, smooth and dark. I've seen many tunnels in regressions before — some narrow and rough, others unsettling — but this one felt inviting.

Inside the mountain, a change was required. I underwent a cleansing — a shower, or perhaps a ritual washing — and was given a white robe. From above, I descended into the heart of a vast crystalline structure. At first, I hadn't realized how large it was, but standing on the floor, its scale revealed itself. It was bright, alive with energy, as if the walls themselves pulsed with light.

From there, I saw a mode of travel — not a cart, not a train, but something magnetic. Two lanes stretched before me. You simply set your intention and it carried you where you wanted to go. I played with it, enjoying the sensation of gliding forward. Soon the tunnel turned dazzling white, stretching far ahead.

Then, the mountain released me into another world. I floated above an ocean so clear I could see the sand below. The shoreline curved gracefully, kissed by waves. I realized then why I've always been drawn to the beach — the memory is ancient. I landed on the far side, where waterfalls cascaded into pools, the water crashing with a sound that seemed to cleanse the soul. Above the ocean, the sun began to set, flooding the horizon with gold and rose light.

At that moment, my first question was answered. My Lemurian healing gifts were meant to be used at sunset, near moving water — ocean waves or waterfalls — never still water. The sound, the motion, the rhythm of the water would weave into the healing itself.

My second question — about speaking Light Language — also received a clear answer: I am already speaking it. The only thing missing was trust.

I remembered a moment after the opening ceremony earlier this week, when I had been driving home after a Light Language activation. Without thinking, I began speaking aloud, moving my hands in patterns I didn't consciously understand. I didn't need to. It wasn't about meaning; it was about sound and vibration.

By the time the meditation ended, I felt I had been given exactly what I asked for. The visions, the instructions, the confirmations — all perfectly aligned.

When I returned home, the energy of the day caught up with me. After so many activations and transmissions, I ate a lot, and rested to ground myself.

48

The Call to the Lemurian Pond

It was my last week in Mount Shasta, and my friend from France—whom I had met earlier at the Mount Shasta Lemurian Life Expo—suggested we spend the day together. Our plan was to drive to Faery Falls.

But in the morning she was meant to come over, a sudden urge swept over me. Instead of Faery Falls, I suggested we visit Hedge Creek Falls. She agreed, but added with a smile, "That is not a big waterfall."

We walked down to the falls, passing through the mist until we reached the small cave tucked behind the curtain of water. We took photos, filmed short clips, and decided we would still make our way to Faery Falls afterward.

I set the GPS and followed its guidance, even when my friend urged me to take a turn onto the freeway. For some reason, I didn't listen. "This road can take us there too," I insisted, not knowing why I felt so sure.

The road wound deep into the forest, becoming narrower and rougher until we were creeping along at ten miles per hour. Then, out of nowhere, a familiar energy stirred inside me. You are so close... The feeling was undeniable. It wasn't Faery Falls calling—it was something else.

We reached a fork in the road. The GPS told me to turn right, but my intuition pulled me left. I checked the map and realized it was leading us toward a place I had visited just a few weeks earlier—a spot I called the Lemurian Pond, known for its high-frequency energy.

I told my friend where we were. She lit up and said, "Let's go."

Within five minutes, we arrived. I often say that my guides love to "play" with my GPS, diverting me exactly where I need to be for an activation—whether it's the first time or a necessary return for a deeper purpose.

We parked and began walking. The moment we approached the river, the air changed. My friend stopped in her tracks, needing a few minutes to adjust to the intensity. As we continued, we came to an old stone wall, the remains of a structure long gone. She pointed up at the stone and said she could see strange faces embedded within it—beings that were not human. She also saw another creature—a dragon—that existed in a higher dimensional layer of the space.

Drawn toward the water, I slipped on my swimsuit. This time, I had come prepared. The first time I visited the Lemurian Pond, the cold water had been merely an introduction, a way for my body and spirit to become familiar with the energy here. Today was different—today was for the full session.

The water was so cold it bit into my skin, but the moment I submerged, the downloads began. I understood that immersing myself here wasn't just a cleansing—it was an activation. Dormant strands of DNA were coming alive. I was told that opportunities like this can unfold over many years if we allow them to, but if we embrace them fully, in the right moment, the process can accelerate exponentially. That day, I chose the fast track. I dipped under the water three times. It felt like hitting the spiritual jackpot.

Afterward, I climbed onto a massive boulder. It wasn't the safest perch, but the view was unmatched. As I sat there, dripping and exhilarated, I scanned the scene for the next message.

That's when I saw her.

A girl, perhaps six or seven years old. She wore a long dress and something delicate adorned her hair. She was turned slightly to the side, hands clasped to her chest, cradling something unseen.

I asked inwardly, What is she holding?

The answer came: True wisdom.

She was my Lemurian daughter—a keeper of knowledge, holding the sacred records of her people. The wall before me became more than stone. It was the division between two dimensions. On the other side lay vast archives of ancient wisdom, accessible only after certain activations.

My friend confirmed what I felt—two distinct energies were emanating from opposite sides of the wall. She told me that in French, the name of this area meant "singing." The word sent chills through me. I have never considered myself a singer; in fact, my sister once teased me as a child for "singing like a goat," and I never sang again. But now, in this place, something inside urged me to sing.

So I did. I let my voice spill out over the water. Vibrations rolled through me, from my feet to the crown of my head. Fear dissolved. Judgment dissolved. My voice was free, and with it, another activation was complete.

We ended our time there in meditation, both receiving torrents of knowledge. The air shimmered with unseen presence, as if the wall itself was humming in quiet agreement: The wisdom is here. Always.

I felt an undeniable pull to cross the rushing water and reach a large stone at the water's edge. The current was icy, the kind of cold that bites at your skin, and the stones beneath the surface were slick, demanding each step be chosen with care. This was the end of the trail—no easy way to that stone except to walk against the flow itself, moving upstream, resisting the push of the water. I stayed close to the side, avoiding the strongest current, until finally I reached it. The moment I stood there, I knew this was part of the activation. But then, standing in the freezing current, a wave of light-headedness washed over me. The energy was so intense it felt as if my body might give way. I turned back, retracing my steps carefully, until I could lower myself onto a large dry rock. Still dizzy, I splashed my face again and again with the cold water, willing myself back into my body. The drums were still there—deep, resonant, echoing from somewhere beneath the water or somewhere else, as if from another dimension entirely. It wasn't just meditation; it was a kind of time travel, a crossing into something ancient. I stayed on that stone, watching the water's relentless flow, letting the energy settle until at last I felt steady again. Only then did I turn toward the shore, ready for our lunch.

We decided to have a small picnic right there beside the rushing water. As we sat eating, the sound of the river wrapped around us—its rhythm constant, its force unrelenting. We shared our experiences from the activation. My friend described hers as a vibrational coding, while my sound had a deep, steady, resonant tone.

Then, something caught my attention.

"Do you hear that?" I asked.

"Hear what?"

"Drums."

She shook her head. "No, I hear different songs—layered melodies, from different dimensions."

We were in the same place, at the same time, yet perceiving entirely different worlds.

I began noticing shapes in the stones: the number 7 again and again, reminding me of the Seven Sisters, the Pleiades, the ancient connection. I saw a heart carved into the rock, with a keyhole in its center. It pulled up a memory from a dream where my grandmother left me a heart-shaped hanger with keys, and I had found the one that fit. Now here it was again, this heart with a keyhole, a sign of another discovery.

Next, I noticed a different shape—another kind of keyhole entirely. My friend's eyes landed somewhere else. "I see the eye of a snake," she said. I didn't see it—it was her message, not mine. The stones spoke to us individually, tailoring their messages to our own paths.

When we left, I asked how long she had been camping. She'd been living out on the mountain for a few weeks. I offered her a shower at my place, and her face lit up. I also told her she could stay the night if she wished. After so long without electricity, internet, or a real bed, she welcomed the offer.

That afternoon, as we chatted, she revealed something unexpected—she remembered a past life as a Queen in England.

I laughed softly and thought, "Well, now we have a full house of queens." I remember my own past life as a Queen of England.

She was the first wife of Henry VIII. Without any regression, the memory was vivid. She recalled the Tower where she was put for isolation and then died.

Her revelation sparked a recognition in me. I double-checked, and yes—Henry's first wife had been Catherine of Aragon, followed by Anne Boleyn, the mother of Queen Elizabeth I. And I knew from my own past-life work that I had lived as Elizabeth I. (I wrote about that past life in my first book *Because I Can Remember*).

Two women, one from France, one from Belarus, meeting in Mount Shasta—not by chance, but to place missing puzzle pieces into the great mosaic of our soul histories. Together, we brought healing to a lineage that had been waiting for it across centuries.

Nightfall at Pluto's Cave

That night was not over yet. After we came back to my home and shared a light salad with fish, I suddenly felt a calling—Pluto's Cave was calling me.

On the way, I suggested we make a quick stop at the Living Memorial Sculpture Garden.

When we arrived, I instantly felt the heaviness of the place. The air was dense, and pressure built in my head. My friend felt it too. After the light and expansive energy of the Lemurian Pond earlier in the day, this heaviness was almost unbearable. I managed to take only a few quick photos before we both agreed we had to leave.

So we continued toward Pluto's Cave.

The moment we arrived, the energy shifted completely—lighter, inviting, almost cleansing. We entered the cave and explored one side, but it felt empty. On the way to the other side my friend stopped and pointed to a specific spot.

"Here," she said. "This is where the energy is strongest."

I stepped into that space, closed my eyes, and without thinking, my hands began to move in the flowing shapes of Light Language. She stood to the side, observing, then began channeling.

"You need to remove bad energy from your knees," she told me.

I focused there, moving the energy with my hands, and suddenly waves of electrical current surged through me—again and again—strong, intense, undeniable. My body responded instinctively. I began to sing in Light Language, letting tones rise from deep within me. She joined in, adding her own frequency, and for several minutes we sang together—our voices and movements weaving in perfect unison.

Then the energy began to recede. I knew the ceremony in that spot was complete. My friend told me, "You need to continue on your own—there's still more."

She moved deeper into the cave to find her own activation point. We each had our own places, our own energies to clear, our own memories to release.

When we finally emerged, the sun had set. The sky was painted in breathtaking colors, and from this vantage point, Mount Shasta revealed herself in a way you can't see from the town—the clear, unmistakable shape of the ancient volcano. She was magnificent.

The ride home was quiet. We were both tired, our bodies still humming from the day's activations. I knew for certain now that Light Language was a living part of me. It had been activated, and I had used it. My friend laughed and said, "If you're already speaking the language and moving your hands, why are you still doubting? You're already doing it."

It had been such a full day—dense with energy, signs, and breakthroughs. By the time we reached home, we simply collapsed into bed. My friend, after so long camping in the mountains, blessed the comfort of a real bed, wrapping herself in warmth.

I lay in the dark, thinking of how this day had unfolded—how each moment had led to the next, how every call had been answered. Nothing about it was random. Not the people, not the places, not the work we did. All of it was part of the path.

49

Trip to Faery Falls

We had planned to visit Faery Falls, but detours, activations, and moments that seemed too precious to cut short, delayed that intention. Today, though, the pull was unmistakable. It was the day for Faery Falls. For once, I wasn't behind the wheel. My friend was driving, and I could sink into the rare luxury of being a passenger—watching the winding road open ahead without needing to focus on every curve. When we arrived, we parked near the trailhead, shouldered our small packs, and began the short hike in. The path was familiar. I walked it a year ago with another friend, yet this return felt different. Then, it had been a discovery. Now, it was a reunion.

When we reached the waterfall, its voice roared in the air—powerful, insistent, alive. I felt an irresistible pull to come closer. The ground under water between me and the waterfalls was a mosaic of stones—small, large, some slick with spray. I slipped off my shoes and began walking barefoot. The first steps were sharp, biting into my soles. Some stones pressed into spots that sent a jolt of pain, almost unbearable. Yet, somewhere in the sensation was release—like finding long-forgotten knots inside myself and letting them dissolve. Years of wearing high heels had numbed parts of my feet, and now each step woke them up with a mix of pain and bliss. It took nearly ten minutes to cover just a short stretch. I paused often, breathing through the intensity, trusting that my body knew why this was necessary. Every stone seemed to press a different pressure point, as if the earth itself were offering me a reflexology session.

Finally, I stood before the falls. Noon sunlight poured down from above, scattering in every droplet. The cascade towered over me, crashing from the cliff with an elemental force that made the ground hum beneath my feet. The voices of other visitors vanished into the roar. As I watched the water, I felt it was more than water—it was a carrier of knowledge. On the surface, a waterfall. In the deeper sense, a stream of information, energy, memory. The longer I stood there, the more I felt lightheaded, as if "downloads" were flowing directly into me from this liquid library of the earth.

When the crowd thinned and my friend and I were left alone, she suggested something unexpected: "Let's try light language," she said. A flicker of hesitation rose in me. It was still so new—what if I was only pretending, making it up? But then I remembered: there are no mistakes. This was about allowing, not forcing.

She began first, her voice weaving through tones and syllables that bypassed ordinary understanding. I took a deep breath. Almost immediately, I felt something strange—a pressure at the crown of my head, like a helmet being placed over my brain. My mind went quiet, numbed, softened, so my subconscious could step forward. When my turn came, the sounds and hand movements came without thought. I didn't need to know what I was saying; I only needed to trust the flow. It felt ancient, familiar, and deeply alive. The vibration itself was healing, not just for us, but for the space we were in. Eventually, the energy faded, the message received. We both sat in stillness, smiling. Healing doesn't always announce itself with fireworks—sometimes it lingers in the quiet, like an aftertaste you can still feel hours later.

Back in the car, I noticed a "Mt. Shasta Sacred Sites Guide Book" on the seat. I picked it up and opened it without thinking, landing on page 32—my favorite number, which also adds up to five, a number that follows me everywhere. The page featured Medicine Lake. "That's it," I said, tapping the page. "Tomorrow—Medicine Lake." It would be a longer drive, but both of us felt the quiet pull. With only a few days left—her leaving Saturday, me on Sunday—it felt like the perfect next step in our closing chapter here. One more journey, one more place to listen, receive, and let the land work its quiet magic on us.

50

Sacred Waters of Medicine Lake

Medicine Lake sits high in the mountains, at 6,700 feet, wrapped in a quiet that feels ancient. The locals say it rests in the crater of an old volcano, one so large it dwarfs even Mount Shasta. I could feel that presence before we even arrived—an unspoken weight in the air, the kind that makes you instinctively lower your voice.

For thousands of years, Native tribes have come here in the summer to pray, to heal, to gather. They say the waters carry medicine—not the kind kept in bottles, but the kind that seeps into your spirit, rearranging things you didn't know needed moving. Some believe these cool, forest-guarded waters can even help restore fertility, returning life where it has been absent.

I didn't come here to test the legends. I came because the lake called.

The map of sacred spaces had opened to page 32 without me trying—my favorite number—and there it was: Medicine Lake.

The road to Medicine Lake felt like a journey into another world. GPS said it would take one hour and twenty-six minutes, but time seemed to move differently as we wound deeper and deeper into the forest. The trees stood tall and proud on both sides of the narrow road, their branches leaning toward each other like old friends whispering secrets above our heads.

We had packed swimsuits and a small picnic, imagining we would spend the afternoon by the water. When we arrived, the view took my breath away. The lake shimmered under the sunlight, a wide expanse of pure stillness framed by green pines.

There were only a few people swimming. We walked to the water's edge with excitement, but the moment the wind brushed against us, reality shifted. It was too cold even to take off our hoodies. So instead, we wrapped ourselves in blankets, the fabric fluttering in the crisp air. The sun was strong, but the wind kept stealing the warmth, blending heat and chill in a way that made the body constantly recalibrate.

After a while, the place quieted us. The chatter faded, replaced by the sound of wind in the trees and the gentle lapping of the water. I dipped my feet in—warmer than the icy waterfall waters I had known, but still touched by mountain chill. My friend closed her eyes, sinking into stillness, and I followed her lead.

Somewhere in that silence, sleep claimed me. It was a deep, effortless nap, the kind where the body feels completely safe and held. When I woke, the world felt softer, and my friend was smiling.

"I see blue water beings in the lake," she said, her voice calm but certain.

I laughed gently. "Do they have a message for us?"

"They say all answers to our questions are inside our hearts."

I grinned. "Something new, maybe? We already know that one."

She closed her eyes again, listening inwardly, and after a moment said, "We need to go tomorrow—hike the mountain from Bunny Flats. Two and a half hours each way."

When she finished channeling, she opened her eyes and asked, "So? What do you want to do?"

Part of me knew I wanted one last journey to the mountain before leaving, but my energy had been unpredictable lately—rising and dipping like the wind on the lake. I told her we'd see how we felt in the morning. Tomorrow was her last full day here; I still had two more.

Before leaving, I gave my quiet blessings to the land, the water, the forest, and the unseen beings who dwell here. I had brought a simple dress with me, and I dipped it into the lake, letting it absorb the medicine of this place. I decided I would not wash it—only let it dry and keep its energy preserved for the day I might need its healing again.

We drove back through the forest as the sun lowered, carrying the wind's chill on our skin, the lake's stillness in our hearts, and perhaps, somewhere behind us, the watchful gaze of blue water beings.

51

Above the Tree Line

That morning we decided to take the trail from Bunny Flat up to
Horse Camp. It promised to be a little shorter than the route we
had originally considered, and something about it felt right. After a
nourishing breakfast, we drove to Bunny Flat, parked the car, and began the ascent.

Horse Camp sits at an elevation of about 7,950 feet—higher than
I had ever climbed on Mount Shasta. The air grew warmer as the sun
rose, and soon the trail was alive with fellow hikers. We passed smiling
faces, many of them older men and women, who moved with surprising grace and joy. I admired them deeply. This is how I want to grow
old, I thought—active, vibrant, smiling, and in love with life.

We stopped to rest along the way, sipping water and nibbling cookies. Yet my single bottle felt far too small for such a hot day. When I
asked a group of three women if there was water ahead, they told me
of a spring at Horse Camp. Just hearing that gave me renewed energy.
Nothing compares to drinking spring water on the mountain—alive,
pure, vibrating with the essence of the Earth itself.

When we finally reached Horse Camp, the sight took my breath
away. Before us stood a stone structure, framed by the mountain's
shoulders and endless sky. It looked like something from an old film,
timeless and enduring. Curious, I first went straight to the spring, fill-

ing my bottle and savoring the cool water. Then I stepped toward the stone building. Out of habit, I called out a cheerful "Hello!" as if entering someone's home. To my surprise, a voice answered back.

Inside was a kind woman who greeted me warmly. She explained that she worked there as a caretaker and told me about the history of the place. The first caretaker, Joseph Macatee "Mac" Olberman, had served from 1923 to 1934. He even built a 950-yard-long flagstone path climbing upward from Horse Camp into Avalanche Gulch. To this day, it remains known as Olderman's Causeway.

Her story inspired us. Though Horse Camp had been our original destination, we couldn't resist the call of that stone path. We set off upward, each step placed on carefully laid flagstones. The stones were all different shapes and colors, some patterned like fabric, as if each one carried its own memory and story. We walked with reverence, careful not to step off the path, knowing the fragile alpine herbs around us could take years to recover if trampled.

Not long after, we came across a massive rock that looked nothing like the others. It resembled a meteorite, dark and powerful. "That's not from this planet," I murmured. My friend laughed, saying it looked more like a friendly dog. We both touched it, petting the "dog rock" with affection, as if acknowledging its silent companionship.

As we continued climbing, the world shifted. Looking back, we realized we had crossed above the tree line. The forest tops lay far below, and beyond them, Lake Siskiyou shimmered like a blue jewel in the distance. Above us stretched a flawless sky—except for one solitary cloud, perfectly shaped like a spaceship. We both smiled knowingly. Someone was watching.

The locals often warn: Never go above the tree line. That's where the mystical things begin to happen. To me, that was exactly the invitation I had been waiting for.

The air changed with each step higher. The heat of the morning gave way to sudden cold, and my friend pulled on a blazer against the chill. Our conversation fell away into silence. The mountain was speaking now, through wind and stone and the vast stillness that surrounded us.

At last, we heard the faint sound of water. A small spring revealed itself, hidden yet alive, trickling from the mountain's heart. My friend suggested we meditate nearby, but she chose the trail while I was drawn directly to the water. I sat on a sun-warmed rock beside the spring, craving the presence of all the elements together—the Sun, the Air, the Earth, and the Water.

For a moment, I felt as though I might drift into sleep right there. Perhaps the mountain was inviting me into a dream. Instead, I ate a handful of nuts, sipped the spring water, and let my energy return. Closing my eyes, I allowed gratitude to flow through me—gratitude for the climb, for the stories of those we met, for the stones beneath my feet, for the water that revived me, for the mountain itself and the unseen beings who tend it.

I sat in quiet bliss, wrapped in the embrace of Mount Shasta, above the tree line where the ordinary world falls away and the mystical begins.

As I sat in gratitude beside the spring, I eventually heard a gentle song drifting toward me. My friend had finished her meditation and was softly calling, asking if I was ready to head down. I was. We began the descent, our hearts still full from the energy of the mountain.

From a distance, the mountain had looked like one great structure, but as we walked, I noticed how it unfolded into countless rises and dips—an endless rhythm of up and down, like stepping between dimensions of peaks and valleys. Each one felt as if it carried its own story. Yet what stood out most was not the shape of the land, but the vibration itself. The higher we had climbed, the higher the frequency had become—something beyond comparison, something that pulsed with pure life.

Back at Horse Camp, I stopped once more at the spring. This time I filled both bottles I had carried, grateful to bring the mountain's water back with me. We thanked the kind caretaker, wished her well, and continued on our way down.

Descending was much quicker than the climb. On the way to the parking lot my friend turned to me with a thoughtful expression.

"When you see beings here—the Lemurians—how do you see them?" she asked.

I told her that I usually don't see them in a physical form. They come to me telepathically, or as tall beams of light. Sometimes pure white, sometimes with a bluish glow. She nodded, then quietly shared what had come to her.

As we walked down, she had received a message. The message told her that she and I already knew each other, in another form. That we were companions—partners—on a spaceship.

Her words sent a ripple of recognition through me. She explained further: this was why, at the Lemurian Life Expo, she had broken her usual habit of sitting in the back. That day, she felt pulled to the very front, and when she did, I came and sat right in front of her. It wasn't a coincidence.

From the very beginning, our connection had felt effortless, natural. Normally I am sensitive to other people's energies, often uneasy with strangers in my home. Yet with her, it was different. Her energy felt like it had always belonged. She felt the same.

And then, as if to seal this truth, the sky gave us a sign. Driving down the winding road toward town, we suddenly saw it between the trees: a vast, ship-shaped cloud, almost identical to the one that had greeted us above the tree line. "Did you see that?" she asked. "They are still watching us."

We both smiled. And then, in a moment, the road curved, the cloud disappeared, and it was gone—as though it had revealed itself only for us, only for a second, before returning to the unseen.

I couldn't help but wonder: Was it us? Was it a reflection of who we are elsewhere, reminding us that we exist both here and there at the same time? Perhaps it was simply an acknowledgment—that we were seen.

52

Until We Meet Again

Six weeks this summer, and four weeks the summer before. Ten weeks in total stretched beyond time itself, as if Mount Shasta opened her arms to me and showed me both who I am and who I am becoming. These two summers feel like lifetimes, each moment woven into a tapestry of connection, synchronicity, and remembrance.

Here, I walked sacred paths, drank from the purest springs, climbed stones that whispered their secrets, and sat beneath trees that held the memory of the Earth itself. Here, I met people who were not strangers, but companions from other times, other places, other worlds.

This morning, one of those companions came to say goodbye. My French friend stopped by on her way out of town, holding a gift in her hands—a sacred geometry drawing, passed to her here on the mountain, now passed to me.

She told me of her vision. She was back on a spaceship, looking at a monitor that showed Earth below. On the screen, countless bodies were rising, ascending, their consciousness aligned with Source, their earthly mission fulfilled. The project was complete. She watched as the monitor went dark. Then, another screen flickered on—this time showing a lush green planet. Someone on the ship turned to her and said, "Your next project."

We smiled at each other when she finished, both knowing without words that we might see each other again—on this Earth, on that spaceship, or on the green planet waiting in the distance. Goodbyes are never final when the soul remembers. They are simply pauses in the endless unfolding of connection.

After my French friend left, I went to a coffee shop to see another friend, just to say goodbye. It was bittersweet—sad in the heart, yet at the same time I felt my mission here was accomplished, at least for now. I knew I would see them again, yet it was no less tender to feel the departure. A quiet sadness also lingered at the thought of returning to Los Angeles, leaving this sacred mountain that had given me so much.

On the way back to my car, I wandered past the Blue Star Child Gallery in downtown Mount Shasta. Something in the window caught my eye—sacred geometry shimmering in the glass. Without even thinking, I stopped, turned, and walked inside. Instinctively, I slipped off my shoes at the entrance.

And then, there she was—the owner.

We began speaking about the mountain, about how everything here unfolds in divine timing, and how connections reveal themselves the moment we are ready. I mentioned that I had once seen a Mantis Being's eyes in one of her drawings, shown on a screen at the Lemurian Life Expo. She smiled and brought out a smaller version of that same drawing.

As I gazed at it, something stirred within me, and the words rose up before thought could catch them:

"Do you have a Divine Feminine Energy Activation in sacred geometry?"

She replied without hesitation: "Of course." Then she brought out three.

The first was connected to Mother Mary. Still, I felt guided to ask again:

"Do you have something about Mary Magdalene?"

And there it was—Mary Magdalene's presence revealed through sacred geometry, her energy woven into the activation codes. I knew instantly this was the piece meant for me, and I bought it, feeling her energy resonating through every line.

In that moment, I remembered my regression session with Jeff, when Mary Magdalene had spoken to me about awakening my Divine Feminine Energy.

When I finally said goodbye, I felt lighter, as though something deep within me had clicked into place. A quiet voice whispered: "Now it is truly accomplished."

As I leave Mount Shasta once again, I carry with me not only the beauty of the land, but the presence of those I met, the visions shared, the activations received, and the quiet assurance that the work here is complete—for now. Mt. Shasta will always be here, a beacon, a portal, a guide.

Until we meet again.

Acknowledgements

With a heart full of gratitude, I honor all the beings—seen and unseen—who have guided me along this soul's journey. To my family, friends, and soul companions, your love, support, and presence have been a light on every step of this path.

I offer deep reverence to the sacred land of Mount Shasta, whose waters, trees, and elements have been both teacher and healer, inspiring and sustaining this work.

I am profoundly grateful to all Quantum Healing Hypnosis practitioners whose sessions enriched these pages, and I especially honor the memory of Jeff Bennett, whose guidance shaped much of my writing.

To my star family, divine guides, and spiritual mentors—Adama, Archangel Michael, my Pleiadian star family, Saint Germain, Dolores Cannon, and Mary Magdalene—thank you for your unwavering guidance, protection, and illumination throughout this sacred exploration of past lives, reincarnation, and spiritual awakening.

To every soul who has walked this path with me, in human form or beyond, each of you reminds me that we are never truly alone, and that this journey is woven with love, light, and eternal connection.

With deepest love and appreciation,
Volha Zhamoitsina

About the Author

Volha Zhamoitsina was born in Belarus and later moved to Hamburg, Germany, to follow her studies in fashion design at the Hamburg University of Applied Sciences. After graduation, she relocated to Los Angeles, exploring paths in the film industry and real estate, yet sensing a deeper calling beyond the material world.

During the global lock down, Volha experienced a profound spiritual awakening that opened the door to her life's true purpose. She graduated with honors from the Hypnosis Motivation Institute (HMI), where she trained in hypnotherapy. Later, she became a certified practitioner of the Quantum Healing Hypnosis Technique (QHHT)®, the method developed by Dolores Cannon.

Today, Volha gently guides souls on journeys of self-discovery, self-healing, and spiritual awakening, helping them reconnect with their higher selves, release limiting patterns, and align with their highest potential. Her work invites individuals to embrace clarity, purpose, and the transformative power of their own inner guidance.

Her journey and teachings have been featured in numerous publications, inspiring countless people and leaving a meaningful impact in the fields of consciousness, spiritual growth, and soul-centered healing.

www.hypnovz.com

Index

10. Emilie A. Frank, Mt. Shasta - California's Mystic Mountain, Third Edition, Copyright 2023 by Jennifer L Middleton, p. 122.

11. Francis Bacon (1561–1626), English Renaissance philosopher.

12. Godfre Ray King, Unveiled Mysteries: Ancient Secrets are Revealed, Start Publishing LLC, Copyright 2012, p. 175, 178.

13. Henry VIII (1491-1547), King of England.

14. Jeff Bennett 1966-2024, Hypnotherapist.

15. Louis XV (1710–1774), King of France.

16. Madame de Pompadour (1721–1764) was the mistress of King Louis XV and a member of the French court.

17. Master Mary - Mary Magdalene (1st century).

18. Peter Mt. Shasta, I Am The Open Door, Pearl Publishing of Mount Shasta, Copyright 1978, p. 84-85.

19. Queen Elizabeth I (1533–1603), Queen of England and daughter of Henry VIII.

20. Robert Dudley (1532–1588), 1st Earl of Leicester, was an English statesman.

21. Saint-Germain, Ascended Master.

22. Sharula Dux (1725- current), Princess of Telos.